Privacy in a Cyber Age

Palgrave Macmillan's Studies in Cybercrime and Cybersecurity

This book series addresses the urgent need to advance knowledge in the fields of cybercrime and cybersecurity. Because the exponential expansion of computer technologies and use of the Internet have greatly increased the access by criminals to people, institutions, and businesses around the globe, the series will be international in scope. It provides a home for cutting-edge long-form research. Further, the series seeks to spur conversation about how traditional criminological theories apply to the online environment. The series welcomes contributions from early career researchers as well as established scholars on a range of topics in the cybercrime and cybersecurity fields.

Series Editors:

MARIE-HELEN MARAS is Associate Professor and Deputy Chair for Security at the Department of Security, Fire, and Emergency Management at John Jay College of Criminal Justice. Maras's research focuses on cybercrime, cybersecurity, digital forensics, surveillance, and counterterrorism. In addition to several peer-reviewed academic journal articles, she has published several books titled *Computer Forensics: Cybercriminals, Laws and Evidence* (now in its second edition); *Transnational Security* (2014); *CRC Press Terrorism Reader* (2013); *Counterterrorism* (2012); and *Exploring Criminal Justice: The Essentials* (2011). Moreover, she is the International Editor for the *Journal of Applied Security Research*.

THOMAS J. HOLT is Associate Professor in the School of Criminal Justice at Michigan State University. Holt's research focuses on cybercrime, criminological theory, and policy, and he is the editor of *Crime On-line: Correlates, Causes and Context* (now in its third edition) and coauthor of *Policing Cybercrime and Cyberterror*, *Cybercrime and Digital Forensics: An Introduction*, and *Cybercrime in Progress: Theory and Prevention of Technology-Enabled Offenses*. He is also a member of the editorial boards of the journals *Deviant Behavior*, the *Journal of Criminal Justice Education*, and the *International Journal of Cyber Criminology*.

Titles:

Privacy in a Cyber Age: Policy and Practice
Amitai Etzioni

Privacy in a Cyber Age

Policy and Practice

Amitai Etzioni

PRIVACY IN A CYBER AGE
Copyright © Amitai Etzioni, 2015.

All rights reserved.

All articles have been modified, some extensively. Texts were originally published in:

"A Cyber Age Privacy Doctrine" used with permission from *I/S: A Journal of Law and Policy for the Information Society*.

"A Cyber Age Privacy Doctrine: More Coherent, Less Subjective, and Operational" used with permission from *Brooklyn Law Review*.

"Eight Nails into Katz's Coffin" used with permission from *Case Western Reserve Law Review*.

"The Privacy Merchants" used with permission from *University of Pennsylvania Journal of Constitutional Law*.

"The Private Sector: A Reluctant Partner in Cybersecurity" used with permission from *Georgetown Journal of International Affairs*: Cyber Edition.

"Liberal Communitarian Approach to Privacy and Security" used with permission from *Homeland & National Security Law Review*.

"The Right to Be Forgotten" used with permission from *The American Scholar*.

"Balancing National Security and Individual Rights" used with permission from *Intelligence and National Security*.

First published in 2015 by PALGRAVE MACMILLAN® in the United States—a division of St. Martin's Press LLC, 175 Fifth Avenue, New York, NY 10010.

Where this book is distributed in the UK, Europe and the rest of the world, this is by Palgrave Macmillan, a division of Macmillan Publishers Limited, registered in England, company number 785998, of Houndmills, Basingstoke, Hampshire RG21 6XS.

Palgrave Macmillan is the global academic imprint of the above companies and has companies and representatives throughout the world.

Palgrave® and Macmillan® are registered trademarks in the United States, the United Kingdom, Europe and other countries.

ISBN: 978-1-137-51358-8

Library of Congress Cataloging-in-Publication Data

Etzioni, Amitai.
   Privacy in a cyber age : policy and practice / by Amitai Etzioni.
      pages cm
   Includes bibliographical references and index.
   ISBN 978-1-137-51358-8 (hardback)
   1. Computer security. 2. Internet—Social aspects. 3. Privacy. I. Title.
QA76.9.A25E89 2015
005.8—dc23
                                                            2014050093

A catalogue record of the book is available from the British Library.

Design by Amnet.

First edition: June 2015

10 9 8 7 6 5 4 3 2 1

Contents

Preface		vii
Acknowledgments		xiii
1	A Cyber Age Privacy Doctrine	1
2	More Coherent, Less Subjective, and Operational	19
3	Eight Nails into *Katz*'s Coffin	49
4	Privacy: A Personal Sphere, Not Home-Bound	61
5	The Privacy Merchants	75
6	The Private Sector: A Reluctant Partner in Cybersecurity	93
7	Liberal Communitarian Approach to Privacy and Security	101
8	The Right to Be Forgotten	113
9	Balancing National Security and Individual Rights	123
10	DNA Searches: A Liberal Communitarian Approach	157
Notes		179
Index		245

Preface

Technological and economic forces are developing at what seems to be an accelerating pace, while our normative and political institutions are lagging ever farther behind. Like the sorcerer who lost command of his apprentice, like the Golem who got out of hand, we are often more buffeted by these instrumental developments than we are able to direct them to serve our higher purposes. We need to regain mastery of our fate, to be in charge again. In a bygone era, this cardinal challenge of modernity was expressed by stating that we need to put "man on top again," though I am far from sure that he ever was. A much better way to express this idea is to hold that we should learn to direct history rather than be subjugated by it, governed by forces we do not understand or control. "Us" is particularly appropriate because there are limits to what we each can accomplish alone; we can achieve more if we come together as a community, reform our institutions, and ensure that they reflect our shared values.

This book examines this challenge in one particular arena: privacy. It is commonplace to hold that technological developments promoted both by the private sector and by the government have greatly undermined our ability to exercise the basic human right to privacy. In asking in which ways we may shore up our right to privacy, I find that we often consider the challenges posed to privacy by new surveillance technologies, new marketing strategies, and social media in moral and legal terms formed before the dawn of the cyber age. Hence, we focus on whether or not *collecting* given categories of personal information should be allowed (the old issue) rather than on the question of to what *use* that information is put (the main new issue). Therefore, the first chapter of this book is devoted to the question of what the key terms, concepts, and assumptions of a privacy doctrine suitable for the cyber age should be. The suggested cyber age privacy doctrine (CAPD) is found to favorably compare to the American "third party doctrine"—which holds that when an individual voluntarily provides a third party with a piece of information, that third party may share the information with government officials without a warrant without triggering a Fourth Amendment violation—and to the European Data Protection Directive, which, at least at first blush, seems to suggest that if anyone seeks to use a piece of information that the user of the information released, they must first seek and gain that individual's explicit consent.

In Chapter 2, I ask how the key three dimensions of this new cyber age privacy doctrine—volume, sensitivity, and cybernation—can be operationalized. That is, I show that these three core concepts are not abstract academic notions, but rather concepts that can be readily employed, for which metrics can be (and in some cases already have been) developed. Also, I discover that there is a strong positive relationship between oversight (or accountability) by government and by civilian bodies and how much license can safely be accorded to those who collect personal information and, above all, those who engage in secondary usages. That is, the more thorough and trustworthy the oversight, the more license we can accord to those who collect, process, and apply information to enhance our security, public safety, and public health.

In reviewing these two chapters, as the book was readied for publication, I was surprised to realize that I am still influenced—more than fifty years after I became an American citizen—by what might be called a "continental" approach. This approach searches for general normative and legal principles from which to derive specific public policies, court rulings, and social norms, rather than drawing on an accumulation of cases or precedents. This is, of course, a major way the European (sans the United Kingdom) and the Anglo-Saxon ways of thought often differ from each other. I believe that the reader will agree that, at least in the study of privacy, the times call for adopting some of the continental approach to render what others have called the crazy quilt of privacy laws into a more systematic, consistent whole. We should cease asking whether or not the authorities should be allowed to use facial recognition technology, thermal imaging, GPS technology, phone tracking, drones, and the numerous other new technologies that seem to be springing up at an accelerated pace. Instead, we should articulate a set of principles that will apply to all these new devices. This is what Chapters 1 and 2 attempt to accomplish.

I am not particularly fond of flashbacks. However, in this book I sought to first put forward a positive case: the case for a privacy doctrine attuned to the cyber age. Hence, in Chapters 3 and 4 I examine two approaches I believe should be allowed to fade away if not be discarded outright. Chapter 3 provides what I consider definitive proof that a conception that plays a major role in American law, the "expectation of privacy" (which draws on the oft-cited court case *Katz v. United States*), is untenable and should be allowed to die, to be replaced by the CAPD presented in Chapters 1 and 2.

Chapter 4 makes the case that focusing privacy protection on what takes place in the home enables domestic violence, as feminists have long pointed out. Moreover, given various recent technological developments, we shall see that there is much that we do in public space that we should be entitled to keep private, as if we were at home. Hence, instead of making our home our castle, we should consider privacy to be a personal sphere that goes with the person wherever he or she travels, whether in private or public space. For instance, if the authorities were to use parabolic microphones to listen to one's political or personal exchanges in a public park, that would be a gross violation of privacy. Indeed it would be a greater violation of privacy than if, say, the authorities were to measure the temperature in one's kitchen. The three criteria of the cyber age privacy doctrine—volume, sensitivity, and cybernation—delineate the personal sphere and thus play a role similar to the one played by the walls of the home in traditional privacy doctrine. They inform us which types of personal information should be especially well-protected and which ones we should be more ready to allow authorities to collect, store, and apply in the service of compelling public interests.

Chapter 5 deals with a major source of the violation of privacy that is usually not included when libertarians and civil libertarians focus on Big Brother (i.e., government intrusions): privacy violations committed by corporations. When I started studying this matter, I realized, of course, that many corporations keep track of what their customers prefer and pitch products tailored to personal tastes. I did not realize, however, the scope and extent of the dossiers that data brokers keep on most Americans. They include some very sensitive information and great amounts of personal data. If the FBI were to keep such dossiers on hundreds of millions of Americans, not only libertarians and civil libertarians but also very large segments of the American public and their elected officials would be up in arms. For various reasons, private sector privacy violations arouse much less ire—even though the source of the information matters little if you want to keep something private and instead find it on the front page of the newspaper or going viral in the blogosphere.

I was stunned when I discovered that data brokers sell access to the dossiers they amass to various government agencies. It seemed to me that if the government was not allowed to violate the privacy of Americans *who were neither* charged with nor even suspected of any crime, neither could private parties that were acting, in effect, as a government proxy. As we shall see in Chapter 5, this is clearly not the case, despite the fact that the government is merely one click away from these private databanks. I therefore lay out an extremely challenging question: If privacy is to be restored, must private sector privacy violators be treated in the same way as government agents? Should we, and could we, read the Fourth Amendment as applying to both the public and the private sectors?

Computer security is obviously a major privacy concern, given that information is, by and large, no longer stored in drawers, files, and ledgers, but rather in databases that can be accessed electronically from anywhere in the world. Therefore, the more strongly this information is protected, all other things being equal, the more strongly privacy is protected. One would expect that the private sector would be keen to protect its databases after experiencing raids by criminals, foreign agents, and hackers that have led to loss of customers' trust and business and have damaged American security. However, as spelled out in Chapter 6, there are ideological and pragmatic reasons the private sector has been slow to adopt the necessary privacy-protecting security measures. The government has responded by focusing on protecting its own computers and networks. However, we shall see that here too the private and public sectors are converging. It is not possible to effectively protect one without achieving a similar level of protection in the other.

The transposition of information from a paper-locked world to a digital one, in which information is electronically freed—a major factor and marker of the advent of the cyber age—is the source of both benefits and losses for individuals and society. To curb the losses, a new individual right has been minted: the right to be forgotten. The argument is that by making it much easier to find out about people's pasts, the cyber age prevents people from having second chances. Therefore some have suggested that people should have a right to erase information about their previous conduct from databases kept by corporations. Chapter 8 explores this suggestion. We shall see that the radical version of this proposal would cause much more harm than good, and its moderate version raises numerous questions that so far remain unanswered.

The right to be forgotten points to a much greater issue: the question of where the balance between individual rights and the common good lies. Clearly, if all "old" information is erased, it would be easier, for instance, for sex offenders to gain jobs at kindergartens. On the other hand, if anyone who smoked a joint as a teenager and was caught is treated—for life— as someone who "has a record," both society and these people would be damaged. Therefore, the issue of balance arises. How far should society tilt toward protecting privacy and other individual rights, and how far should society advance the common good, especially security, public safety, and public health? (For a discussion of this balance as it applies to privacy and security, see Chapter 7.)

This issue is first explored in general terms, drawing on the communitarian philosophy that underlies all the parts of this volume. Communitarianism is a body of thought that focuses on the social and moral foundations of society, ranging from small local communities to the nascent global one.

Although only a very small number of philosophers and public intellectuals formally adopt the communitarian label, there are strong communitarian elements in the Old and New Testaments, in Islam's concept of "shura," in Confucianism, in Catholic social thought, in moderate conservative thought (e.g., Edmund Burke's "little platoons"), and in democratic socialism (e.g., Fabianism). In short, communitarian elements can be found in most religious and secular belief systems.

The term "communitarian" was first used in the 1840s to refer to those who experimented with unusually communal lifestyles. It was rarely used in the generations that followed. In the 1980s, the term became associated with the work of a small group of political philosophers who argued for the importance of a shared formulation of the good, as opposed to the liberal position that each individual should define the good for himself or herself.[1]

In 1990, a group composed of academics and public leaders called "responsive communitarians" formulated a platform that contained a public philosophy.[2] (More recently, the term "liberal communitarian" is more often used to refer to the same line of thinking.) This group's main thesis is that people face two major sources of normativity—individual rights and the common good—neither of which should be a priori privileged over the other. Liberal communitarians hold that all societies must heed the moral claims of two core values: the dignity of the individual, which is the foundation of individual rights, and the importance of the common good. These communitarians believe that societies tend to tilt toward one core value or the other and need to be pulled toward a balanced center to make a good society. Thus, Japan is depicted as strongly dedicated to the common good but in need of strengthening the rights of women, minorities, and the disabled; meanwhile, the United States under President Ronald Reagan—and the United Kingdom under Prime Minister Margaret Thatcher—was diagnosed as too individualistic.

Throughout this volume, this line of thinking is applied to the standing of privacy versus the common good. It raises questions such as whether, in a particular era (e.g., post-9/11) and a particular country (in this volume, the United States), security as a common good has unduly undermined the right to privacy, and what markers or criteria one should employ to determine where the proper balance rests. (For a detailed theoretical analysis of the liberal communitarian approach to privacy, see Chapter 7.)

The question of balance is then explored by examining two US National Security Agency (NSA) programs (Chapter 9) and the police use of DNA profiles (Chapter 10). The NSA's programs provide a fine way to examine the issues at hand. One's evaluation of them depends a great deal on the weight one accords the common good involved, namely protecting the homeland from terrorism and other security threats; on the extent to which one finds that NSA programs actually violate privacy (e.g., Do they actually examine the content of messages, or only the metadata, and does the NSA shadow only foreigners and their American agents or keep a tab on millions of innocent Americans?); and the extent to which these programs are subject to close oversight, and by whom.

By contrast, the study of the increasing use of forensic DNA profiles by law enforcement authorities makes for a very unusual case study of the balance between the common good and individual rights, particularly privacy. We shall see that not only are the concerns raised about the threat DNA profiles pose to privacy mainly based on misunderstandings (e.g., confusing samples with profiles) and overstated, but also that DNA profiling makes very important contributions to both public safety *and* a most fundamental individual right.

Privacy is not dead, and it should not be allowed to die. To protect it from all those who would violate it, whether they are government agents or private corporations, we must focus our analysis and new tools (e.g., computerized audit trails) on protecting privacy instead of allowing it to be further undermined. To proceed, though, we must simultaneously take into account the need to serve the common good. This book seeks to stimulate a dialogue that will lead to new shared moral understandings and legal, political, and social expressions of the same in order to cope with this age-old issue in a new age: the cyber age.

A.E.

December 2014

Washington, DC

Acknowledgments

All articles included in this volume that were previously published were revised, extended, and updated.

Chapter 1

Amitai Etzioni. "A Cyber Age Privacy Doctrine: A Liberal Communitarian Approach." *I/S: A Journal of Law and Policy for the Information Society* 10(2), 2014.

I am indebted to Ashley McKinless for extensive research assistance on this article, as well as to Alex Platt, Steven Bellovin, Shaun Spencer, and Marc Blitz for comments on a previous draft.

Chapter 2

Amitai Etzioni. "A Cyber Age Privacy Doctrine: More Coherent, Less Subjective, and Operational." *Brooklyn Law Review* 80(4), 2015.

I am indebted to Peter Swire, Joris van Hoboken, and Daniel Pesciotta for profound comments on a previous draft, and to Thomas Rory Donnelly for editorial comments on a previous draft.

Chapter 3

Amitai Etzioni. "Eight Nails into *Katz*'s Coffin." *Case Western Reserve Law Review* 65(2), 2015.

I am indebted to Rory Donnelly for research assistance on this article.

Chapter 4

I am indebted to Erin Syring for research and editing assistance on this article.

Chapter 5

Amitai Etzioni. "The Privacy Merchants: What Is to Be Done?" *University of Pennsylvania Journal of Constitutional Law* 14(4), 2012.

Chapter 6

Amitai Etzioni. "The Private Sector: A Reluctant Partner in Cybersecurity." *Georgetown Journal of International Affairs* 15(3), 2014.

Chapter 7

Amitai Etzioni. "Liberal Communitarian Approach to Privacy and Security." *Homeland and National Security Law Review* 1(1), 2014.

I am indebted to Jesse Spafford for his extensive research assistance on this paper and to Ashley McKinless and Erin Syring for comments on a previous draft.

Chapter 8

Amitai Etzioni. "Second Chances, Social Forgiveness, and the Internet." *The American Scholar*, Spring 2009.

This article was co-authored by Radhika Bhat, a research and outreach assistant at the Institute for Communitarian Policy Studies at The George Washington University.

Chapter 9

Amitai Etzioni. "NSA: National Security vs. Individual Rights." *Intelligence and National Security*, 2014.

I am indebted to Jesse Spafford for his extensive research assistance on this paper, as well as to Danielle Kerem for the research that she contributed.

Chapter 10

This chapter was not previously published. I am indebted to Erin Syring for research assistance as well as for final editing on the whole manuscript.

I
A Cyber Age Privacy Doctrine

A. Introduction

1. Focus on Use

A privacy doctrine built for the cyber age must address a radical change in the type and scale of violations that the nation—and the world—face, namely that the greatest threats to privacy come not at the point that personal information is collected, but rather from the secondary uses of such information. Court cases such as *Katz, Berger, Smith, Karo, Knotts, Kyllo*—and most recently *Jones*—concern whether the initial collection of information was legal. They do not address the fact that legally obtained personal information may nevertheless be used later to violate privacy and that the ways such information is stored, combined with other pieces of information ("collated"), analyzed, and distributed often entail very significant violations of privacy.[1] Whereas a considerable number of laws and court cases cover these secondary usages of information, they do not come together as a coherent doctrine of privacy—and most assuredly they do not address the unique challenges of the cyber age.[2]

True, collected personal information was subject to secondary abuses even when it was largely paperbound (e.g., in police blotters or FBI files). Indeed, when Warren and Brandeis published their groundbreaking 1890 article in the *Harvard Law Review*, considered the "genesis of the right of privacy,"[3] they were not concerned about gossip per se (a first order privacy violation), but about the wider distribution of intimate details through the media (a secondary usage).[4] However, the digitization of information, the widespread use of the Internet and computers, and the introduction of artificial intelligence systems to analyze vast amounts of data have increased the extent, volume, scope, and kinds of secondary usages by so many orders of magnitude that it is difficult to find a proper expression to capture the importance of this transformation.[5] The main point is not that information can now be processed at a tiny fraction of the cost and at incomparably faster speeds than when it was paper bound, which is certainly the case, but that modes of analysis that divine new personal information out of personal data previously collected are common today, but were inconceivable when most personal information was paper bound.[6] In other words, preventing excessive intrusiveness required less recourse to the Fourth Amendment when most personal information was paper bound because very often it was simply impossible to accrue and analyze large amounts of personal information—but much expanded protections are necessary now that these abilities have much increased. Because this observation is critical to all that follows, and because the term "secondary usages" (which implies usages less important than the first or primary ones) is a rather weak one, I employ from here on the infelicitous term "cybernation" to refer to the process of storing information, combining it with other pieces of information ("collating"), analyzing it, and distributing it. Cybernated data can be employed in two distinct ways, and both represent a serious and growing threat to privacy. A discrete piece of personal information, collected at one point in time ("spot" information) may be used for some purpose other than that for which it was originally approved, or the fruits of spot collection may be pieced together with other data to generate new information about the person's most inner and intimate life. (For a more complete definition of spot collection, see Chapter 2.)

The cyber age privacy doctrine must lay down the foundations on which the U.S. Congress can develop laws and the courts can accumulate cases that will determine not just what information the government may legally collect, but what it might do with that data. According to some legal scholars, the D.C. Circuit's decision in *Maynard* and the concurring opinion authored by Justice Samuel Alito in *Jones* provide the building blocks for this new edifice, which is sometimes referred to as a mosaic theory of the Fourth Amendment, and under which "individual actions of law enforcement that are not searches for Fourth Amendment purposes may become searches when taken together *en masse*."[7] This observation is based on Justice Alito's argument that the GPS tracking of a vehicle on a public highway constituted a search because of the length of time over which the monitoring took place (i.e., 28 days). This opens the door to take into account the volume of information collected and presumes that, while limited amounts of collection may be permissible, large amounts could constitute a violation of privacy. *Jones*, however, still only deals with collection. Hence, most of the work of laying down the foundations for the protection of privacy from cybernated information remains to be carried out.

2. But Not Back to the "Castle"

While the time has come to leave behind the reasonable expectation standard, this is not to say that the courts should revert to pre-*Katz* Fourth Amendment analysis, which gave considerable weight to the home as the locus of privacy. (For more on this subject, see Chapter 4.) In *Katz* the majority ruled that "the Fourth Amendment protects people, not places," rejecting the "trespass" doctrine enunciated in *Olmstead*. However, even after this, the home remained largely inviolable in the eyes of the courts. It seems *Katz* did not detach Fourth Amendment safeguards from the home but rather extended the sphere of privacy beyond it to other protected spaces. Information collected about events in one's home is still often considered a priori a violation of privacy, while much more license is granted to the state when it collects information about conduct in public and commercial spaces. As Justice Antonin Scalia put it, drawing heavily on *Silverman v. United States*, "'At the very core' of the Fourth Amendment 'stands the right of a man to retreat into his own home and there be free from unreasonable governmental intrusion.' With few exceptions, the question whether a warrantless search of a home is reasonable and hence constitutional must be answered no."[8] This idea has deep roots in American and English common law: "The zealous and frequent repetition of the adage that a 'man's house is his castle,' made it abundantly clear that both in England and the Colonies 'the freedom of one's house' was one of the most vital elements of English liberty."[9] In *Dow Chemical Company v. United States,* the court established that the expectation of privacy was lower in an industrial plant than in a home because the latter "is fundamentally a sanctuary, where personal concepts of self and family are forged, where relationships are nurtured and where people normally feel free to express themselves in intimate ways."[10]

The inviolability of the home and the private/public distinction in privacy law has been roundly criticized by feminist scholars. Catharine MacKinnon writes the problem with granting the home extra protection is that "while the private has been a refuge for some, it has been a hellhole for others, often at the same time."[11] Linda McClain points out that freedom from state interference in the home "renders men unaccountable for what is done in private—rape, battery, and other exploitation."[12]

There is good reason to assume that the private/public distinction is rapidly declining in importance in general[13] and with regard to privacy in particular.[14] Marc Jonathon Blitz related this to the cyber age and hence is quoted here at some length:

> The 1969 case Stanley v. Georgia forbade the government from restricting the books that an individual may read or the films he may watch "in the

privacy of his own home." Since that time, the Supreme Court has repeatedly emphasized that Stanley's protection applies solely within the physical boundaries of the home: While obscene books or films are protected inside of the home, they are not protected en route to it—whether in a package sent by mail, in a suitcase one is carrying to one's house, or in a stream of data obtained through the Internet.

However adequate this narrow reading of Stanley may have been in the four decades since the case was decided, it is ill-suited to the twenty-first century, where the in-home cultural life protected by the Court in Stanley inevitably spills over into, or connects with, electronic realms beyond it. Individuals increasingly watch films not, as the defendant in Stanley did, by bringing an eight millimeter film or other physical copy of the film into their house, but by streaming it through the Internet. Especially as eReaders, such as the Kindle, and tablets, such as the iPad, proliferate, individuals read books by downloading digital copies of them. They store their own artistic and written work not in a desk drawer or in a safe, but in the "cloud" of data storage offered to them on far-away servers.

Therefore, it follows that privacy is best viewed as a personal sphere that surrounds an individual irrespective of location. This is a version of what Christopher Slobogin calls the protection-of-personhood version of privacy, which "views the right to privacy as a means of ensuring individuals are free to define themselves."[15] Privacy plays the same role whether one is in the home or out in public: "Because a substantial part of our personality is developed in public venues, through rituals of our daily lives that occur outside the home and outside the family, cameras that stultify public conduct can stifle personality development."[16] If the government uses a long distance "shotgun mic" to eavesdrop on the conversation of two people walking in a public park, such a search would be more intrusive than if the government were to measure the temperature of their kitchens. This is the case because conversations are much more revealing about an individual than his or her preferred temperature, because the former can include their medical condition, political views, and so on. (I discuss later the question of whether information revealing that one is committing a crime deserves extra protection.) In short, privacy should not be home bound. (For a more thorough discussion of this point, see Chapter 4.)

3. A "Social Policy" Model of the Fourth Amendment

The cyber age privacy doctrine concerns the normative principles that underlie both the evolving interpretations of the Constitution and the laws enacted by Congress, both of which reflect changes in the moral culture of the society. It therefore deals with both the Fourth Amendment and public policy. Such normative changes have occurred in other areas. For instance, the civil rights movement led to changes in the position of the Supreme Court (e.g., from *Plessy v. Ferguson* to *Brown v. Board of Education*) and to acts of Congress (e.g., the Voting Rights Act of 1965). More recently, changes were introduced both by the courts and by various legislatures reflecting changes in the characterization of same sex marriage in the moral culture. Now such a change is called for in regard to the concept of privacy. This chapter next discusses the normative principles of such a reconstituted concept. (For a philosophical discussion of these normative principles, see Chapter 7.)

(i) In seeking to base a privacy doctrine not on the usual foundations of expectations or location, this chapter draws on a liberal communitarian philosophy that assumes that individual rights, such as the right to privacy, must be balanced with concerns for the common good, such as those about public health and national security. By contrast, authoritarian and East Asian communitarians tend to be exclusively concerned with the common good or pay mind to rights only to the extent that they serve the rulers' aims. And at the opposite end of the spectrum, libertarians and several contemporary liberals privilege individual rights and autonomy over societal formulations of the common good. (Although the term "common good" is not one often found in legal literature, its referent is rather close to what is meant by "public interest," which courts frequently recognize, and a similar concept is found in the U.S. Constitution's reference to the quest for a "more perfect union.")

The Fourth Amendment reads: "The right of the people to be secure in their persons, houses, papers, and effects, against *unreasonable* searches and seizures, shall not be violated" (emphasis added). This is a prime example of a liberal communitarian text because it does not employ the absolute, rights-focused language of many amendments (e.g., "Congress shall make *no* law"), but recognizes on the face of it that there are reasonable searches, which are understood to be those in which a compelling public interest takes precedence over personal privacy.

(ii) This book assumes that the communitarian balance is meta-stable. That is, for societies to maintain a sound communitarian regime—a careful balance between individual rights and the common good—societies must constantly adjust their public policies and laws in response to changing external circumstances (e.g., 9/11) and internal developments (e.g., FBI overreach). Moreover, given that societal steering mechanisms are rather loose, societies tend to oversteer and must correct their corrections with still further adjustments. For example, in the mid-1970s, the Church and Pike Committees uncovered "domestic spying on Americans, harassment and disruption of targeted individuals and groups, assassination plots targeting foreign leaders, infiltration and manipulation of media and business." As a result, Congress passed the Foreign Intelligence Surveillance Act of 1978 (FISA) and created the Foreign Intelligence Surveillance Court to limit the surveillance of American citizens by the U.S. government. After 9/11 several reports concluded that the reforms had gone too far and had blocked the type of interagency intelligence sharing that could have forestalled the terrorist attacks. As a result, the Patriot Act was enacted in a great rush and, according to its critics, excessively sacrificed privacy in order to enhance security and "correct" what were considered to be the excesses of the reforms the Church and Pike Committees set into motion. Since then, the Patriot Act itself has been recalibrated.[17]

At each point in time, one must therefore ask whether society is tilting too far in one direction or the other. Civil libertarians tend to hold that rights in general and privacy in particular are inadequately protected. The government tends to hold that national security and public safety require additional limitations on privacy. It is the mission of legal scholars, public intellectuals, and concerned citizens to nurture normative dialogues that help sort out in which direction corrections must next be made.[18] (Note that often some tightening in one area ought to be combined with some easing in others. For instance, a case can currently be made that the Transportation Security Administration's (TSA) screening regulations are too tight, while the monitoring of whether visitors and temporary residents who have committed to leaving the United States actually do so is too loose.)

Orin Kerr and Peter Swire engage in an important dialogue on whether the issues presented here are best suited for treatment by the courts or by Congress, and whether they are largely viewed through the prism of the Fourth Amendment or congressional acts. The following discussion treats both as if they were an amalgam.

(iii) *Four criteria* help specify the liberal communitarian approach to privacy.[19] First, a liberal democratic government will limit privacy only if it faces a *well-documented and large-scale threat* to the common good (e.g., to public safety or public health), not merely a hypothetical threat or one limited to few individuals or localities. (I avoid the term "clear and present danger," despite the similarity in meaning, because it has a specific legal reference not here intended.) The main reason this threshold must be cleared is that modifying legal precepts—and with them the ethical, social, public philosophies that underlie them—endangers their legitimacy. Changes, therefore, should not be undertaken unless there is strong evidence that either the common good or privacy has been significantly undermined.

Second, if the finding is that the common good needs shoring up, one had best establish *whether this goal can be achieved without introducing new limits on privacy.* For instance, this can be achieved by removing personally identifying information (e.g., names, addresses and Social Security numbers) when researchers need medical records, which would make it possible to allow access to previously inaccessible data (e.g., Medicare databanks). Various technical difficulties arise in securing the anonymity of the data. Several ingenious suggestions have been made to cope with this challenge.[20] Conversely, if privacy needs shoring up, one should look for ways to proceed, such as introducing audit trails, that impose no "losses" to the common good.

Third, to the extent that privacy-curbing measures must be introduced, they should be *as minimally intrusive as possible*.[21] For example, many agree that drug tests should be conducted on those, such as school bus drivers, directly responsible for the lives of others. Some employers, however, resort to highly intrusive visual surveillance to ensure that the sample is taken from the person who delivers it. Instead, one can rely on the much less intrusive procedure of measuring the temperature of the sample immediately upon delivery.

Fourth, measures that *ameliorate the undesirable side effects* of necessary privacy-diminishing measures are to be preferred over those that ignore these effects. Thus, if contact tracing is deemed necessary to fight the spread of infectious diseases in order to protect public health, efforts must be made to protect the anonymity of those involved. A third party may inform those who were in contact with an affected individual about such exposure and the therapeutic and protective measures they ought to next undertake without disclosing the identity of the diagnosed person.

Applying these four balancing criteria helps determine which corrections to a society's course are both necessary and not excessive. This article focuses on the third criterion and seeks to address the question: what is least intrusive?

B. Privacy as a Three-Dimensional Cube

In this section I attempt to show that to maintain privacy in the cyber age, boundaries on information that may be used by the government should be considered along three major dimensions: the level of sensitivity of the information, the volume of information collected, and the extent to which it is cybernated. These considerations guide one to the lowest level of intrusiveness holding constant the level of common good.

1. Sensitivity

One dimension is the *sensitivity* of the information.[22] Information is generally considered sensitive if, based on the cultural values of the society in question, it is viewed as a significant violation of the prevailing norms to reveal or seek the information sans a preexisting relationship of affect or specific business, such as the relationship between spouses or between an individual and her doctor. For instance, data about a person's medical condition would be considered highly sensitive, as would information about one's political beliefs and conduct (e.g., voting) and personal thoughts. Financial information would be ranked as less sensitive than medical information, with publically presented information (e.g., license plates) and routine consumer choices even less so.

These rankings are not based on "expectations of privacy," what this or that judge divines as societal expectations, or acts of Congress.[23] Rather, they reflect shared social values and are the product of politics in the good sense of the term, of liberal democratic processes, and of moral dialogues.[24] (Individual nations may rank differently what they consider sensitive. For example, France strongly restricts the collection of information by the government about race, ethnicity, and religion, even though its rationale is not the protection of privacy but rather a strong assimilationist policy and separation of the state and church.) For those who analyze the law in terms of the law and economics paradigm, disclosure of sensitive data causes more harm to the person by objective standards than does the disclosure of data that is not sensitive. Thus, disclosure of one's medical condition may lead one to lose one's job or not be hired, to be unable to obtain a loan, or to incur higher insurance costs, among other harms. By contrast, disclosure of the kinds of bread, cheese, or sheets one buys may affect mainly the kind and amount of spam one receives.

A reexamination of *Kyllo* helps highlight this principle. If one goes by *Katz*, the legality of conducting thermal imaging from outside the home depends on what one presumes personal and societal expectations to be. At least in middle class American suburbs, people may consider such a heat reading to be a violation of their expectations. If one clings to the idea that "my home is my castle," measuring the heat inside the home is indeed a major violation of privacy. However, if one goes by the cyber age privacy doctrine here outlined, such readings rank very low on sensitivity because they reveal nothing about the resident's medical, financial, or political preferences, let alone their thoughts. In effect, they detect an extremely low bandwidth of information (the term "bandwidth" here refers to a measurement of the number of different types of information collected). The information revealed is less consequential than what kind of cereal or which brand of coffee the person purchased.

One may argue that information about the temperature inside a home is actually particularly sensitive because it can reveal that a crime is being committed. Preventing crime obviously contributes to the common good.

And given that in 2011 fewer than half of violent crimes and less than 20 percent of property crimes in the United States were resolved, some may well hold that public authorities are not excessively indulged when dealing with crime.[25] As for harm to the individuals involved, they would be harmed only if they had a right to commit a crime. The arguments against the notion that crimes committed in a home (e.g., spousal abuse) deserve more protection than ones committed in public have already been discussed. What is new here is that historically, when the Constitution was written, searching a home required a person to enter or peep, which would entail a high level of intrusiveness because the intruder could not help but note other potentially sensitive information besides whether a crime was being committed. However, technologies that have a very narrow and crime-specific bandwidth (e.g., dogs that sniff for bombs or sensors that measure abnormal levels of heat) and are, hence, minimally intrusive should be allowed. One may disagree with this line of analysis but still accept the basic point that the less-intrusive collection of insensitive information should be tolerated, while the collection of highly sensitive information should be banned.

Many court cases treat the voluntary release of information to others as if the information disclosed—including phone numbers dialed,[26] copies of written checks,[27] documents given to an accountant,[28] newspaper records,[29] and even papers held by a defendant's attorney[30]—all had the same level of sensitivity.[31] A privacy doctrine that follows the principles here outlined would grant persons more say about the secondary usages of sensitive information, while recognizing that the less sensitive information may be used and passed on without the individual's explicit consent.

Over the years, Congress has pieced together privacy law by addressing the protection of one kind of sensitive information at a time, rather than treating all kinds in a comprehensive fashion. Thus, in 1973, the Department of Health, Education and Welfare developed the Code of Fair Information Practices to govern the collection and use of information by the federal government. The principles of the code were incorporated in the Privacy Act of 1974, which "prohibits unauthorized disclosures of the records [the federal government] protects. It also gives individuals the right to review records about themselves, to find out if these records have been disclosed, and to request corrections or amendments of these records, unless the records are legally exempt."[32] The Privacy Act applies only to the federal government and has not been expanded to include records kept by the private sector. In 1986, the Electronic Communications Privacy Act (EPCA) restricted wiretapping, regulated government access to electronic communication stored by third parties, and prohibited the collection of communications content (i.e., what was said, not who was called) by pen registers. After the Supreme Court ruled in the 1976 case *United States v. Miller* that there was no reasonable expectation of privacy for records at financial institutions, Congress passed the Right to Financial Privacy Act,[33] which extended protection to these records. As required by the 1996 Health Insurance Portability and Accountability Act (HIPAA), in 2002 the Department of Health and Human Services published the final form of "the Privacy Rule," which set the "standards for the electronic exchange, privacy and security of health information."[34] This accumulation of privacy protections includes laws covering specific sectors—or responding to specific events—but not any overarching design. A well-known case in point is Congress's enactment of the Video Privacy Protection Act after the video rental records of Supreme Court nominee Judge Robert Bork were obtained by a Washington, D.C., newspaper.[35]

Congress could help to establish a privacy doctrine for the cyber age by reviewing what by now has been fairly called an incomplete "patchwork of federal laws and regulations" and providing a comprehensive overall ranking of protections based on the sensitivity of the data.[36]

2. Volume

The second dimension from which a cyber age privacy doctrine should draw is the volume of information collected. "Volume" refers to the total amount of information collected about one person by one agency or actor. Volume reflects the extent of time surveillance is applied (the issue raised in *Jones*), the amount of information collected at each point in time (e.g., only e-mails sent to a specific person or all e-mails stored on a hard drive?), and the bandwidth of information collected at any one point in time (e.g., only the addresses of e-mail sent or also their content?). A single piece of data deserves the least protection and a high volume of information should receive the most.

Under such a cyber age privacy doctrine, surveillance and search technologies differ in their intrusiveness. Least intrusive are those that collect only discrete pieces of information of the least sensitive kind. These include speed detection cameras, toll booths, and screening gates, because they all reveal, basically, one piece of information of relatively low sensitivity. Radiation detectors, heat reading devices and bomb- and drug-sniffing dogs belong in this category, not only because of the kind of information (i.e., low or not sensitive) they collect, but also because the bandwidth of the information they collect is very low (i.e., just one facet, indeed a very narrow one, and for a short duration). These volume rankings must be adapted as technologies change. The extent to which combining technologies is intrusive depends on the volume (duration and bandwidth, holding sensitivity constant) of information collected.

Typical CCTVs—privately owned and mounted on one's business, parking lot, or residential lobby—belong in the middle range because they pick up several facets (e.g., location, physical appearance, who one associates with), but do so for only a brief period of time and in one locality. The opposite holds for Microsoft's Domain Awareness System, first tested in New York City in 2012. The program makes data—such as that from the city's CCTV cameras, arrest records, 911 calls, license plate readers, and radiation detectors—easily and instantly accessible to the police. While the system does not yet utilize facial recognition, it could be readily expanded to include such technology.

Phone tapping—especially if continued for an extended period of time and not minimized—and computer searches collect more volume. (This should not be conflated with considerations that come under the third dimension: whether these facts are cybernated.)

Drones are particularly intrusive because they involve much greater bandwidth and have the potential to engage in prolonged surveillance at relatively low costs compared to, say, a stakeout.

When the issue of extending privacy protection beyond spot collection arose in *Jones*, several legal scholars, in particular Orin Kerr, pointed to the difficulties of determining when the volume of collection was reasonable and when it became excessively intrusive. Kerr writes: "In *Jones*, the GPS device was installed for 28 days. Justice Alito stated that this was 'surely' long enough to create a mosaic. But he provided no reason why, and he recognized that 'other cases may present more difficult questions.' May indeed. If 28 days is too far, how about 21 days? Or 14 days? Or 3.6 days? Where is the line?"[37] In response, one notes that there are numerous such cutoff points in law, such as the number of days suspects may be detained before they must be charged or released, the voting and driving ages, the number of jurors necessary for due process, and so on. One may say that they reflect what a "reasonable" person would rule. Actually, they reflect what judges consider a compromise between a restriction that is clearly excessive and one that's clearly inadequate—a line that has been adjusted often. There is no reason the volume of collection should not be similarly governed.

3. Cybernation: Storage, Analysis, and Access

The third dimension seems to be the one that is increasing in importance and regarding which law and legal theory have the most catching up to do. To return to the opening deliberations of this chapter, historically, much attention was paid to the question of whether the government can legally collect certain kinds of information under specific conditions. This was reasonable because most violations of privacy occurred through search and surveillance that implicated this first-level spot collection. True, some significant violations also occurred as a result of collating, storing, analyzing, and distributing information. However, to reiterate, as long as records were paper bound, which practically all were, these secondary violations of privacy were inherently limited when compared to those enabled by the digitization of data and the use of computers.

To illustrate this cardinal transformative development, a comparison: In one state, a car passes through a tollbooth, a picture of its license plate is taken, and then this information is immediately deleted from the computer if the proper payment is made. In another state, the same information, augmented with a photo of the driver, is automatically transmitted to a central data bank. There, it is combined with many thousands of other pieces of information about the same person, from locations they have visited based on cell tower triangulation to their magazine subscriptions and recent purchases and so on. Artificial intelligence systems regularly analyze the information to determine if people are engaged in any unusual behavior, which places of worship they frequent (flagging mosques), which political events they attend (flagging those who are often involved in protests), and if they stop at gun shows. The findings are widely distributed to local police and the intelligence community and can be gained by the press and divorce lawyers.

Both systems are based on *spot collection*, that is, the collection of pieces of information that pertain to a very limited, specific event or point in time and that typically are of little significance in and of themselves—as in the case in the first state. However, if such information is stored, combined with other information, analyzed, and distributed—that is, if such information is cybernated—as depicted in the second scenario, it provides a very comprehensive and revealing profile of one's personal life. In short, the most serious violations of privacy are often perpetuated not by surveillance or information collection per se, but by combination, manipulation, and data sharing—by cybernation. The more information is cybernated, the more intrusive it becomes.

C. Limiting Intrusion by Cybernation

1. *Third Party and the Europeans*

There are in place two major systematic approaches to dealing with privacy violations that result from secondary uses: the third-party doctrine and the EU Data Protection Directive (DPD). The third-party doctrine holds that once a person voluntarily discloses a fact to another party, that party is free to disclose the information to the government without the exchange constituting a Fourth Amendment search. (For more information about the third-party doctrine, see Chapter 2.)

This approach is challenged by critics who note that in the cyber age much of our private lives are lived in a cyber world operated by third parties like Google and Facebook. Thus, Matthew Lawless writes:

> The third party doctrine gives effect to the criticism often aimed at the "reasonable expectation of privacy" principle, by holding that individuals can only reasonably expect privacy where the Court gives them that privacy. Because the third party doctrine fails to address true societal expectations of privacy (as evident by its failure to protect any information entered into a search engine), it reinforces the privacy norms of a politically and temporally insulated judiciary: once people know their searches are exposed, then—by the time these cases are contested—there will, in truth, be no expectation of privacy.[38]

However, even without drawing on whatever the societal expectation of privacy is, one notes that considerable harm will come to people and that core societal values will be violated if the third-party doctrine is given free rein. This observation is strengthened by the fact that various exceptions to the third-party doctrine are already in place, such as special rules for medical and financial information. However, according to Greg Nojeim, these rules do not provide the same level of protection granted by the Fourth Amendment. He notes that "privacy statutes that protect some categories of sensitive personal information generally do not require warrants for law enforcement access."[39]

The European Union's DPD in effect takes the opposite view, namely, that any secondary use of personal information released by a person or collected about him requires the explicit a priori approval of the original individual "owner" of the information, and that this consent cannot be delegated to an agent or machine.[40] The details of the DPD are complex and changing.[41] For instance, it made exceptions to this rule for many areas, such as when the data is needed for the purposes of research, public health, or law enforcement, among others. In January 2012, the European Commission passed draft legislation that would update the existing data protection law. This legislation includes an "opt-in" provision. "As a general rule, any processing of personal data will require providing clear and simple information to concerned individuals as well as obtaining specific and explicit consent by such individuals for the processing of their data."[42] Data shows that information about a person is used many times each day by a large variety of users. Hence, if such a policy were systematically enforced, each

Internet user would have to respond to scores if not hundreds of requests each day even for uses of nonsensitive information. It seems that in this area, as in many others, the way the DPD rules survive is by very often not enforcing them. Whenever I meet Europeans, and following public lectures in the European Union, I ask if anyone has been ever requested to consent to the use of personal information that they had previously released. I have found only one person so far. He said that he got one such request—from Amazon. Other sources indicate that compliance is at best "erratic."[43] The penalties for violating the DPD seem to be miniscule and rarely collected. No wonder a large majority of the EU public—70 percent—fears that their personal data may be misused.[44]

In short, neither of these approaches is satisfactory.

2. Mending the Crazy Quilt

There are a large number of laws, regulations, and guidelines in place that deal with limited particular usages of personal information beyond the collection point. However, a very large number of them deal with only one dimension of the cube and often with only one element of cybernation, limiting either storage, analysis, or distribution. The laws reflect the helter-skelter manner in which they were introduced and do not provide a systematic doctrine of cyber privacy. They are best viewed as building blocks, which, if subjected to considerable legal scholarship and legislation, could provide the needed doctrine. They are like a score of characters in search of an author.

One of the key principles for such a doctrine is that the legal system can be more tolerant of the primary point spot collection of personal information (a) the more limited the volume (duration and bandwidth) of the collection[45] and (b) the more limited and regulated cybernation is—holding constant the level of sensitivity of the information. (That is, much more latitude can be granted to the collection and cybernation of insensitive information, stricter limitations can be placed on highly sensitive information, and a middle level of protection can be established in between). The same holds for the threat level to the common good.

In other words, the cyber age privacy doctrine can be much more tolerant of primary collection conducted within a system of laws and regulations that are effectively enforced to ensure that cybernation is limited, properly supervised, and employed for legitimate purposes—and much less so, if the opposite holds. One may refer to this rule as the *positive correlation between the level of permissiveness in primary collection and the strictness of controls on secondary usage of personal information.*

Another key principle is a ban on using insensitive information to divine the sensitive (e.g., using information about routine consumer purchases to divine one's medical condition), because this is just as intrusive as collecting and employing sensitive information.[46] This is essential because currently such behavior is rather common.[47] Thus, under the suggested law, Target would be prevented from sending coupons for baby items to a teenage girl after the chain store's analysis of her recent purchases suggested she might be pregnant.[48]

Kerr correctly points out that it would be exceedingly difficult to cover the private sector by drawing on the Fourth Amendment and points, instead, to the 1986 Electronic Communications Privacy Act (ECPA) to show that Congress can enact laws that protect people from intrusion both by the government and by private actors.[49] To further advance the cyber age privacy doctrine, much more attention needs to be paid to private actors. Privacy rights, like other rights, are basically held to be a source of protection against the government, to protect people from undue intrusion by public authorities. However, cybernation is increasingly carried out by the private sector. There are corporations that make shadowing Internet users—and keeping very detailed dossiers on them—their main line of business. According to Slobogin,

> Companies like Acxiom, Docussearch, ChoicePoint, and Oracle can provide the inquirer with a wide array of data about any of us, including: basic demographic information, income, net worth, real property holdings, social security number, current and previous addresses, phone numbers and fax numbers, names of neighbors, driver records, license plate and VIN numbers, bankruptcy and debtor filings, employment, business and criminal records, bank account balances and activity, stock purchases, and credit card activity.[50]

And these data are routinely made available to the government, including the FBI.[51] Unless this private cybernation is covered, the cyber age privacy doctrine will be woefully incomplete.[52]

Given that private actors are very actively engaged in cybernation and often tailor their work so that it might be used by the government (even if no contract is in place and they are, hence, not subject to the limits imposed on the government), extending the privacy doctrine beyond the public/private divide is of pivotal importance for the future of privacy in the cyber age. Admittedly, applying to the private sector similar restrictions and regulations that control the government is politically unfeasible. However, as one who analyzes the conditions of society from a normative viewpoint, I am duty bound to point out that it makes little sense to maintain this distinction.[53] Privacy will be increasingly lost in the cyber age, with little or no gain for the common good, unless private actors—and not just the government—are more reined in. To what extent this may be achieved by self-regulation, changes in norms, increased transparency, or government regulation is beyond the scope of this chapter.

For this doctrine to be further developed, laws and court rulings ought to be three-dimensional.[54] Laws and court cases must specify not only whether a particular collection of personal information is a "search," but also what level of sensitivity can be tolerated and to what extent the information may be stored, massaged, and distributed. This may seem—and is—a tall, if not impossible, order. However, as is next illustrated, a considerable number of measures are already in place that are, in effect, at least two-dimensional. However, these suffer from the fact that they have been introduced each on their own and do not reflect an overarching doctrine of privacy; hence, they reveal great inconsistencies that need to be remedied. I cannot stress enough that the following are only selective examples of such measures.

One should note that a very early attempt to deal with the issue—basically, in terms here used, by banning a form of cybernation—utterly failed. In 2003, Congress shut down the Pentagon's Total Information Awareness (TIA) program, which was created to detect potential terrorists by using data mining technologies to analyze unprecedented amounts of personal transaction data. However, a report by the *Wall Street Journal* in 2008 revealed that the most important components of the TIA were simply "shifted to the NSA" and "put in the so-called black budget, where it would receive less scrutiny and bolster other data-sifting efforts."[55]

Minimization is one way of addressing the volume issue, as pointed out by Swire in his groundbreaking article on *Jones* and mosaic theory.[56] Accordingly, when the FBI taps a phone, even for an extended period of time, the intrusion can be reduced significantly if the FBI either stops listening when it hears that the conversation is not relevant to the investigation (e.g., a child is calling the suspect under surveillance) or locks away those segments of the taped correspondence that turn out to be irrelevant.[57] For this rule to be integrated into the doctrine, it may be waived for insensitive information. That is, there would be no need to minimize if the child asked, say, to watch TV, but there would be a need to minimize if she asked, say, about medical news concerning a family member.

Another example of a safeguard against excessive privacy intrusions is the requirement that certain content be *deleted* after a specific time period. Most private companies that utilize CCTV erase video footage after a set number of days, such as after a week. Admittedly, their reasons for doing so may be simply economic; however, the effect is still to limit the volume of collection and potential for subsequent abuse. Note that that there are no legal requirements to erase these tapes. However, such laws should be considered. (Europeans are increasingly recognizing a "right to be forgotten.") It would be in the public interest to require that footage be kept for a fixed period of time, as it has proven useful in fighting crime and terrorism, but also to ban under most circumstances the integration of the video feed into encompassing and cybernated systems of the kind Microsoft has developed.

The treatment of private local CCTVs should be examined in the context of the ways other such spot collection information is treated. Because the bandwidth of information collected by toll booths, speed cameras and radiation detectors is very narrow, one might be permitted to store it longer and feed it into cybernated systems. By contrast, cell phone tracking can be utilized to collect a great volume and bandwidth of information about a person's location and activities. People carry their phones to many places they cannot take their cars, where no video cameras or radiation detectors will be found, including sensitive places such as political meetings, houses of worship, and residences. (These rules must be constantly updated as what various technologies can observe and retain constantly changes.)

Regulations to keep information *paper bound* have been introduced for reasons other than protecting privacy, but these requirements still have the effect of limiting intrusiveness. For example, Congress prevents the Bureau of Alcohol, Tobacco, Firearms and Explosives (ATF) from computerizing gun records when such information is collected during background checks.[58] In 2013, an amendment to the anti-insider trading STOCK Act exempted 28,000 executive branch staff from having to post their financial disclosure forms "online in a searchable, sortable and downloadable format."[59] These bans remind one that not all the privacy measures that are in place are legitimate and that some are best scaled back rather than enhanced.[60]

A related issue is raised by the cybernation of arrest records. Arrest records should be but are not considered highly sensitive information. When these records, especially those concerning people who were subsequently released without any charges, were paper bound, the damage they inflicted on most people's reputations was limited. However, as a result of cybernation, they have become much more problematic. Under the suggested doctrine, arrest records of people not charged after a given period of time would be available only to law enforcement officers. The opposite might be said about data banks that alert the public to physicians that have been denied privileges for cause, a very high threshold that indicates serious ethical shortcomings.

Many computer systems ("clouds" included) encrypt their data and a few have introduced audit trails. The cyber age privacy doctrine might require that all data banks that contain sensitive information be encrypted and include at least some rudimentary form of an audit trail.

Technologies can be recalibrated to collect the "need to know" information while shielding extraneous but highly sensitive information from observation. For example, when law enforcement collects DNA samples from convicted criminals or arrested individuals, FBI analysts create DNA profiles using so-called "junk DNA" "because it is not 'associated with any known physical or medical characteristics,' and thus theoretically poses only a minimal invasion of privacy."[61] Storing these "genetic fingerprints" in national databases is much less intrusive than retaining blood samples, which contain the entirety of an individual's DNA sequence. In 2013, the TSA stopped its use of body scanners that revealed almost-nude images, using instead scanners that produce "cartoon-like" images on which the scanners mark places hidden objects are found.[62] This did not affect the volume of collection, but lessened the sensitivity of the content.

Other measures must address the fact that often data can be "re-identified" or "de-anonymized." In 2006, AOL released the search records—stripped of "personal identifiers"—of over 600,000 people. An investigation by the *New York Times*, however, demonstrated that intimate information—including names and faces—can be gleaned from such purportedly anonymous data. This risk is mitigated by the development of statistical methods that prevent such undertakings, such as "differential privacy," which allows curators of large databases to release the results of socially beneficial data analysis without compromising the privacy of the respondents who make up the sample.[63]

Many more examples could be provided. However, those noted here may suffice to show that, while there are numerous measures in place that deal with various elements of the privacy cube, these have not been introduced with systematic attention to the guiding principles needed for the cyber age.

2

More Coherent, Less Subjective, and Operational

In Chapter 1, I outlined a a cyber age privacy doctrine, or a CAPD, that seeks to account for important differences between the paper age and the digital one.[1] This chapter attempts to show that the CAPD provides a coherent normative doctrine that can be employed by the courts and legislatures and that is more systematic, less subjective, and at least as operational as the prevailing privacy doctrines. It deals with the right to privacy vis-à-vis the U.S. government rather than as a protection from intrusions by private actors such as corporations. Section A summarizes and develops the previously published doctrine. Section B compares the coherence and objectivity of the CAPD to those of other doctrines and indicates the ways the CAPD can be operationalized.

A. The Cyber Age Privacy Doctrine Revisited

The advent of the cyber age—also referred to as the digital revolution—requires a new privacy doctrine. The main—although not the only—reason for this requirement is that the proportion of privacy violations that result from secondary usages of personal information compared to those that result from primary collection has radically changed. Most privacy violations in the paper age resulted from primary collection; most violations in the cyber age result from secondary usages of information that has been legally collected. If a collection was deemed legal in the paper age, there were very sharp limits, at least in practice, on the additional uses of the information.[2] Thus, the danger that permission would be abused was relatively limited. In the cyber age, functional limits on data abuse are fewer and secondary usages proliferate.

The difference in the extent of secondary usages between the paper age and the cyber age is of such magnitude that one is hard put to find a measurement or analogy to express it. The difference is much greater than the difference between the impact of a hand grenade and that of a nuclear bomb. Indeed, most secondary analyses conducted via the Internet within a very short period of time could not be carried out at all in the paper age. Because this point is crucial to all that follows, and because people have become so accustomed to the cyber age's information facilities, a simple example follows to illustrate the transformation's scope. Interpol's database of lost and stolen travel documents includes more than 39 million entries reported by 166 countries.[3] When travelers pass through airport security, authorities can determine in a split second whether the passports they carry are on the Interpol list.[4] Such an operation would have been unimaginable as recently as two decades ago. Peter Cullen, Fred Cate, Viktor Mayer-Schönberger, and Craig Mundie, among others, have pointed to the rising problem posed by secondary usages of personal information and have suggested ways forward for governments and the private sector.[5]

However, most relevant court cases in the United States deal mainly with the primary collection of personal information, much of which falls into the category of "spot collection." (This chapter uses the term "spot collection" to mean the collection of a very small amount of information about one limited facet of an individual's conduct that is neither stored nor cybernated in any other ways—for instance, the information collected by tollbooths that immediately erase data once the computer has established that the proper toll has been paid.) These cases concern whether the collection of information through drug testing, wiretaps, screening gates at airports, DNA sampling, breathalyzers, and so forth constitutes a search in Fourth Amendment terms; that is, they concern whether collection should be freely allowed or should require authorization by a distinct institution following given procedures. Notable cases include *Katz v. United States*,[6] *Terry v. Ohio*,[7] *United States v. White*,[8] *United States v. Knotts*,[9] *United States v. Karo*,[10] *Kyllo v. United States*,[11] *United States v. Jones*,[12] and *Florida v. Jardines*,[13] among others. The courts, in these and other such cases, do not address the fact that information that has been legally collected may be used later to harm the privacy of the individuals involved. A privacy doctrine suitable for the cyber age must address both primary collection and subsequent secondary usages of information. Details follow, but as a general principle the government can allow some kinds of personal information to be freely collected and used without causing undue risks to privacy. Some other kinds of information might be considered private and therefore should not be collected or used unless a specific authority, following specific procedures, grants an agent a license to do so. In other cases, collection of some information should be allowed, but the ability of the government to carry out secondary usages should be limited or banned. To express this notion in terms of the expectation of privacy, an individual suspected of a crime should expect to be questioned by the police but should also be able to expect that their answers will be locked away if they are found innocent.

Several overarching legal doctrines do address the issues raised by secondary usages and cybernation. This chapter addresses two of these. First, the third-party doctrine holds that once a person has knowingly relayed information to a third party, sharing this information with law enforcement officials by the intermediate party does not constitute a Fourth Amendment search and therefore requires no warrant. The Supreme Court ruled in *United States v. Miller*[14] and *Smith v. Maryland*[15] that business records such as financial documents and records of phone numbers dialed are not protected from warrantless collection by law enforcement agencies under certain circumstances.[16] The Court also held that law enforcement's collection of the content of conversations between suspects and third-party informants is not presumptively unconstitutional, because those third parties could pass along the information to the police even without technological assistance.[17] Richard A. Epstein summarizes the third-party doctrine as follows: "The received judicial wisdom is that any person who chooses to reveal information to a third person necessarily forfeits whatever protection the Fourth Amendment provides him."[18]

The third-party doctrine is particularly problematic in an age of cybernation, because third parties can share information with others and combine it with still more information, resulting in detailed and intimate dossiers of innocent people unsuspected of crimes. Given that more and more information about people is in the hands of third parties due to the extensive number and scope of transactions and communications carried out in cyberspace and stored in the cloud,[19] if the third-party doctrine is allowed to stand, precious little will prevent the government from intruding on the privacy of American citizens. Individuals constantly leave behind them a trail of data with every click of a mouse; "data exhaust" akin to the vapors left behind a car.[20] Will Thomas DeVries points out that one of the key characteristics of the "digital revolution" for privacy is that "every interaction with the Internet, every credit card transaction, every bank withdrawal, every magazine subscription is recorded digitally and linked to specific individuals. [...The] impact of the digital age is so deep and pervasive that expansion of a single area of privacy law is unlikely to adequately address the problems. Since the digital age affects every aspect of privacy, it requires an evolution not just in the existing framework, but in the very conceptual and legal status of privacy."[21] (Many other scholars have also criticized the third-party doctrine. [22])

Another doctrine that speaks to the cybernation challenge in effect takes the opposite tack. It assumes that personal information belongs to the person to whom it applies, that the individual has a right to keep this information private that extends beyond primary collection, and that only the person can agree to secondary usages of the information—even when they have already consented to primary collection.[23] (Some refer to this doctrine as the fundamental rights approach; others refer to it as the information as property approach.) Europeans often cite this doctrine, which is at the foundation of the European Data Protection Directive and the European General Data Protection Regulation[24]; for this reason, this chapter refers to it as the European approach.

At first blush, it may seem that the European approach governs a wholly different area of privacy than the CAPD, which, to reiterate, deals with the right to privacy vis-à-vis the government rather than vis-à-vis private actors such as marketers and data brokers. The European model is nonetheless relevant because it turns out that, to generalize, governments regularly use personal information collected by private actors. Thus, the limitations imposed on private actors affect the scope of government intrusions. To illustrate: It is difficult to imagine the conditions, short of an extreme national emergency, under which the U.S. government could require all American citizens to turn over to law enforcement records of their purchases on the Internet, their e-mails, and their other transactions. However, because the same American citizens "disclose" this information to private corporations, and these corporations aggregate this information, the government, in effect, can use the resulting databases without seeking permission for these secondary usages.[25]

The drafters of the European approach, however, realized that if the European Union were to follow its limitations on secondary usages, many common goods would suffer greatly. They hence introduced a large number of areas in which secondary usages of personal information do not require consent.[26] According to the European approach, the government need not ask the consent of those whose personal information it collects and uses if the collection is for a considerable list of public purposes, such as public health or security. Thus, the Data Protection Directive excludes from its requirement that "controllers" gain personal consent to record and process personal information in any instance in which "the processing is carried out under a contract, or in the context of a quasi-contractual relationship of trust, with the data subject and is necessary for its discharge," when "the data come from sources generally available to the public and their processing is intended solely for correspondence purposes," and when "the controller of the file is pursuing a legitimate interest, on condition that the interest of the data subject does not prevail."[27] According to Joris van Hoboken, "The exceptions have to become the rule, which means that the meaning of the fundamental right, even if one would want to more categorically protect certain core interests, is eroded."[28] Moreover, the European approach survives only because it is infrequently enforced. And privacy statements provided by businesses and other agents that rely on the collection of consumer data are frequently extensive and draw on legal terminology, making them incomprehensible to most users. Consent means little if those who give it cannot possibly understand what they are allowing.[29] In short, the European approach seems not to provide a sound foundation for dealing with secondary usages. In other words, it is hardly a sound approach.

If the third party doctrine is truly followed, it leaves little privacy; if the European approach is truly followed, it undermines the common good.[30] It seems clear that a different doctrine dealing with cybernation is needed—one that is neither as permissive as the third-party doctrine or as strict as the European approach. This monumental task, for which I can provide at best a first approximation, is what this chapter sets out to chart in the following pages.

Moreover, even initial collection, including limited spot collection, calls for a new doctrine. Since *Katz v. United States* (1967), the courts have relied on both individual and societal expectations of privacy to determine which types of primary collection are constitutional. For reasons spelled out in my original paper on this topic,[31] the expectation of privacy is an indefensible basis for such judgments. Briefly, the expectation-of-privacy test is tautological: If a judge rules that a person's expressed claim to an expectation of privacy meshes with the judge's ideas about what a "reasonable" individual might expect, then the expectation of privacy exists. If the judge rules otherwise, the person should not have "reasonably" expected to have privacy.[32] Thus, whether or not Mr. Katz, a gambler, expected or did not expect to have privacy when he placed bets in a public phone booth is immaterial; he had a reasonable expectation of privacy if a court divined that he had a reason to have it, and he had no such expectation if a court ruled otherwise.

The societal expectation of privacy is also subjective. The test presumes that the courts can evaluate such expectations, yet judges have no way of knowing what a "reasonable" person would actually expect—and reasonable people differ greatly in their expectations. (For more about the tautology of the "reasonableness" concept, see Chapter 3.)

The need for a new privacy doctrine stands out in particular when one reviews the major court cases that currently provide the basis for deliberations on privacy by the public, law enforcement authorities, policy makers, and courts. Each case seems to rely on a different rationale; some of these rationales are obsolete, and some are surprisingly idiosyncratic. (A harsher critic would call them capricious.) One case ruled unconstitutional the planting of a GPS device because it constituted trespassing; another ruled unconstitutional the use by law enforcement of a thermal imaging device on the grounds that it was not a technology then in common public use; others have referenced the "special needs exception"; yet another held that the presence of a police narcotics dog at the door of a residence was sufficiently dissimilar to the act of a private citizen knocking on the door as to be unconstitutional without a warrant. Whatever limitations the preliminary CAPD outlined below has, it is surely less subjective than judges' intuitions as to what constitutes a reasonable expectation of privacy and is surely more systematic than the curious amalgam of court cases that currently govern the field.

The liberal communitarian philosophy—which holds that individual rights, including privacy, have the same fundamental standing as the common good and that neither a priori trumps the other, and which is described more fully in the first chapter of this book—provides an excellent normative foundation for just such a new doctrine. Each society works out a balance between the two claims, which is often adjusted to take into account changes to the society's international environment, domestic social developments, and changes in technology. (For another discussion of this balance as it applies to privacy and security, see Chapter 7.)

As Chapter 1 mentions, the Fourth Amendment exemplifies the liberal communitarian approach because it prohibits only *unreasonable* searches and seizures and provides a mechanism for according rights or the common good priority.

The following analysis focuses exclusively on one of the two elements of liberal communitarianism: individual rights, in particular the right to privacy. It seeks to outline the principles that should guide the courts and legislatures in determining the type and scope of intrusions by the government that should be tolerated, banned, or allowed only with prior authorization. The analysis holds constant the level of contribution to the public good accomplished by these intrusions and studies only changes in the level of privacy violation. This "control" is necessary because, as already indicated, if there were a significant change in the threats facing the common good—whether an increase or a decrease—the balance between privacy and security (and other common goods) would have to be recalibrated. I have explored this subject elsewhere, including in Chapter 7 of this book.[33]

B. Operationalization of the Key Principles

1. *Key Considerations*

Before proceeding to specify the CAPD, it is necessary to outline a few major considerations that underlie the endeavor. First, during a discussion of the original paper, several colleagues asked whether the suggested doctrine is a proposed means of interpreting the Constitution or a framework for passing legislation and formulating public policy. They inquired whether the CAPD is a means of interpreting the Fourth Amendment or a public policy model. After all, as these legal scholars pointed out, a world of difference exists between the former, which deals with the courts, existing case law, and the ways in which judges deliberate, and the latter, which involves the democratic processes of the legislature.[34]

While there are indeed significant differences between these two institutions, the CAPD is an articulation of normative principles that apply to and affect both. That changes to normative precepts affect both institutions is highlighted by developments in other arenas. In the wake of changes to the United States' moral culture precipitated by the civil rights movement, the Supreme Court overturned *Plessy v. Ferguson* in the landmark case *Brown v. Board of Education*, and Congress passed the Voting Rights Act of 1965. Recent changes to the moral culture, in which libertarian principles led some to take similar positions to those held by liberals regarding same-gender marriage, have led to court cases, most notably *United States v. Windsor*,[35] in which the Court ruled that interpreting the words "marriage" and "spouse" to apply only to heterosexual couples violates the Due Process Clause. This decision was followed by legislation by various states. Furthermore, the same moral shift has led to changes in federal administrative rules regarding the extension of tax and other benefits of marriage to same-gender couples. A similar sea change must now take place with respect to the normative conceptualizations of privacy and its application by the courts and legislatures. Several preliminary steps in this transformation are outlined below.

Second, an important thesis underlying the following is that as a privacy doctrine is adapted to the grand transformation of information from the paper age to the cyber age, society can become more tolerant of spot collection of personal information if at the same time it becomes more restrictive of secondary usages—that is, if it restricts cybernation of the information collected—without suffering a net increase in privacy violations. This is true of all circumstances except for limited conditions, such as the arrival of a tyrant. There is an inverse relationship between the two elements: The less cybernation, the more primary collection is possible without causing an increase in privacy violations. The more cybernation is allowed, the less collection can be tolerated if the demands of the common good do not call for a net increase in intrusions.[36]

Third, the challenge my colleagues posed when asking me to specify the new doctrine is completely justified, indeed essential, if the courts and legislatures are to apply this doctrine. However, the law often functions without taking definitions to the third decimal point and by leaving much interpretation to the discretion of law enforcement authorities, lower courts, and regulators. For example, in cases of drunk driving, the moment a suspect has actually been taken into custody and must be read her Miranda rights seems to remain unclear.[37] The Bill of Rights defines the right of a U.S. citizen to be tried by an "impartial" jury rather than merely a judge in criminal cases; however, the definition of "impartial" is far from specified.[38] These examples illustrate that the courts function more or less effectively without excessive precision. In short, specification is essential, but the law functions quite well without carrying it to the level demanded by the sciences. This is particularly the case given that, to reiterate, only a first approximation of the new doctrine is here attempted.

Above all, this chapter will attempt to show that the CAPD is more coherent and less subjective than the prevailing doctrines.

2. The Three Dimensions of the Cyber Age Privacy Doctrine "Cube"

The new doctrine draws on three principal criteria: the volume, level of sensitivity, and degree of cybernation of information collected. Together, these dimensions form a cube; a conceptualization that contrasts with the idea of information collection as a "mosaic."[39]

i. Volume
Volume concerns the total amount of information collected about a person by one agency or actor. The measurement refers to one agency or actor because the law should differentiate between that which *one* agent may collect and that which may be collected in total by *multiple* agents. The law may greatly limit, for example, the information a health inspector, an OSHA specialist, or an IRS agent may individually collect about a given restaurant—but the total amount they and others are allowed to collect will obviously be much more extensive.

This dimension of the CAPD is relatively easy to operationalize, and it encompasses two components. The first of these is *quantity*, which simply concerns the amount of information collected, whether this is measured in terms of e-mails, phone records, text messages, or, better yet, in terms of megabytes of information.[40] The length of time of a wiretap is in effect a crude but useable measurement of quantity. It is crude because there is no strong correlation between the amount of time a tap is in place and the amount of information collected; parties under surveillance may vary a great deal in the extent to which they use a tapped phone. At the same time, the metric is useable because it may not be practical to allow the authorities to collect a specific number of calls or bytes of information. There are many precedents for this approach. For example, at present the courts limit wiretap orders to thirty days and grant additional thirty-day extensions in accordance with the Wiretap Act.[41]

In the case of e-mails and similar data, the Electronic Communications Privacy Act of 1986 dictates that upon receiving a preservation request from law enforcement officials, telecommunications providers shall "take a 'snapshot' of available electronic records in the account which is held pending legal process (such as a search warrant, court order, or subpoena). [This information is] held for 90 days until legal process is obtained and submitted to the provider. The 90 day preservation can be extended once more for an additional 90 days."[42] In short, there is ample precedent for using time as a crude approximation for determining whether a collection of personal information is acceptable or excessive.

Taking volume into account rather than merely asking whether a single collection constitutes a search finds precedent in *United States v. Jones*. This case concerned the installation of a GPS tracking device on Jones's car after a warrant obtained by the state had expired. The GPS tracking device was activated constantly for twenty-eight days. The majority opinion did not address the length of the GPS surveillance, but the concurring opinion by Justice Alito stated that the length of the surveillance was a factor in his ruling that this tracking constituted a Fourth Amendment search. Alito wrote, "The use of longer-term GPS monitoring in investigations of most offenses impinges on expectations of privacy. For such offenses, society's expectation has been that law enforcement agents and others would not—and indeed, in the main, simply could not— secretly monitor and catalogue every single movement of an individual's care for a very long period. In this case, for four weeks, law enforcement agents tracked every movement that the respondent made in the vehicle he was driving. We need not identify with precision the point at which the tracking of this vehicle became a search, for the line was surely crossed before the four-week mark."[43]

For the first approximation purposes attempted here, it is unnecessary to provide specific numbers to limit various information collection operations. (For a brief discussion of the difficulties associated with arriving at such specific numbers, see Chapter 1.) This is a task for another time. This chapter instead recognizes the most significant difference regarding volume: the difference between "spot collection," the one-time collection of one or very few discrete pieces of information over a very short period of time, such as those carried out by speed cameras at intersections, Transportation Security Administration (TSA) agents during airport security screenings, and many CCTV cameras—and prolonged collections, including wiretaps or continuous GPS tracking.[44] Those familiar with these issues may protest that certain spot collection programs are relatively comprehensive because they capture all individuals who walk through an area, for example. However, as will be emphasized later, a large quantity of information can be collected without meaning being divined from the information through cybernation.

The second concept of relevance to the dimension of volume is bandwidth, a term here used to refer to the collection of different types of information from or about a single subject. Collection of only one type of information, such as the metadata associated with an individual's phone calls, e-mails, or locations, constitutes narrow bandwidth collection. By contrast, the collection of several kinds of information—say, phone call content *and* voice data *and* text message content *and* e-mail content—constitutes broad bandwidth collection. Bandwidth is important because when it is broad it allows law enforcement to gain a much more comprehensive profile of the person under surveillance than when it is narrow, and diminishes privacy much more.

One might argue that when high quantities of data are collected, even on a narrow bandwidth as is the case with "big data," a comprehensive picture of the individual's private life is created. However, these concerns do not take into consideration the limits on cybernation proposed by this chapter; limits that would apply particularly strongly to sensitive information. These limits—including a ban on cybernating insensitive information in order to divine sensitive information—would restrict, legally speaking, the ability to create such comprehensive pictures when they would be detrimental to privacy. For the CAPD to be effective, all three dimensions—volume, sensitivity, and cybernation—must be applied simultaneously. Considering high-volume collections without simultaneously considering the sensitivity of the information involved and the level of cybernation to which it is subjected produces an incomplete picture of the privacy violations—or lack thereof—caused by a particular collection. Unbounded "big data" may well blur the difference between collection and cybernation; however, "big data" limited by the suggested restrictions would be much less prone to damaging privacy.

Just as the length of time surveillance is conducted or the number of messages collected by a search are crude but still useable measures of volume, so is the number of collection methods a crude but useable measure of bandwidth. This is the case because some surveillance methods are able to gather many more types of information about an individual than others; for instance, taping phone conversations (which captures the complete content of a call and thereby potentially includes many kinds of information) is a much broader bandwidth method than the collection of phone records (which captures who called whom, at what time, and from where). For traffic control purposes, it is possible to measure the speed at which a vehicle travels in public places without taking a picture of the person sitting next to the driver in the front seat. (Incidentally, for this reason, speed cameras are set lower, at the level of license plates.) A more sophisticated measure of bandwidth could take these differences into account.

ii. Sensitivity
The concept that some kinds of information are more sensitive than others has been often articulated by privacy scholars and operationalized by lawmakers, albeit using a variety of terms. Additional terms that have been applied include "intimate information" or "revealing information," and some scholars have defined them in terms of the level of risk or the extent of harm to one's privacy.[45]

Two levels of distinction between types of information must take place in order to enable the development of a nuanced understanding of sensitive information. The first level of distinction is very basic; it establishes the realm of information to be considered, distinguishing personal information from other forms of information that either do not deal with persons or have been de-identified or anonymized in ways that are presumed to be irreversible.[46] (Paul M. Schwartz and Daniel J. Solove note that "numerous federal statutes turn on [the distinction between personally-identifiable information (PII) and other forms of information]."[47]) Briefly, all nonpersonal information is inherently not sensitive. Revealing the amount of rain that falls in Spain, for example, endangers no one's privacy. The issue of sensitivity concerns the second level of distinction, which distinguishes among the various kinds of personal information.

Quite a few leading privacy advocates rail against all collection of personal information by the government. In response to the introduction of airport screening gates to prevent skyjackings, an American Civil Liberties Union (ACLU) staff counsel wrote that "the new [general] passenger screening regulations are completely inconsistent with the values safeguarded by the fourth amendment."[48] The ACLU has also opposed speed cameras at traffic intersections, calling them "extreme,"[49] as well as the use of cookies on federal government websites[50]—without which many Internet activities might well be impossible. (In fact, the ACLU website itself now uses them.[51]) Some strong privacy advocates concede that exceptional conditions exist under which surveillance and other forms of personal information collection might be justified, but they hold that the onus is on the government to prove such conditions are in place.[52] They furthermore set a very high bar that must be cleared before they consider an intrusion to be justified.

Instead, the CAPD and many others hold that not all personal information can or should be accorded the same level of protection, and that the more sensitive the information an agent seeks to collect, the more measures to protect privacy should be implemented and the higher the public interest must be before collection of the information is legitimated.

What should determine the sensitivity of a piece of information? Measurements of sensitivity should reflect the values of the society in question. Some societies, for example, consider expressions of affection or intimacy, let alone sexual relations, highly sensitive and private matters, while other societies take a less constricted approach. For instance, Americans consider women's breasts to be highly private, while many Europeans consider it acceptable to go bare on the beaches. In another example, some societies hold that disputes should be resolved in private, while the Mambila people of Nigeria consider it important to "act within the sight of everyone" because "[only] witches act secretly, eating behind closed doors or conducting financial transactions at night . . . [and quarrels] held in public are seen as dangerous since witches may 'hide' behind them."[53] This is not to say that any particular society's standards of privacy are superior, merely that they are affected by the particular normative culture of the given society and are a major factor in determining what the legal system considers sensitive personal information.

In each society, the legislatures and courts operationalize these differences in the normative standing of different kinds of information. In the United States, this ranking has been mainly brought about by Congress enacting piecemeal a series of specific laws. In 2003, for example, Congress enacted the US Health Insurance Portability and Accountability Act of 1996 (HIPAA). This law treats protected health information (PHI)[54]—the identifying information that would associate an individual with records of their medical conditions—as highly sensitive, with restrictions on the disclosure of psychotherapy notes being especially tight.[55] The Department of Health and Human Services' description of HIPAA's Privacy Rule states that HIPAA "creates, for the first time, a floor of national protections for the privacy of [consumers'] *most sensitive* information—health information."[56]

Following the Supreme Court's decision in *United States v. Miller*,[57] Congress passed the Right to Financial Privacy Act, which restricted financial institutions' ability to share "any record [...] pertaining to a customer's relationship with the financial institution."[58] Several other specific kinds of information have been deemed sensitive enough to protect through federal law. Records of video rentals were protected, for example, through the Video Privacy Protection Act of 1988 following the revelation of a list of movies rented by the family of Supreme Court nominee Robert H. Bork.[59] Additional types of information entitled to a higher level of protection include education records (Family Educational Rights and Privacy Act), genetic information (the federal Genetic Information Nondiscrimination Act of 2008[60]), and journalistic sources (Privacy Protection Act of 1980[61]). The FTC has issued guidelines indicating that sensitive data includes five categories of information: financial information, health information, Social Security numbers, information collected from children, and geo-location information such as the information gleaned from cell phone tracking.[62] Legislation has been advanced—but not yet passed—to grant this status to information about race and ethnicity, religious and political beliefs, sexual orientation, and "unique biometric data."[63] In all these cases, the kinds of information considered sensitive were denoted rather than defined. That is, lists of examples rather than defining attributes defined each category. To illustrate with a more concrete example, listing the names of all qualifying cities would constitute denotation, whereas stating that any population center with more than 100,000 people would constitute definition.

When Congress seeks to classify particular types of personal information as more sensitive than others, it often relies on the rationale that privacy law should prevent economic or physical harm; that is, sensitive information is defined as information the unauthorized disclosure of which could cause tangible harm.[64]

Sensitivity has also been operationalized through enumeration of the specific kinds of information that are or are not sensitive rather than through the articulation of a defining attribute. HIPAA, for example, defines protected healthcare information as that which "is maintained or transmitted in any form ... and relates to the past, present, or future physical or mental condition of an individual; provision of health care to an individual, or payment for that health care; and identifies or could be used to identify the individual."[65] The Fair Credit Reporting Act of 1970 likewise regulates the disclosure of "consumer reports," which encompass any information "that bears on a consumer's credit worthiness or personal characteristics when used to establish the consumer's eligibility for credit, insurance, or for a limited set of other purposes."[66]

The courts have also contributed to the categorization of sensitive information. In *United States v. Jones,* Justice Sotomayor joined the majority opinion and issued her own concurring opinion, in which she articulated that even short-term GPS monitoring impinges on privacy rights because it "reflects a wealth of detail about . . . familial, political, professional, religious, and sexual associations."[67] The courts also have limited government powers to obtain information on individuals' book purchasing histories beginning with *United States v. Rumely*, famously in the case of *In re* Grand Jury Subpoena to Kramerbooks & Afterwords, Inc., in which the government unsuccessfully attempted to subpoena Monica Lewinksy's purchase records.[68]

There is a need for Congress to review these myriad laws and more systematically and consistently categorize the types of personal information that should be better protected than others. However, for the purpose of a first approximation, there is little question that sensitivity can be operationalized, and there is an extensive categorization of the sensitive types of most personal information from this viewpoint.

iii. Cybernation

Cybernation is the most novel component of the CAPD. Sensitivity was a full-blown factor in the paper age; volume was also an issue in the paper age, although it was of much less pressing importance due to practical limitations. However, the kinds of processing and secondary usages of personal information engendered by cybernation, as well as their effects on privacy, were inconceivable in the paper age. Cybernation is also the most consequential factor of the three dimensions because it is the one directly tied to the grand shift from focusing on primary collection to prevent privacy violations to focusing on the privacy violations caused by secondary uses. Cybernation includes storing, "collating," analyzing, and distributing items of information.

Privacy is much better protected if the information collected is not *stored*. If a tollbooth payment system immediately erases the information that a given car was at the booth at a certain point in time once the computer has verified payment of the toll, the risk that the information will be abused to violate privacy is very limited compared to a situation in which the same information is stored. The same is true for speed cameras that erase the car's identifying information once it has been established that it traveled below the speed limit. (Although CCTV maintains information somewhat longer, and what they collect has greater bandwidth, they too could neither store nor share the information and in fact should erase it after short periods of time.)

By contrast, all data banks, which keep records about even a single particular personal item—what magazine the person reads, which bar the person frequents—pose a higher risk to privacy than nonstoring mechanisms.

This element of cybernation can be operationalized, as a first order of approximation, by determining whether or not the information is stored or instantly erased. As a second order of approximation, if information is stored, the degree of cybernation can be approximated by determining the length of time the information is kept.

In regard to the collation of information about the same person, especially when building dossiers is involved, the risk to privacy increases when information collected and stored by one agent is combined or linked with information collected and stored by other agents. For example, some civil rights advocates much prefer state or regional databases to federal ones, not taking into account that these local databases are often linked to each other and thus in effect act like one central database. Although the volume of information in each state or local database may well be lower than the amount stored in a national database, that the state and local databases are linked to each other means that those who have access to them have access to the same amount of information that would be gathered in a national database. Many civil rights advocates would also be greatly concerned if the FBI amassed information on most Americans, including those who have not been charged with any crime or are under any suspicion—but they pay less mind to data brokers who keep such information and sell access to the FBI.[69] The law must adapt to these technological developments, treat all linked databases as if they were one, and impose limits on collection accordingly.

The risk to privacy is also lower when personal information is merely stored and collated than when the same information is analyzed to ferret out other information and draw conclusions about the person not revealed by the raw data. For first approximation purposes, this dimension can be operationalized by considering whether such analysis is carried out at all; that is, analysis is contrasted with the mere use of raw information. Additional measurements are needed to establish how much and what kinds of new information are gained through analyses. In particular, it is essential that when the collection and use of sensitive information is banned, so too should analysis that is used to divine the same information from insensitive information be banned. It seems that no such bans are yet in place. They are clearly needed because without them limits on collecting and cybernating sensitive information face the grave danger of being eroded.

Finally, risks to privacy are fewer when information collected by one party such as a hospital or the IRS, even information that has been analyzed or compiled into dossiers, is *inaccessible* to other parties or is only made available to other parties under special circumstances. The Federal Privacy Act of 1974, for instance, limits the conditions and the degree to which information collected, stored, and analyzed by a given federal agent may be shared with other federal agents or other parties. Distribution and access are two facets of the same process; sharing information captures both forms of cybernation. Here, the relevant measures are (1) the scope of limits set by laws and by regulations; (2) the volume of information that is shared; and (3) the number of agents with whom the information is shared. For instance, Social Security numbers were initially meant to be used only by the Social Security Administration and were not meant to be shared with other federal agents—let alone other parties. However, their wide use today makes it easier to collate personal information from different sources and draw a much more comprehensive and therefore privacy-violating picture of an individual.

To complete the analysis, it is essential to add a variable that at first blush seems rather different; one might well hold that it should be treated as a fourth dimension that would turn a cube composed of volume, sensitivity, and cybernation into a four-dimensional tesseract. For first approximation purposes, this additional variable is treated as negative cybernation and is referred to as *accountability*. All the various "places" from which personal information is collected, stored, and analyzed have at least some barriers to use by unauthorized parties. These include simple devices such as passwords and locks on computers as well as more powerful ones such as firewalls and encryption. Although all of these have a technological element, human factors are also involved. Audit trails, for example, are useless if no one reviews the records detailing who accessed the data or determines whether the information has been inappropriately employed.

All accountability measures limit one element of cybernation or another. Some limit sharing, such as making Medicare data inaccessible; others limit storage by ensuring that data stored for longer than a given period is erased; others limit analysis, such as by de-identifying the information. The more extensive and effective accountability measures are, the less cybernation occurs and the better privacy is protected. It follows that the stronger the accountability measures associated with a given database, the fewer privacy violations will occur even if the volume of information is high, the information's sensitivity is considerable, and a significant degree of collation and analysis takes place. Conversely, if accountability is deficient, more violations of privacy will occur even if volume is relatively low, information is relatively insensitive, and collation and analysis are not particularly extensive. This demonstrates once again that collection is less important in the cyber age than the scope of—or limits on—secondary usages, a ratio that is expected to continue to grow significantly due to improvements in artificial intelligence.[70]

That the level of accountability can be operationalized can be gleaned from various debates about whether it is sufficient. For instance, it has been widely argued that the Foreign Intelligence Surveillance Court (FISC) is much too lenient because it has reportedly declined a mere 0.03% of the government's requests for court orders authorizing intentional electronic surveillance of individuals in the United States.[71] Defenders of the Foreign Intelligence Surveillance Act, which governs such courts, argue that the number is low because FBI agents, fearing damage to their careers if their requests are rejected, file only well-justified requests or because the FISC often returns requests for reassessment rather than rejecting them outright.[72] This debate suggests that the data used to assess the FISC's strictness need to be fine-tuned but also shows that accountability can be operationalized.

In June 2013, Gen. Keith Alexander, director of the National Security Agency (NSA), testified to the House Intelligence Committee that the surveillance programs revealed by Edward Snowden had contributed to averting "potential terrorist events more than 50 times since 9/11."[73] However, an investigative report by the New America Foundation found that in the 225 cases of "individuals recruited by al-Qaeda or a like-minded group or inspired by al-Qaeda's ideology, and charged in the United States with an act of terrorism since 9/11" the NSA's collection of phone metadata belonging to U.S. persons was of minimal help.[74] More specifically, the phone metadata collection program "appears to have played an identifiable role in initiating, at most, 1.8 percent of these cases," while surveillance of non-US persons was helpful to 4.4 percent of the cases, and "NSA surveillance under an unidentified authority" was helpful to 1.3 percent.[75] At *most*, therefore, NSA bulk surveillance programs may have substantially contributed to 7.5 percent of these investigations—or 16 cases in 12 years.[76]

A report released by the Justice Department in 2004 held that 179 convictions or guilty pleas stemming from 310 investigations of terrorism were materially helped by the Patriot Act.[77] However, a later investigation by *The Washington Post* found that despite President Bush's claims that "federal terrorism investigations have resulted in charges against more than 400 suspects, and more than half of those charged have been convicted," only 39 individuals were by June 2005 actually convicted of terrorism or other crimes against national security.[78] Of the 1,755 delayed-notice search warrants authorized by the Patriot Act from 2006 to 2009, only 15 (or 0.8%) were related to terrorism investigations.[79] More than 1,600 warrants were related to drug investigations.[80]

To see the utility of these kinds of data for the operationalization of accountability, one only has to imagine that the figures ran the opposite way and demonstrated that the collections prevented a considerable number of significant terrorist attacks. That is, if the evidence instead showed that the various acts by U.S. authorities that entailed privacy intrusions served to abort many major terrorist attacks, most Americans would see them as justifiable. In any case, the data clearly allow citizens and their elected officials to assess threat levels, the value of countermeasures, and the effectiveness of accountability.

3. Combined Considerations

The next step is to combine and apply the three key considerations. One may argue that such an application of the CAPD reveals that this is a much more complex doctrine than the expectation of privacy rule. This is indeed a valid observation. However, given the explosive growth of the role of information in our private and public lives, its complexity, and the continued expansion of cybernation, a doctrine of privacy of commensurate complexity seems unavoidable. Not all possible permutations are reviewed here, as this chapter is merely a first attempt to operationalize the CAPD; however, the main ones are considered on a first approximation basis. Moreover, while one day it may well be possible to numerically score each of the elements of the cube, for the preliminary purposes at hand it will suffice to evaluate each in terms of "zones," referring to each variable as "low" or "high." In the process it shall be seen that while the CAPD often leads to rulings and legislation similar to those currently in place, in some cases it calls for reversing the prevailing law. Moreover, in all cases the CAPD provides a rationale for court rulings and legislation concerning privacy that is much less subjective and much more systematic than the rationales now in place. This is an audacious claim; however, it is one that is surprisingly easy to document.

Only select sub-cubes are next examined, given that the application of the approach to the other sub-cubes seems self-evident.

i. Low Volume, Low Sensitivity, No Cybernation
The CAPD holds that low volume, low sensitivity, noncybernated personal information collection should be tolerated at the current level of common good because the risks to privacy are low and the contributions to the common good engendered by such collection are very often middling to high. (By "tolerated," I mean that the law should allow such collection of information unless there are specific reasons to object to it; the default should

The Cyber Age Privacy Doctrine "Cube"

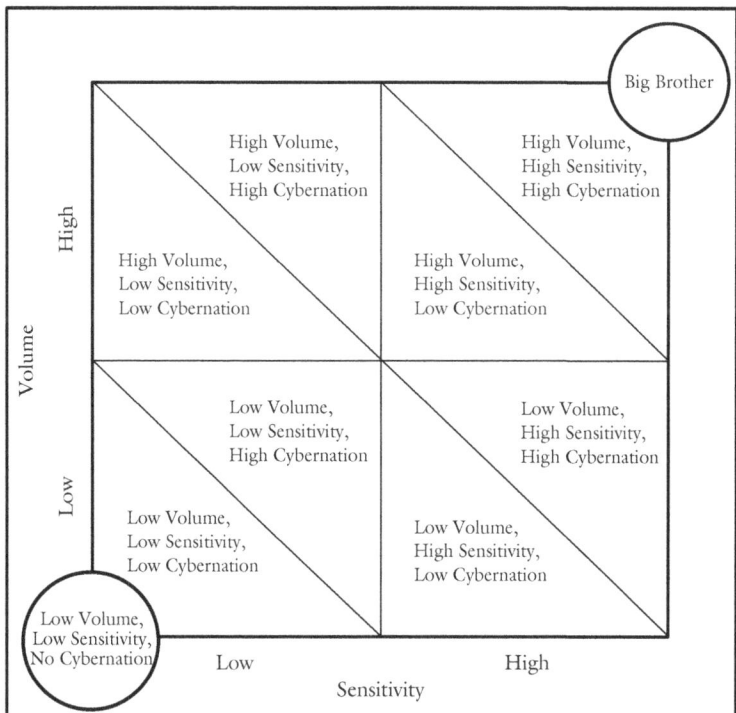

1. Low Volume, Low Sensitivity, No Cybernation: Tollbooths
2. Volume, Low Sensitivity, Low Cybernation: Collection of phone records
3. Low Volume, Low Sensitivity, High Cybernation: Household purchases of specific, routine consumer goods
4. Low Volume, High Sensitivity, Low Cybernation: Airport screening devices that reveal the body
5. High Volume, Low Sensitivity, High Cybernation: Select cloud storage
6. High Volume, High Sensitivity, Low Cybernation: Health records
7. Low Volume, High Sensitivity, High Cybernation: Leaks of the names of CIA agents
8. High Volume, High Sensitivity, High Cybernation: The sale of data brokers' "dossiers" to the government

be an a priori permission to proceed. In colloquial terms, one might say that "you do not have to love it to allow it.") Courts should allow the collection of such personal information and Congress should pass laws along the same lines. Examples include tollbooths,[81] license plate readers,[82] police body cameras,[83] airport screening gates,[84] breathalyzers,[85] general traffic stops,[86] random mandatory drug testing,[87] health and safety inspections, and many others. (Note that components of all of these examples have been contested by civil libertarians.)

In many of these situations as a rule, no cybernation takes place due to informal practices, the technological limitations of collection mechanisms, or lack of a motive for cybernation—not necessarily because cybernation is banned unless authorized by a judge. This at least used to be the case for many tollbooth and speed camera operators who had no reason to keep the information, let alone combine it with other information or analyze it. However, typically the statutes and court rulings stemming from the prevailing privacy doctrine contain nothing to prevent secondary usages of such information.[88] The absence of cybernation is either driven by custom or economic motives that are easily reversed if data brokers, the press, or even divorce lawyers seek access to the information. The CAPD indicates that points of collection should be required to erase information immediately after primary use or after a given period of time and should be banned from sharing it. An exception should be included for situations in which public authorities declare a state of emergency, such as after a terrorist attack, during the commission of a crime, or if a child has been kidnapped. Even during such a period of exception, sharing should be limited to the relevant public authorities. To reiterate, this is often already the de facto practice; however, for each category of information collection, it should be made law.

Before turning to the examination of a similar category—that of high volume, low sensitivity, and low cybernation collection—that requires distinct treatment, this chapter shall show that the CAPD provides a more systematic rationale for cases of information collection than does the odd assortment of prevailing rationales employed by the courts to deal with the very same cases. The courts provide different rationales for different cases that seem highly similar from the CAPD point of view, because they all concern low volume, low sensitivity, noncybernated information—and should therefore be allowed.

In *Schmerber v. California* the court ruled that blood tests used to evaluate a suspect's blood-alcohol content are not an undue imposition on an individual's privacy per se; although the collection of a blood sample constitutes a Fourth Amendment search, there was justification for the police officer to arrest the defendant and collect a sample, on the grounds that "the test chosen to measure petitioner's blood-alcohol level . . . *imposed virtually no risk, trauma or pain*, and was performed in a reasonable manner by a physician in a hospital."[89] In *Kyllo*, the Court ruled that because the thermal imaging device used to survey the temperature in a private home was not yet in general public use, the use of that device without a warrant under the circumstances constituted an unreasonable search. In the Court's words, "where, as here, the Government uses a device that is not in general public use, to explore details of a private home that would previously have been unknowable without physical intrusion, the surveillance is a Fourth Amendment 'search,' and is presumptively unreasonable without a warrant." This represents yet another rationale and includes an undefined term—"general public use"—as pointed out by Justice Stevens's dissent, which held, "the Court's new rule is at once too broad and too narrow, and it is not justified by the Court's explanation for its adoption.... [How] much use is general public use is not even hinted at by the Court's opinion, which makes the somewhat doubtful assumption that the thermal imager used in this case does not satisfy that criterion." A great deal depends on the nature of the device. If it is able merely to establish the temperature in select rooms of the house and thus determine whether it was abnormally high—which may indicate the presence of a marijuana "grow room"—the device's bandwidth is quite narrow. By contrast, thermal imaging that produces detailed images of the interior of the house based on temperatures—showing where individuals are sitting, whether they are in bed, and so forth—would be considered to have a high bandwidth. The former should be allowed; the latter should not.[90] There is no inherent reason to cybernate this information for the purposes of divining additional information about that individual if nothing incriminating is found.

Still another rationale was used by the Supreme Court in their ruling in *Florida v. Riley*,[91] which examined the question of whether aerial surveillance from a helicopter constituted a violation of Riley's Fourth Amendment rights. The Court held that, because Riley had no reason to believe that his criminal activity was not visible from the air by a private citizen operating an aerial vehicle from a height of 400 feet, Riley had no reasonable expectation of privacy in this situation.[92] The height of 400 feet was selected because this was the height at which the police helicopter in the case flew over Riley's property; the Court ruled that it was entirely possible that "any member of the public" could have flown at that height over the property. It is at least implied that had a lower-flying plane been used, privacy might have been granted.

Moreover, the special protection for private residences is of less value than it used to be. In the cyber age, one can violate privacy just as much or more in public spaces (e.g., by using parabolic microphones to eavesdrop on conversations in a public park) as in the home (e.g., by using a thermal device or narcotics sniffing dogs to measure temperatures or detect the presence of controlled substances in a private residence). For this reason, the CAPD should be applied as if privacy were a bubble that surrounds a person and that is carried wherever he or she goes.[93] Although many sensors are being added daily to the home—such as smart thermostats, computers, security cameras, and smart televisions—the tapping of these sensors by the government becomes excessively intrusive on privacy only when the information collected is either inherently sensitive or is considered jointly, or cybernated. It is only by examining all of these streams of information that the government can piece together a comprehensive picture of the activities of the individuals contained within.

Moreover, the bubble should be extended to the digital person—that is, to dossiers or profiles kept by the government. This deserves some elaboration. An individual in a remote ranch in Montana may be free from most physical surveillance by speed cameras, CCTVs, and other technologies. However, his communications and Internet transactions could still be used to form an invasive profile. The CAPD therefore holds that the personal bubble—including personal information amassed by the government—should only be legally penetrated if law enforcement follows given procedures and is authorized by specified authorities, in line with the very communitarian Fourth Amendment or if only low volumes of narrow-bandwidth information, low in sensitivity, are collected and subjected to low or no cybernation. *In other words, the CAPD should extend the right to privacy to the virtual person.*[94] The right to privacy should encompass both parts of the person—the virtual and the offline. (Calling the offline "real" disregards the increasing importance to more and more people of the virtual part of life.)

In *Jones* the Court drew on two considerations. First, attaching the GPS to a car, considered a private space, amounted to trespassing. The CAPD would not accept this consideration for reasons previously indicated. Second, the Court opened the door to the CAPD by suggesting that the surveillance undertaken in *Jones* was too long. However, given the narrow bandwidth of information collected and its relatively low sensitivity, the CAPD would allow the surveillance at issue in *Jones* if cybernation was properly limited.

In *Katz v. United States*, the Court used yet another rationale to find that Katz had a reasonable expectation of privacy in a public telephone booth. By contrast, the CAPD would hold that the police should be allowed to install surveillance equipment on telephone booths on the grounds that the amount of information collected is low, the bandwidth of the information collected is limited (and could be further curtailed by using the same procedures used in wiretaps and other methods of intelligence collection subject to minimization techniques[95]), and the information collected is not of a sensitive nature. The CAPD would be more concerned if, even if Katz was found innocent, law enforcement were to keep and share a record that he was a suspect; the CAPD would therefore allow this kind of warrantless tapping only if proper accountability measures were in place to ensure this information is not shared inappropriately.

In *Florida v. Jardines*, the Court ruled that the use of a narcotics-sniffing dog to detect illegal drugs in a suspect's home was a search per the Fourth Amendment because the dog was brought onto the private property—albeit only onto the porch. The Court found that unlike a law enforcement official knocking on the door, the act of introducing a police dog into the area was different from the typical, expected actions of a private citizen and was therefore a search. In the majority opinion, Justice Scalia wrote,

> We have accordingly recognized that "the knocker on the front door is treated as an invitation or license to attempt an entry, justifying ingress by solicitors, hawkers and peddlers of all kinds." This implicit license typically permits the visitor to approach the home by the front path, knock promptly, wait briefly to be received, and then (absent invitation to linger longer) leave. Complying with the terms of that traditional invitation does not require fine-grained legal knowledge; it is generally managed without incident by the Nation's Girl Scouts and trick-or-treaters. Thus, a police officer not armed with a warrant may approach a home and knock, precisely because that is "no more than any private citizen might do." But introducing a trained police dog to explore the area around the home in the hopes of discovering incriminating evidence is something else. There is no customary invitation to do *that*."[96]

A court following the CAPD would arrive at the opposite conclusion, given that the information collected was of low volume and very narrow bandwidth. Concern with cybernation would be the same as with *Katz*. Once again it must be emphasized that the CAPD views the home as no more inherently private than the public sphere—or, more precisely, the CAPD seeks to protect information, not places. The premise of the CAPD is that sensitive information derives its status not from where it is revealed, but from the content contained in the revelation. A great many things that occur in the home may be sensitive, but this is not due to their occurrence in the home. Measuring the level of air pollution in a home would entail much less of a privacy violation then reading a person's e-mails, even if they were sent from a bench in a public park. Of course, the opposite may also take place; much more highly sensitive information could be collected from the home than from speed cameras. The key variables are the volume, the level of sensitivity, and the extent of cybernation—not where the information was first collected.

United States v. White concerns the use of a government informant wearing a hidden microphone to record conversations. The Court ruled that this act does not constitute a Fourth Amendment search because the suspect has no reasonable expectation that the undercover informant would not pass along the information to law enforcement—a still different rationale than those offered in other Fourth Amendment cases. A court following the principles of the CAPD would come to the same conclusion as long as the authorities set limits on the length or number of conversations recorded, no other modes of surveillance were used simultaneously, and cybernation of the resulting information was properly limited through accountability measures.

The CAPD would also recognize a broad category of administrative and safety "searches" that collect a low amount of narrow bandwidth information but furnish critical contributions to a public good. Health inspections at restaurants fit into this category; the information collected by the health inspector is of low volume, with very few searches happening per year and specific types of information sought. The information collected is also of low sensitivity—indeed, most of it is not personal. Finally, there is little need to cybernate the information as long as the restaurant is in compliance with food safety laws; in the case of noncompliance, the information would only be cybernated with other health inspection information from the same restaurant to track progress. If kept for the purposes of public policy analysis, the information's identifying markers would be removed. This rationale seems more coherent, more systematic, and less subjective than the myriad diverse reasons given by the courts for authorizing administrative searches. Indeed, many legal scholars have bemoaned the complexity of administrative search jurisprudence in particular, calling it "incoherent," "abysmal," "devoid of content," a "conceptual and doctrinal embarrassment," and "chaotic at best."[97]

It is therefore clear that the criteria employed by the CAPD can be as operationalized as the criteria now used by the courts. It is similarly clear that the CAPD provides a much more systematic and less subjective set of criteria for distinguishing those intrusions that do not constitute a search in the Fourth Amendment sense from those that do.

ii. High Volume, Low Sensitivity, Limited Cybernation
The collection of information about a person over longer periods of time and at a high bandwidth should be tolerated as long as the information is lowly sensitive and cybernation is limited, in particular by strong accountability measures, because violations of privacy will be limited in these cases. This category includes the planting of beepers, tracking the location of cell phones, the long-term use of GPS tracking devices, and similar law enforcement projects. Again, it is useful to consider the similarities and differences between courts instructed by the prevailing privacy doctrine and a court whose rationale stems from the CAPD.

Consider, for example, the case of *Smith v. Maryland*. In this case, the police, without a warrant, installed a pen register that recorded all of the numbers that connected to the phone of a robbery victim who had begun receiving calls from her attacker. The Court ultimately ruled in this case that the suspect's expectation of privacy had not been violated, because the numbers he dialed had been passively received by the phone company, a third party. In this case, a court applying the CAPD would reach the same ruling—albeit with a different rationale for doing so. Such a court would find that the information collected was of low sensitivity because it does not include the content of the calls.

U.S. police departments sometimes use technology that "aggregates and analyzes public safety data in real time."[98] Developed by Persistent Surveillance Systems (PSS), helicopters or small planes are equipped with cameras that scan large parts of a city continuously and feed the images into a command center.[99] The planes also carry infrared cameras that can track people and cars under foliage and in some buildings.[100] The information is kept and analyzed in the command center maintained by the company. *The Washington Post* reported that "[the company that sells the system] has rules on how long data can be kept, when images can be accessed and by whom. Police are supposed to begin looking at the pictures only after a crime has been reported. Fishing expeditions are prohibited."[101] The amount of information this technology collects, its bandwidth, and its cybernation are significantly higher than those of tollbooths, speed cameras, and other similar technologies included in the previous category. The information's sensitivity is, generally, relatively low. The main privacy effects of this technology concern the scope and kind of cybernation involved. If the company's self-imposed rules are codified in the law—and the law is effectively enforced—the privacy implications of this and other such technologies would be limited and tolerable. If these conditions are not met, the use of such technologies should be prohibited because their use amounts to subjecting all people all the time to fishing expeditions. The main variable that differentiates that which can be tolerated from that which should be banned is not collection but rather the level of cybernation. (To reiterate, this chapter focuses on the harms to privacy of various government acts rather than on their contributions to the common good. Both elements must be considered, per liberal communitarianism, but this study holds constant the contributions to the common good accomplished by a particular use of surveillance.)

An even more telling case is that of Microsoft's Domain Awareness System (DAS), a technology that "aggregates and analyzes existing public safety data streams" from cameras, license plate readers, radiation detectors, and law enforcement databases.[102] The technology helps police keep an eye on suspects by providing their arrest records, related 911 calls, and local crime data, as well as by tracking vehicle locations. The DAS also makes it possible to tap into and rewind the city's thousands of CCTV camera feeds.[103] The DAS may also be expanded in the future to gain access to many additional CCTV cameras as well as to encompass facial recognition, cell phone tracking technologies, and even social media scanners.[104] The data assembled is cybernated in order to identify particularly suspicious individuals, their contacts, and their modi operandi. Data are to be deleted within five years, but material deemed to have "continuing law enforcement or public safety value or legal necessity" may be retained indefinitely.[105] The New York City Police Department has some accountability measures in place to limit access, with the "type of data each officer can view" being "tailored to their job duties,"[106] but it also shares "data and video with third parties not limited to law enforcement."[107] Oakland, California, has already operationalized the first phase of a similar system, and Baltimore, Maryland, and the United Kingdom already use similar technologies.[108]

The CAPD here alludes to the same conclusions drawn from the case of Persistent Surveillance Systems. The main difference between PSS's technology and the DAS is that the amount and bandwidth of information collected by the DAS is much greater. The critical variable is whether accountability measures sufficiently limit cybernation by guaranteeing no fishing expeditions occur and information is not unduly shared or abused.

The NSA's collection of phone call metadata raises numerous complex issues that cannot be adequately explored here.[109] However, the ways the CAPD would approach the program are illustrative. First of all, much discussion by those who follow the prevailing privacy doctrines has focused on the question of collection and on suggestions that the government should cease to collect this information and instead rely on phone companies to keep it. The CAPD would focus much more attention on the usages of the information. *If* it is true that the NSA collects only metadata and refrains from collecting the content of calls; that it collects a large volume of information of very narrow bandwidth and relatively low sensitivity, akin to addresses on envelopes; that the NSA has to gain approval of an FISC judge in order to examine the records associated with any particular individual; and that FISC is indeed strict in granting such permissions only when there is a compelling case, cybernation is well-limited and the program seems to pass muster. If one or more of these suppositions are not valid, it becomes much more difficult to justify the program given the United States' current security needs. To reiterate, the goal here is *not* to evaluate the program but rather to call attention to the key variable that should be employed in judging it—the extent of cybernation, which includes an assessment of the level of accountability that is in place.

iii. High Volume, Low Sensitivity, High Cybernation
The courts, in accordance with their focus on primary collection rather than on secondary usages, have allowed surprisingly high quantities of

wide bandwidth, highly sensitive, highly cybernated personal information to be collected by law enforcement. Once again, the discussion that follows assumes a constant level of threat to the public good and holds constant the benefits of surveillance programs.

The increasing use of drones by public authorities (privacy violations by private actors are beyond the subject of this chapter[110]) raises still more complex issues. On one hand, drones are mainly engaged in primary collection. From this viewpoint, if one applied *Jones*, the use of drones would constitute a search in Fourth Amendment terms because they collect large quantities of information. The CAPD would add that drones provide information that is of a much broader bandwidth than the information provided by a GPS. At the same time, drones are often used for purposes such as finding lost children or skiers or delivering help to stranded victims of earthquakes and floods—all acts for which consent by those involved can be presumed. What about their deployment for routine police surveillance? This issue is now being sorted out by regulatory agencies and the courts.

In one case, the court ruled wireless surveillance did not constitute a search, coming up with a different rationale than the ones previously used in the courts; in the course of events that led to this court case, the government used unmanned aerial vehicles in addition to wireless surveillance technologies. The case concerned a group of far-right extremists known as the Montana Freemen that issued in 1995 a "citizens declaration of war" against the U.S. government, occupied a 960-acre ranch in Montana following its foreclosure, and initiated an armed standoff with law enforcement.[111] The resulting case, *United States v. McGuire*,[112] held in part that federal agents had not violated the Freemen's right to freedom from unreasonable searches and seizures. "FBI agents could not have conducted on-site surveillance of the Freemen property because of its remote, rural location and group members' alertness to law enforcement activities, which created grave dangers. Agents also would have faced risks in executing any search warrant at the compound, because of the group's known violent propensity and undisputed possession of assault weapons. Federal agents would have had difficulty infiltrating the group with FBI informants [and interviewing] witnesses would have helped little."[113] Because direct surveillance posed a danger to the agents working on the case, and there were no alternative reasonable options available to the agents, the court ruled a number of search techniques constitutional under the circumstances, namely electronic surveillance. (The agents also used aerial surveillance to monitor the ranch.[114]) The CAPD would reach the same conclusion, but a court following the CAPD would hold that given the high amount and considerable bandwidth of the information collected, even of low sensitivity, drones should be allowed only if cybernation is limited.

iv. High Volume, High Sensitivity, Must Limit Cybernation
According to the CAPD, highly sensitive information should be collected only if there is a compelling public interest to do so. Here, too, the main issue is limiting cybernation rather than collection. The Social Security Administration, the Department of Health and Human Services, and the IRS all hold considerable amounts of sensitive personal information on the 300 million (mostly) innocent U.S. citizens. However, that their databases have been very rarely abused and the harm caused by violations has been limited shows that a considerable level of collection and cybernation of sensitive information can be tolerated when accountability is very high.

The same cannot be said about the databases kept by the FBI, local police departments, and the Department of Homeland Security. These all have been abused, as revealed by the Church and Pike committees and various leaks to the media. Some consequently argue that these collections should be greatly curtailed, if not abolished entirely. Civil libertarians have often objected to the details (or even the very existence) of such databases, including the Terrorist Screening Database—which includes the "No Fly List"[115]—and the federal DNA profile database, NDIS.[116] Although the rationales for these objections differ, they often reflect—aside from specific concerns, such as the belief that DNA profiles are particularly sensitive information—a sense that the government cannot be trusted. Even if the *current* government is trustworthy, many civil libertarians say, future governments may abuse the databases, and it is therefore best if no collection or storage occurs.

Discussion of the CAPD has so far focused on one of the two core elements of a liberal communitarian approach—rights, in particular the right to privacy—and has held constant the other element: the common good. This is necessary because a society that faces higher demands for the common good in the face of an epidemic or some other threat may well permit greater intrusions on individual liberties than a society that faces lower or declining demands for the common good. However, it must be noted in closing that the analysis is incomplete without accounting for the contributions to the common good called for in a given society at a particular moment in history. To stay with the present example, given that many crimes in the United States remain unsolved and that DNA databases help to close a growing number of such cases, DNA databases should be maintained or expanded with the caveat that accountability measures should be improved. Numerous suggestions to this effect have been made and need not be explored here.[117] (That accountability can be effectively operationalized has already been demonstrated.)

Some have expressed fear that a future government might remove such protective measures and abuse the information held in databases. This is best addressed not by ceasing collection and storage, but by building up the foundations of civil society, public education, and voluntary associations and by ensuring that public goods are provided. The greatest threats to democracy have historically arisen not from abuses of databases but from fearful populations that sought stronger authorities because the existing ones did not adequately protect them from violent crime, civil war, and external enemies. Russians suffering from a breakdown of law and order welcomed Vladimir Putin. In Egypt, the citizens restored a military regime. Many Iraqis increasingly yearn for stronger, more authoritarian leadership. New Yorkers and Angelenos, suffering from high rates of violent crime in the 1980s, supported police departments that made short order of individual rights, as well as the commissioners and mayors who appointed them. After 9/11, a majority of Americans favored adopting more limited interpretations of the Constitution in order to protect the nation from further attacks.[118]

All this suggests that a doctrine concerned with protecting privacy should allow for sufficient security—and other public goods, such as public health in the face of a pandemic—and should permit the collection and cybernation of the data necessary to do so, so long as the usages of this data are properly supervised and curbed. Prohibiting all collection is not the answer.

C. In Conclusion

The prevailing privacy doctrines—of which this chapter has discussed two—reflect concepts suitable to the paper age, in which the main issue was whether primary collection of information unduly intruded on individuals' privacy. Such intrusions required court authorization in line with the Fourth Amendment. This chapter has argued that, since the advent of the cyber age, many more risks to privacy emanate from the secondary usages of personal information—regardless of how it is collected. No prevailing privacy doctrine of which I am aware addresses this pressing issue. The notions of a "reasonable expectation of privacy" and affording special status to the home are obsolete. The CAPD would take into account the risks to privacy posed by the collection of high volumes of information of high sensitivity, paying particular attention to the extent to which the information is cybernated—processed, analyzed, and shared. The CAPD would also consider the degree to which various accountability mechanisms impose limitations on cybernation. This analysis has focused exclusively on one of the two core elements of a liberal communitarian philosophy—namely, the effects on the right to privacy, holding constant the contributions to the common good. Several illustrations have been provided to demonstrate that such an analysis can be operationalized and that the CAPD provides a much less subjective and more systematic rationale for the courts and legislatures to consider when creating law than the rationale presently available. Such a doctrine would form part of a long-overdue refinement to the concept of privacy, allowing it to stay relevant in the cyber age.

3

Eight Nails into *Katz*'s Coffin

The U.S. courts keep drawing on *Katz v. United States* in their rulings about whether or not privacy has been violated, which, from a social science viewpoint, is difficult to comprehend. The case is clearly based on untenable sociological and psychological assumptions. Moreover, many fine legal scholars have laid out additional strong reasons that establish beyond a reasonable doubt that it is unreasonable to draw on "the reasonable expectation of privacy" as a legal concept. Continuing to draw on this concept, especially in the cyber age, undermines the legitimacy of the courts and hence of the law. This chapter reviews these arguments in order to further nail down the lid on *Katz*'s coffin so that this case—and the privacy doctrine that draws on it—can be allowed to rest in peace.

1. *Katz* Is Tautological

The reasonable expectation of privacy standard is tautological and circular. Both the individual and the societal expectations of privacy depend on judicial rulings—and judges, in turn, use these expectations as the bases for their rulings. Mr. Katz had no reason to assume a conversation he conducted in a public phone booth would be considered private or not until the court ruled that he had such an expectation. In other words, when the court holds that it heeds the vox populi—it actually follows the echo of its own voice. Several leading legal scholars find *Katz*'s tautological nature highly problematic. Richard Posner, for example, notes that "it is circular to say that there is no invasion of privacy unless the individual whose privacy is invaded had a reasonable expectation of privacy; whether he will or will not have such an expectation will depend on what the legal rule is."[1] Richard A. Epstein maintains that it is "all too easy to say that one is entitled to privacy because one has the expectation of getting it. But the focus on the subjective expectations of one party to a transaction does not explain or justify any legal rule, given the evident danger of circularity in reasoning."[2] Anthony G. Amsterdam points out that the "actual, subjective expectation of privacy . . . can neither add to, nor can its absence detract from, an individual's claim to Fourth Amendment protection. If it could, the government could diminish each person's subjective expectation of privacy merely by announcing half-hourly on television that [. . .] we were all forthwith being placed under comprehensive electronic surveillance."[3]

Jed Rubenfeld adds wisely that if expectations of privacy are "tied to what a citizen ought to know about the norms specifically governing policemen, Fourth Amendment law becomes a self-validating logical circle in which any police practice can be justified (through its own adoption) and in which any judicial decision will vindicate reasonable expectations of privacy (because the judicial decision will itself warrant the expectations or lack of expectations it announces)."[4] By this logic, he concludes, a totalitarian society with government informants in every workplace and household would satisfy the current interpretation of the Fourth Amendment as long as citizens knew of the informants' existence.

Richard Seamon extends this criticism, arguing that a "reasonable expectations" test that concludes certain government privacy intrusions do not count as searches "for Fourth Amendment purposes" is "not just circular" but causes a "downward spiral" in which restrictions on searches and seizures are reduced over time by virtue of the Court's semantics, thereby undermining the "purpose of the Fourth Amendment's guarantee against unreasonable searches."[5] According to Seamon, the reasoning used by the Court in *Kyllo v. United States* (2001) demonstrates that the justices are aware of and struggling to deal with this dilemma.[6] The majority admitted, "The Katz test—whether the individual has an expectation of privacy that society is prepared to recognize as reasonable—has often been criticized as *circular, and hence subjective* and unpredictable."[7]

A social scientist finds it difficult to comprehend why the well-established observation that *Katz* is tautological is not itself sufficient to lay *Katz* to rest. One may argue that it is not tautological, because it is not just an "expectation of privacy" that the Court recognizes but rather a "reasonable expectation of privacy." However, it is far from clear what "society" or a particular segment thereof would consider "reasonable" in any given situation, and the Court is left to again rely on its own shadow by deciding on a case-by-case basis whether an expectation of privacy is one "society is prepared to recognize as reasonable." An expectation of privacy is reasonable (or unreasonable) if the Court rules that it is.

2. *Katz* Is Subject to Institutional Influence

The reasonable expectation of privacy standard is not only highly malleable by the courts but also subject to influence by various institutions. Statements made by elected officials, especially the president; laws enacted by Congress; and normative positions developed by religious authorities and public intellectuals all affect what people consider private or an open book.

Along these lines, Shaun Spencer points out that the "expectation-driven conception of privacy" facilitates the erosion of privacy overall by "large institutional actors."[8] That is because powerful institutions can influence the social practices that affect the expectations of privacy by "changing their own conduct or practices, by changing or designing technology to affect privacy, or by implementing laws that affect society's expectation of privacy." When employers monitor their employees' computer use, for example, they "diminish the expectation of privacy in the workplace," and when "merchants routinely sell consumers' personal data, they diminish the expectation of privacy in one's transactional information."[9]

Jed Rubenfeld shows that the reasonable expectation of privacy test would allow a simple government announcement that "all telephone calls will henceforth be monitored" to deprive people of their "reasonable expectations of privacy in such calls," retroactively justifying the decree.[10] Put simply by Erwin Chemerinsky, the government "seemingly can deny privacy just by letting people know in advance not to expect any."[11] Richard Julie adds importantly that the ability of legislation and regulation to affect the scope of the Fourth Amendment in this way violates "the core principle of constitutional law, that the legislature may not alter the Constitution by an ordinary statute."[12]

The fact that the vox populi is affected not only by the courts but also by myriad other institutions hardly makes it a more reliable, trustworthy, or independent criterion for determining a reasonable expectation of privacy.

3. Surveys to the Rescue?

Assuming judges try to live up to the standard they have set and seek to figure out what reasonable people consider private beyond looking into their own innards, to whom should they turn? There are some 318 million Americans. Even if one excludes minors and others whose opinion, for one reason or another, the law excludes, a very hefty number remains. There is no reason, and even less evidence, to hold that they all will have the same expectations.

Some have suggested that using opinion surveys could make the reasonable expectation of privacy test less circular and subjective by actually finding out what people believe.[13] Christopher Slobogin and Joseph Schumacher, for example, have suggested that the Supreme Court should factor empirical sources such as opinion surveys into the *Katz* test.[14] Henry Fradella et al. likewise hold that survey data would provide "a far richer and more accurate" basis for determining whether an expectation of privacy is "objectively reasonable."[15]

Actually, social scientists tend to agree that such surveys may not provide a reliable and appropriate tool on which the courts can rely. Survey results vary depending on who is surveyed, the ways the questions are worded, the sequence in which the questions are asked, the context in which they are asked (e.g., at home versus at work), and the attributes of those who ask the questions. Even when the same question is asked of the same people by the same people twice—rather different answers follow.[16] These inherent problems are magnified when one seeks opinions about complicated, abstract issues like "privacy" and "surveillance."[17]

People tend to give answers they believe are expected of them, especially regarding issues that are politically or ideologically loaded. Respondents tend to exaggerate their income, popularity, happiness, and political engagement.[18] Merely changing the phrasing of a question yields rather different results. A 2003 poll, for example, found that a strong majority (68 percent) of Americans favored invading Iraq, but this number fell to a minority (43 percent) if the question mentioned the possibility of American military casualties.[19] Along the same lines, a medical study found that patients were almost twice as likely to reject surgery when the predicted outcome was phrased in terms of "mortality rate" rather than "survival rate."[20] These issues present formidable obstacles.[21] Although social scientists have developed ways to mitigate them,[22] the technological transition from land lines to cell phones and e-mail, coupled with the declining response rate to polls, has made accurate polling increasingly difficult.[23]

Particularly problematic is which "society" the court has in mind when it seeks to determine the societal expectation of privacy.[24] Katz's peers? The members of his gambling community? Or the United States of America?

4. Expectation or Right?

Drawing on the societal expectation of privacy in effect amounts to drawing on consensus. This raises a preliminary question: How much agreement is needed to qualify as "societal" expectation? Full (100 percent) consensus is not found in any complex society, even in ones much smaller than the United States. Is 80 percent agreement enough? 66 percent?

Much more important is the question of whether the courts should be guided by consensus even when it can be accurately determined. True, consensus has a prudential value. The courts should not stray too far from public consensus, lest they lose their legitimacy or stray into a bitter culture war of the kind that occurred around reproductive rights (i.e., decisional privacy). However, consensus has no standing from a normative viewpoint when rights are at stake. Thus, if an overwhelming majority of Americans agrees that women are second-class citizens or that "fishing expeditions" by the police are fully acceptable because "those who did nothing wrong have nothing to hide," this does not mean that a court should accept this consensus and allow it to trump the court's judgment as to what the Constitution entails and what is just and right. In short, from a normative viewpoint, the expectation of the public as to what and who may or may not be searched should matter little.

Because this point is crucial, an elaboration follows. *Katz* runs roughshod over the elementary but essential fact that the political system of the United States is not a simple democracy but a liberal democracy. (Others call it a republic; I would prefer the term constitutional democracy.) The essence of this regime is that it combines two very distinct principles. The first is majoritarianism: when we differ, we choose our course based on which position garners more votes. The other is liberalism: the Constitution deliberately ensconces a set of rights, which makes them so difficult to amend that one should usually take them as a given. To put it differently, the majority can decide what it prefers as long as this preference does not entail violating anybody's rights to speak freely, to worship, to assemble, to petition, and so on. The right to privacy is one of these rights. Therefore, if the courts were to decide whether or not a particular situation is covered by the right to privacy based on what the masses told a pollster or what the judges somehow determine the societal view to be—the courts would in effect turn a right, which is sacrosanct and etched in stone, into a mass-driven, pliable, ephemeral, ever-changing concept.

Thus, Americans showed very little concern for privacy in the months that followed the 2001 attacks on the American homeland and much more concern when no new major attacks took place over the next ten years.[25] They are sure to change their collective mind one more time if another attack occurs. If one bases a constitutional right on such a foundation, one might as well tie it to a weather vane. In short, if *Katz* is allowed to stand and the courts continue to follow it, the result would be to reduce the right of privacy at best to a mere matter of democratic majority rule.

I write "at best" because *Katz* is not more aligned with the democratic half of the United States regime than it is with the liberal/constitutional half. In deciding those public policy issues that are not covered by rights and are subject to majority rule, the United States counts noses. That is, each person has a vote—whether or not the person is reasonable. *Katz* is decided without any actual votes by the public; the people's views are merely divined.

In short, *Katz* is either a convenient fiction or a serious violation of the most basic principles of our polity and should be allowed to expire, the sooner the better.

5. Two Is Less Than One

Originally, the *Katz* test consisted of two "prongs" used jointly to determine whether a "reasonable expectation of privacy" existed. In the words of Justice Marshall Harlan, "[T]here is a twofold requirement, first that a person have [sic] exhibited an actual (subjective) expectation of privacy and, second, that the expectation be one that society is prepared to recognize as 'reasonable.'" Of course, such a dual standard raises the question: what is a court to do when the two standards conflict? If the courts ignore the first standard on the grounds that every defendant will claim an expectation of privacy in the matter at hand—why introduce two prongs in the first place? In practice, courts have increasingly ignored the first prong as a "practical matter," for "defendants virtually always claim to have a subjective expectation of privacy" and such claims are difficult to disprove.[26] Thus, David Cunis notes that the Court "summarily dismissed" the first prong of the *Katz* test in *California v. Greenwood*, *California v. Ciraolo*, *Oliver v. United States*, and *Maryland v. Smith*.[27] Thus, the expectation of privacy test relies almost exclusively on an objective determination of society's "reasonable" expectations. Among all *Katz*'s flaws, this two-pronged approach is a relatively minor one; it merely adds one more reason to allow this legal concept to fade away.

6. *Katz* Is Confronted by the Cyber Age

The reasonable expectation of privacy standard is further undermined by recent technological developments. The rise of social media, Facebook in particular, is a prime example of this trend. Originally intended and promoted as a social networking tool for college students, Facebook's privacy implications have expanded in line with its broadening user base and functionality. There are numerous documented instances of employees being fired over material they, not expecting to share it with their employer, had posted on Facebook.[28] A 2012 survey found that more than a third of employers use Facebook and similar sites to screen candidates,[29] while

70 percent of business managers admitted ruling out candidates based on information found online.[30] Although such evaluations are typically done through Internet searches or mutual friends, in some cases employers and universities demand Facebook passwords from current or prospective employees and students, a practice that, despite controversy, remains legal in the majority of United States.[31] On the other hand, evading this scrutiny by restricting access to or removing personal information from Facebook may also hurt one's job prospects.[32] In addition, Facebook is monitored by intelligence[33] and law enforcement agencies.[34]

Following *California v. Greenwood*, in which the Supreme Court determined that material left outdoors in trash bags was accessible to the public and thus could not reasonably be expected to be private,[35] the Supreme Court has tended to find it reasonable to expect privacy only in acts or spaces unobservable to the general public.[36] As shown by Facebook, however, the evolution and mass adoption of new communications and other technologies tends over time to increase the public visibility of acts people consider private. The Supreme Court has in effect held in recent rulings such as *Dow Chemical Co. v. United States* that "the effect of modern life, with its technological and other advances, serves to eliminate or reduce a person's justified expectation of privacy."[37] Along these lines, Helen Nissenbaum notes that the "expectation of privacy" test prevents the Court from ruling against increasingly prominent practices of public surveillance, which include online public records, consumer profiling, data mining, and the use of location technologies such as radio frequency identification (RFID). This is because the test defines movement or activity in public arenas as "implicitly" abandoning "any expectation of privacy."[38] Nissenbaum views this as evidence that "prominent theoretical approaches to privacy, which were developed over time to meet traditional privacy challenges, yield unsatisfactory conclusions in the case of public surveillance."[39]

7. *Katz* Is Undercut by the Third-Party Doctrine

Katz is further damaged by the combination of recent technological developments with the "third-party doctrine." As stated in *United States v. Miller*, this doctrine asserts that the "Fourth Amendment does not prohibit the obtaining of information revealed to a third party and conveyed by him to Government authorities" and that "issuance of a subpoena to a third party does not violate a defendant's rights."[40] While it originally justified the police subpoena of a suspect's bank records, the third-party doctrine has since become a serious impediment to Fourth Amendment restrictions on new surveillance technologies due to the essential role third parties play over the Internet. As a result, argues Stephen Henderson, the "reasonable expectation of privacy" test in its current form threatens to "render the Fourth Amendment a practical nullity."[41] Whereas the Fourth Amendment requires a warrant for surveillance of personal paper mail, for example, the third-party doctrine leaves e-mail without similar protection.[42] This impelled Congress to legislate protection for e-mail with the 1986 Stored Communications Act, but advances in technology quickly rendered that law obsolete.[43] Likewise, Peter Swire warns that increasing use of the Internet, and thus third parties, to conduct phone calls may render the "expectation of privacy" test ineffective even for phone call wiretapping—the original subject of the *Katz* ruling.[44] In today's era of "big data," which Craig Mundie points out is characterized by the "widespread and perpetual collection and storage"[45] of personal information by third parties and in which individuals and businesses increasingly store information "in the cloud" rather than on their own devices, a traditional privacy paradigm based on secrecy is no longer relevant or useful. Several Supreme Court justices have acknowledged this flaw in Katz jurisprudence.[46]

8. *Katz* Stays Home

Katz will be mourned much less than one might expect given the excitement with which its arrival was greeted. At the time, *Katz* was said to be a "revolution"[47] and a "watershed in fourth amendment jurisprudence,"[48] and consensus quickly emerged that it was a "landmark decision that dramatically changed Fourth Amendment law."[49] This was, at least in part, because prior to *Katz* the boundary between that which was private (in the Fourth Amendment sense of requiring a warrant to be searched) and that which was not was largely based on the legal concept that one's home was one's castle, while that which was out in public was fair game for the state. *Katz* was held to have redefined this boundary such that, in the words of the majority opinion of the Court, whatever a person "seeks to preserve as private, even in an area accessible to the public" is protected by the Fourth Amendment, whereas that which "a person knowingly exposes to the public, even in his own home or office, is not." Yet the assertion that "the Fourth Amendment protects people, not places" did not create the expected privacy bubble that accompanies a person wherever she or he goes. In an important qualification, Justice Harlan noted from the onset that "what protection [the Fourth Amendment] affords to those people [...] requires reference to a place."[50]

Most important, as *Katz* was used as a precedent in case after case that followed, time and time again the courts recognized a reasonable expectation of privacy when the intrusions concerned the home—but not when the person or their communications were in public spaces, in effect reintroducing the property-based definition of privacy through a back door! As Daniel Pesciotta points out, the Supreme Court used *Katz* to maintain "steadfast support of citizens' privacy rights in the most private of all places—the home.[51] In the *Katz* ruling itself, the argument that Katz had a reasonable expectation of privacy in a phone booth hinged on the fact that he "occupie[d]" the phone booth and "[shut] the door behind him."[52] According to Justice Harlan, this made the phone booth a "temporarily private place," raising an implicit comparison to the only permanently private place: the home. In *United States v. Karo*, the Court justified denying the use of a tracking device within a house on the "basic Fourth Amendment principle" that "private residences are places in which the individual normally expects privacy."[53]

Justice Antonin Scalia's majority opinion in *Kyllo v. United States*, which denied the use of infrared technology to evaluate the contents of a house, made the case for a return to the home even more strongly. Justice Scalia drew heavily on an earlier 1961 case, *Silverman v. United States*, in writing that the "right of a man to retreat into his own home and there be free from unreasonable governmental intrusion" forms "the very core" of the Fourth Amendment, which "draws a firm line at the entrance of the house" based on "roots deep in the common law" that reveal the "minimal expectation of privacy."[54]

In the same post-*Katz* period, cases dealing with surveillance technology outside the home have rarely favored privacy interests. Such cases include *Smith v. Maryland*, which held there was no "expectation of privacy" for lists of phone numbers dialed; *United States v. Knotts*, which allowed the use of a tracking device in public;[55] and *California v. Ciraolo* and *Dow Chemical Co. v. United States*, which allowed aerial surveillance of a backyard[56] and a chemical plant,[57] respectively.

Some legal scholars find some support for the transformative view of *Katz* in the Supreme Court's 2012 ruling in *United States v. Jones*, the first Fourth Amendment technology case in a decade.[58] They cite this case as revealing *Katz*'s potential to reconcile technology and privacy by protecting "a defendant's Fourth Amendment rights in his public movements."[59] However, the majority in *Jones* held that a GPS device surreptitiously attached to a suspect's vehicle violated his privacy rights based on the pre-*Katz*[60] "property-based approach" of a "common-law trespassory test" rather than the "reasonable expectation of privacy" test.[61]

In fact, a close reading of the *Jones* ruling reveals that the Court agreed on the drawbacks of the "reasonable expectations" test. Justice Samuel Alito's concurrence, backed by three other justices, spent several paragraphs discussing *Katz*'s flaws, including its "circularity," its subjectivity, and especially the erosion of privacy expectations in the face of technology.[62]

Justice Sonia Sotomayor's own concurrence went even further and took the opportunity to criticize the third-party doctrine as "ill suited to the digital age" despite the lack of third parties in the actual case at hand. Justice Scalia's majority opinion sidestepped these issues by resurrecting the property-based standard and treating the vehicle in question as akin to a home because trespassing, a term usually used for homes and here applied to a person's car, was involved. Alito's concurrence criticized Scalia's application of "18th-century tort law" as being unsuited to "21st-century surveillance" and pointed out the ruling's "[d]isharmony with a substantial body of existing case law," emphasis on the "trivial" matter of a physical device rather than the central issue of privacy, and irrelevance to non-physically intrusive electronic surveillance.[63] Scalia responded to this criticism by warning that relying "exclusively" on Katz "eliminates rights that previously existed."

The issue stands out if one puts aside for a moment the language of legal discourse, going beyond "this court stated" and "this court ruled," and examines the issue in layperson's terms. Compare two situations: In the first, the government suspects that a person is illegally growing marijuana in his home, but the suspicion does not rise to the level that would convince a judge to grant a warrant. How much violation of privacy occurs if the government uses a thermal device to find out the temperature in that home's den—and it turns out that the person was innocent, cooking nothing more than dinner? Or consider a police dog trained to detect bombs and contraband that approaches the home from a side most visitors do not. The Court has ruled that both cases are intrusions on the home and thus violate a reasonable expectation of privacy. Now, compare these to a situation in which cameras follow a person in public, all day and all night—to bars, clinics, Alcoholics Anonymous sessions, political meetings, rendezvous with a lover—and collect and analyze all this information to make it available to the government. Such systems are not science fiction, but rather are an increasing reality in major US cities; notable examples include Persistent Security Systems[64] and Microsoft's Domain Awareness System.[65] Or consider the use of parabolic microphones to eavesdrop on private conversations in a public area such as a park. If one accepts the principle that some privacy should exist even in public areas, these modes of surveillance represent much broader, deeper, and more indiscriminate violations of privacy than the limited and situational intrusions of a drug-sniffing dog or an infrared scanner penetrating the home.

In short, *Katz* moved the United States no more than, at best, a baby step toward privacy protection outside the home. *Katz* excessively privileges the home, while the United States needs a doctrine of privacy that protects privacy in both realms against unreasonable search and seizure.

A psychologist may argue that the legal community is holding on to *Katz* because it does not want to regress to the property-based, home-centered privacy doctrine—but, in effect, *Katz* does little to move the protection of privacy beyond the home's walls. The time has come to develop a cyber age privacy doctrine that focuses on secondary use rather than on primary collection of personal information, a subject that deserves a separate treatment.[66]

4

Privacy: A Personal Sphere, Not Home-Bound

A. Introduction

"[T]he Fourth Amendment protects people, not places. What a person knowingly exposes to the public, even in his home or office, is not a subject of Fourth Amendment protection. But what he seeks to preserve as private, even in an area accessible to the public, may be constitutionally protected." So stated the Supreme Court majority in *Katz v. United States*[1] in 1969. This chapter builds on this statement and attempts to show that it has generally gone unheeded in Fourth Amendment case law since 1969, and that sweeping and significant technological advances mean that the statement is more valuable than ever.

In this chapter, I suggests criteria upon which to build a coherent standard for evaluating the legitimacy of privacy claims, one that applies regardless of a person's location—whether he is at home or in public space—and does not require assessing what a person "expects" or does "knowingly." The following sections briefly review the historical association between privacy and the home, outline scholars' criticisms of this association, and point to technological developments that greatly blur the difference between the private and public realms. I then examine a means of moving away from using the walls of the house (and of other physical spaces such as cars and those encompassed by containers) to separate the areas in which privacy ought to be privileged. After suggesting that a major previous attempt to accomplish this, based on the well-known case *Katz v. United States*, has failed, I outline a new foundation for defining a sphere in which a person's privacy should be privileged that would accompany the person to any location, either public or private.

B. The Historical Association between Privacy and the Home

Western culture has long held that the home is a sovereign place in which privacy is highly protected. The Code of Hammurabi held the home as sacrosanct; even the slightest uninvited intrusion into the home was punished—on par with robbery and kidnapping—by death: "If a man makes a breach into a house, one shall kill him in front of the breach and bury him in it."[2] An early record of a right to privacy is contained in the Mishnah, a compilation of ancient Jewish oral law collected circa 200 CE, which constitutes the core of the Talmud.[3] In ancient Greece, privacy existed only on private property and within the family, and although Rome had more expansive notions of privacy it was most important and best protected in the house.[4] In the 1500s this normative position was distilled in the phrase "a man's home is his castle."[5] English common law offered the house especial protections against intrusions by the government.[6]

In the modern era, social science research added further rationales to the long historical association between privacy and the home. Psychological research indicated that the ability to exclude unwanted others from one's private spaces was essential for individuality and "personhood" to develop.[7] Biologists observed that many animals have a natural urge to seek privacy, and to establish this privacy through the creation of controlled spaces separated by buffer zones analogous to houses, which have physiological benefits.[8]

The Supreme Court has repeatedly held that warrantless government intrusions into the home are presumptively unreasonable unless they fall into one of a handful of exceptions.[9] Indeed, the Fourth Amendment to the U.S. Constitution explicitly names "houses" as a domain in which citizens have a right to be secure.[10] Moreover, the Court has held on numerous occasions that the house stands apart from and above other secure domains.[11] Legal scholars describe the home as practically "sacred" in Fourth Amendment jurisprudence.[12] (It should be noted that of course "secure" and "private" are not synonymous; however a major way privacy is promoted is by making a space secure from intrusion. It is hard to imagine a person not gaining at least some privacy if he or she is secure, and difficult to conceive of anyone feeling secure without privacy.)

Importantly, in *Olmstead v. United States* the Supreme Court stated that the secure home was essential to civilization and liberty itself: "A sane, decent, civilized society must provide some such oasis, some shelter from public scrutiny, some insulated enclosure, some enclave, some inviolate space which is a man's castle."[13] In *Johnson v. United States*,[14] the Court held that "the right of officers to thrust themselves into a home is also a grave concern."[15] In *Silverman v. United States*,[16] the Court observed that,

"At the very core [of the Fourth Amendment] stands the right of a man to retreat into his own home and there be free from unreasonable governmental intrusion."[17] And in *Payton v. New York*,[18] the Supreme Court wrote that "physical entry of the home is the *chief evil* against which the wording of the Fourth Amendment is directed"[19] and "freedom from intrusion into the home or dwelling is the archetype of the privacy protection secured by the Fourth Amendment."[20] In *Payton*, the Court found that the home's "unambiguous physical dimensions" facilitated the drawing of a bright line to secure against even the smallest government intrusion.[21] One scholar points out that the Supreme Court has suggested in its rulings that the security of the house is central to the exercise of First Amendment rights as well as the liberty associated with exercising control over decisions not specifically regulated by the Constitution.[22]

The Supreme Court held, for instance in *Smith v. Maryland*,[23] that a Fourth Amendment search was defined by a physical government intrusion into one or more constitutionally protected interests—that is, persons, houses, papers, and effects.[24] One may hence argue that the Constitution refers to "houses" as merely one of four protected interests, the privacy of which is entitled to special protection. However, considerable evidence supports the thesis that the courts and others have viewed houses as entitled to exceptional protection. (Indeed, legal scholars see a direct line connecting the normative idea that the house was sovereign and inviolate to the writers of the Bill of Rights. As one of them put it, because "most of the language and structure of the Fourth Amendment was primarily the work of one man, John Adams," understanding his views is critical to the task of grasping the framers' intent.[25] Adams was closely acquainted with the concept that "a man's home is his castle"—and he held this concept in the foreground of his thoughts when drafting America's founding documents.[26])

Moreover, the Fourth Amendment, which was ratified in 1791, is reported to have originated as a protection against writs of assistance; these were general warrants that authorized British customs officers to search houses or other personal property to find and seize unspecified smuggled goods.[27] Writs of assistance were first used in the colonies in 1755; they replaced a system of search warrants issued by colonial governors that "authorized search only in places set forth in the warrant and upon information given on oath that smuggled goods were hidden there."[28] *Semayne's Case* (1603), James Otis's famous challenge to writs of assistance (1761),[29] *Wilkes v. Wood* (1763), *Entick v. Carrington* (1765), and judges' resistance of the Townsend Act (1767) collectively laid the foundation for opposition to general warrants in the colonies.[30] The grievances advanced in each of these cases specifically concerned homeowners and searches of houses.[31] That the Fourth Amendment grew out of these cases and opposition to writs of assistance suggests that it was intended to especially prevent the type of intrusions—namely, those into the home—that so troubled American colonists.

Finally, several legal scholars support the conclusion that the Fourth Amendment's original intent was explicitly to protect the home.[32] They suggest that the security of persons, papers, and effects was intended to be *secondary* to the security of the home against government intrusion. An early treatise on constitutional law published in 1868—that is, eighteen years prior to *Boyd*—explicitly stated that the original intent of the Fourth Amendment was to protect the home from government intrusion, and separated this from a second goal of protecting persons, papers, and effects.[33]

C. Criticisms of "Housing Exceptionalism"

Scholars have argued that housing exceptionalism is flawed for two main reasons. First, the prioritization of the house *underprotects* a wide swath of activities that ought to be free from public intrusion. Second, the sanctity of the home *overprotects* many activities that ought to be regulated by the state. Feminist scholars as well as advocates for the homeless have advanced strenuous criticisms of housing exceptionalism on the former grounds, while second wave feminists have levied the latter criticism. These two approaches are two sides of the same coin—they both fundamentally hold that the public-private distinction is a rhetorical tool that extracts power from certain groups of people and awards it to other groups. For this reason, critics of this tool seek to vacate or fundamentally recast it.

1. Protection of Domestic Abusers

Feminist scholarship has offered criticism of housing exceptionalism based on feminist academic analysis of the public-private dichotomy in the 1970s.[34] One scholar calls "attacking the public[-]private line . . . one of the primary concerns (if not *the* primary concern) of feminist legal theorizing for over two decades" spanning 1980 to 2000.[35] Another writes, "Perhaps no concept has been more influential in the field of women's history than that of the distinction between public and private spheres."[36] Another held that the public-private dichotomy is "the source of women's oppression."[37] Carole Pateman, one of the most influential feminist scholars to study the dichotomy, called it "what the feminist movement is about."[38]

Feminist legal scholars pointed out that the liberal division of the world into public and private spaces—a broad distinction that encompasses the dichotomies between political-apolitical, freedom-interference, accessible-inaccessible, and society-individual, among other conceptualizations,[39] and that is represented in law as a "boundary which the law (and its agents) cannot cross absent special circumstances"[40]—is highly gendered. In particular, women were historically legally precluded from participating in numerous political, social, and public activities, including voting and property ownership.[41] Prior to the Industrial Revolution, women were largely limited to the realm of family and household work;[42] after the Industrial Revolution, paid labor was no longer frequently conducted within the house but rather elsewhere, and thus breadwinning became a public activity from which the "ideal" woman was typically barred. Moreover, the liberal social contract enshrined in English common law and, eventually, the Fourth Amendment of the U.S. Constitution depended on this exclusion: To offer (white) men sovereignty over the home required that the home include subjects who had already been precluded from participation in the public sphere—that is, women—and to offer (white) men a refuge from public space required that someone—again, women—make that private sphere a comfortable retreat by cooking, cleaning, and caring for children. Feminists therefore argue that the public-private dichotomy is artificial,[43] a rhetorical tool of power. There is no difference between the public and the private, but language to the contrary reflects a false belief in such a difference; the linguistic or conceptual distinction solidifies itself and structures social conditions to women's disadvantage.[44]

Another criticism of spatial privacy concerns some more specific power implications of this distinction. "Women may be victims of men's privacy,"[45] insofar as spatial privacy protects from state interference violent or oppressive acts of men against women that take place within the home. Catherine MacKinnon famously wrote, "For women the measure of intimacy has been the measure of oppression. This is why feminism has had to explode the private."[46] Until the 1970s, for example, marital rape was not a crime in most of the United States, and marital rape remained legal in North Carolina until 1993.

To redress these problems, feminist legal scholars argue for the rejection of the home as an inherently private sphere into which the state may not intrude, writing that "the state must cross the private boundary of home and family and regulate the distribution of power within that sphere."[47]

Feminist scholars also attest that the public-private dichotomy and women's formal and informal exclusion from the public realm has other negative impacts on women. For example, the exclusion of "proper" women from paid work decreased their economic power and independence.[48] Women, especially unskilled women, are now encouraged to take lower-paying jobs such as nursing, cleaning, child care, and secretarial work, which typically involve significant affective labor and are devalued precisely because of their resemblance to private *housework*.[49]

It is worth noting that some feminist scholars have argued that the public-private distinction can be rehabilitated and used as a tool of feminism.[50] For example, several feminist scholars have proposed alternate spatial divisions predicated on intimacy and a right to exclusion, which are not tied to specific physical locations infused with patriarchal gender symbolism. (These scholars include Elshtain and Iris Marion Young.[51])

2. *Underprotecting the Poor and Vulnerable*

First, legal scholars have argued that the exceptions to the inviolate home permitted by law—namely administrative searches and consent—structurally underprotect specific segments of the population. For example, where a special need beyond law enforcement can be demonstrated and the government intrusion can be characterized as "principally benevolent," the intrusion may not even constitute a search at all. This was the conclusion reached by the Supreme Court in a case regarding mandatory home visits to recipients of welfare benefits.[52] This decision effectively designated impoverished individuals—the recipients of government benefits—as a group uniquely less protected against government intrusions. A persistent belief in the United States that poverty is the product of moral deficit has been used to justify a long series of warrantless intrusions into the houses of impoverished individuals by various government agencies.[53] Similarly, parolees and probationers have been held by the Supreme Court to lack the same privacy rights granted to other citizens,[54] as have undocumented immigrants whose houses are raided by Immigration and Customs Enforcement agents.[55] Given that, in 2011, 23.1 percent of Americans (roughly 71,610,000 people) received some form of welfare benefits,[56] this underprotection affects a very large number of people.

Second, several scholars have pointed out that privileging the house over persons, papers, and effects by the Supreme Court subjects those who do not own a home into which to retreat to more government intrusions.[57] In the United States in 2013, more than 600,000 Americans were homeless "on any given night."[58] One author writes, "[O]ur Fourth Amendment doctrine has not been able to fully escape this archaic entanglement with property [the concept of basing rights on one's ownership of property] because it has evolved under the assumptions that each citizen has a 'house' and that each person has some minimal access to personal property."[59] Most people who do not own property recognized as a "house" by the Court live in the open fields—"park benches, steam grates, alleyways, areas beneath bridges, and other shelterless habitats lacking any significant degree of enclosure"[60]—which have been explicitly recognized by the Court as a sphere of legitimate government intrusion without a warrant. Even homeless persons who attempt to enclose their living space are unknot protected against government intrusion; the relative solitude of public spaces such as tunnels does not negate the ability of the government to intrude at will, and homeless persons who "squat" in abandoned buildings are still less protected by virtue of the fact that they are actually trespassing.[61]

D. Technological Changes

Much public discourse in the West assumes a sharp difference between the "public" and "private" realms, most obviously about the relative merits of government programs and regulations compared to private economic and social activities, between liberal and conservative philosophy. In a previous study, this author showed that these differences are often vastly overstated.[62] For instance, privacy may be violated not only by the government, but also by corporations that specialize in collecting vast amounts of personal information about Americans to form detailed dossiers on them, including information about intimate aspects of their lives. These corporations not only intrude on their own, but also sell their data to various government agencies that include the FBI and IRS.[63] The difference between public and private databanks is thus merely a check and a click. Can one protect privacy (or national security, for that matter) in one realm without also undertaking parallel steps in the other? To highlight the scope of the normative and legal challenge this question poses, in effect the question is, "Should not the Fourth Amendment also apply to private actors?"

The issue is made more acute by several major technological developments. The most prominent of these is the rise of the personal computer and the Internet. It makes less and less difference whether a person accesses information in the privacy of their home or in public, because it is increasingly possible to discern the information a person is accessing at home, from outside the home. Moreover, if the individual reads, say, a physical copy of a radical political text on a public bench, only passersby or passing authorities could learn of it. By contrast, in the Internet age, the same observation can be made by any hacker, gangster, intelligence agency, or curious (or controlling) lover traveling on another continent. Moreover, information stored by the person, including correspondence, love letters, financial information, and medical records, was once locked in a drawer at home, but is very likely these days to be found on "the cloud." The individual may well be unaware whether his personal information is stored on his hard drive or in the cloud, and he may be further unaware of the difference it makes in terms of ease of access by others and legal protection of privacy. The law requires a warrant for the government to tap a phone under most circumstances. In the past, in the days that all phones used landlines, people mainly had phones in their homes and in enclosed offices. These days, most calls are made on cell phones—over 70 percent of 911 calls, for example, are made from cell phones[64]—that people carry in and out of private and public spaces, largely eroding the difference between the two realms. The same blurring of the realms is evident in e-mails and communication of photos. Moreover, cell phones, whether at home or in public space, can be turned into listening devices even when turned off, and computer cameras can be turned on to provide visual surveillance in either space.

Moreover, new technologies such as high-power binoculars, aerial surveillance tools such as drones, and thermal measurement devices make it possible to learn details about the interior of a home or its curtilage without ever physically entering either space. While the Court banned the warrantless use of thermal imaging devices in *Kyllo v. United States*, one must expect that in the near future technologies will be able to detect increasingly small amounts of chemicals or electromagnetic radiation emanating from homes. These technologies will enable private individuals, corporations, and government agents to learn about matters in the home as if they were conducted in open and public space.

All of this shows that the most important consideration when it comes to protecting privacy in an age of exponential technological growth is not *where* a person is, but rather *what kind* of information is collected. This chapter next shows that if the information collected about an individual is limited in *volume*, not *sensitive*, and not *stored or combined* with other pieces of information, such collection will amount to a limited intrusion that the courts should tolerate, even if the information is collected inside private space by a public actor. By contrast, if the information collected is of great volume, sensitive, and extensively stored and combined with other information, the collection is likely to violate one's privacy even if the collection is only carried out in public. Such collection should be barred unless there is a particularly pressing threat to the public. Before spelling out these criteria for determining the scope of the personal privacy sphere, I examine one previous attempt to form such a sphere on markedly different grounds—an attempt that failed.

E. A Failed Foundation for a Personal Sphere of Privacy

As discussed briefly in Chapter III, in 1967, the Supreme Court departed from its home-centric approach to Fourth Amendment cases in *Katz v. United States*. This case concerned an FBI investigation in which the agents did not obtain a warrant before attaching an electronic device to record the sounds that escaped through the walls of a public telephone booth. Using this device, the FBI obtained six telephone conversations in which Charles Katz placed illegal bets across state lines.[65] The Court held that the FBI's actions constituted a violation of Katz's Fourth Amendment rights. In one of the most oft-cited excerpts in Fourth Amendment jurisprudence, the Court stated that "the Fourth Amendment protects people, not places. What a person knowingly exposes to the public, even in his home or office, is not a subject of Fourth Amendment protection. But what he seeks to preserve as private, even in an area accessible to the public, may be constitutionally protected." In so doing, the Court placed the first major cracks in housing exceptionalism's armor.[66] The Court viewed Americans as entitled to assert a sphere of privacy outside of the home, one that is not tied to a physical location. Justice Harlan's concurring opinion did much of the work of outlining a replacement for the physical trespass standard by establishing a two-pronged test for determining whether the government had breached an individual's reasonable expectation of privacy. First, the individual must "have exhibited an actual (subjective) expectation of privacy," and second, this expectation must be a "reasonable" one.[67]

Several Court rulings that followed held that one could have a reasonable expectation of privacy outside of the home—for example in closed, portable containers and in vehicles. Discussion of a few such examples follows. One should note, though, that these rulings often rely on the idea that the protected area is in some way *similar* to or an artificial extension of the home,[68] and thus *Katz* and the rulings that followed in effect continued to draw on the rationale of housing exceptionalism. (Stephanie Stern originated the term "housing exceptionalism"; the following lines benefited much from her contributions.)

The Court thus recognized an expectation of privacy when it comes to sealed, portable containers. What has been labeled the "container doctrine"—"that police officers with probable cause to believe contraband or evidence of a crime is within a container may seize the container, but cannot open and search it without first obtaining a warrant," even in public space—dates to the 1970s.[69] Charles Lee, who has written on this subject, points out that the Court overwhelmingly held for some time that government officials would need a warrant to constitutionally search "any object capable of holding another object," which includes pockets and cars, regardless of the physical location of the container.[70] The Court ruled that a government official who *opened* a sealed packet he found in an arrestee's pocket and found illicit drugs violated the arrestee's Fourth Amendment rights. It also held that government officials may not open luggage without a warrant when dealing with travelers on a public bus. Moreover, it ruled that governmental officials may not access "papers," namely sealed communications, without a warrant, but that they may access unsealed communications such as postcards.[71]

The Court has also recognized that automobiles moving through public space may be protected against certain kinds of government intrusions. In *United States v. Jones*, for example, the Court ruled that installation of a GPS monitoring device on the defendant's car without a valid warrant constituted a physical trespass on Jones's effects, even though the car was in a public space when the GPS device was installed. In so doing, the majority recognized protection against government intrusion into non-home but home-like roving objects.

In short, *Katz* and the cases that followed provided precedents for moving beyond housing exceptionalism and beyond associating the highest level of privacy with the "inviolate home." However, as we have seen, the Court has largely maintained the distinction the home (and home-like spaces) and the public realm.

F. Introducing the Personal Sphere of Privacy Standard

To define a personal sphere of privacy, it is necessary to lay out criteria for determining which behaviors are encompassed in the sphere, and which are to be excluded. These criteria are needed to replace the role played by walls in the home-centric privacy doctrine. That is, drawing a clear line between protected and unprotected behavior (or at least more and less protected behavior); in other words, marking the boundaries of the sphere of privacy.

Three criteria come to mind[72]: the volume of information collected, its sensitivity, and the extent to which it is "cybernated"—that is, the extent to which the information is stored, combined with other information sources ("collated"), analyzed, and distributed. Each of these criteria should be considered a continuous rather than dichotomous variable, and they should be considered jointly when determining whether a particular government action constitutes a privacy violation.

Volume concerns the total amount of information collected about one person by one agency or actor. It encompasses two components. The first of these is the quantity of information collected. Quantity is measured in number of e-mails, phone records, text messages, or, better, megabytes of information.[73] The second component is bandwidth, a term here used to refer to the collection of different types of information from or about a single subject. (For a more complete discussion of the concepts of quantity and bandwidth, see Chapters I and II.)

In *Jones*, Justice Alito held that the collection, which lasted 28 days, was too long. Of course, the courts have ruled that a person cannot be held longer than a given number of hours or days without being charged. And in *Riley v. California*,[74] the Court ruled that the warrantless search of the contents of a smartphone incident to arrest constitutes a Fourth Amendment violation because the volume and bandwidth of information contained on smartphones is much higher than the information contained on other sources. The Court wrote, "many of these devices are in fact minicomputers that also happen to have the capacity to be used as a telephone. They could just as easily be called cameras, video players, rolodexes, calendars, tape recorders, libraries, diaries, albums, televisions, maps, or newspapers."[75] Their storage capacity is far beyond physical storage capabilities, and most people now carry around "a cache of sensitive personal information" in the form of a smartphone. Cell phones that contain vast quantities of data, the Court held, are thus qualitatively and quantitatively different than physical containers the Court had previously analyzed.[76] In short, there are some precedents for using volume as a criterion.

Sensitivity is the second criterion. Privacy scholars and lawmakers have often articulated and operationalized the observation that some kinds of information are more sensitive than others, albeit using a variety of terms including "intimate information" and "revealing information." In the United States, Congress has ranked many types of information according to sensitivity. An individual's medical information is granted a high level of protection; financial information is not regarded as sensitive but nearly so. Additional types of information entitled to a relatively high level of protection include education records (Family Educational Rights and Privacy Act), genetic information (twenty-seven state legislatures had regulated the disclosure of identifiable genetic information in some way as of 2008[77]), and journalistic sources (Privacy Protection Act of 1980[78]). The FTC has classified five categories of information, namely financial information, health information, social security numbers, information collected from children, and geo-location information, as sensitive data.[79] The result of this piecemeal consideration is a crazy patchwork quilt. However, given that many kinds of information have already been ranked, it would not take a great deal of legislation to systematically rank the level of sensitivity of all the major kinds of information.

Cybernation is the third criterion. It concerns the scope of processing and secondary uses of information. It includes storing, collating, analyzing, and distributing discrete items of information in concert with numerous others. To demonstrate this difference, an example that encompasses all three criteria follows. First, consider a situation in which the volume of information collected is low, the sensitivity of that information is low, and the information is only minimally cybernated. This occurs when private enterprises employ CCTV to enhance their security. The footage contains a low volume of information; basically only whether a given person was at a given space at one point in time. The information collected is typically of low sensitivity; it merely reveals the kind of information people readily display in public; whether they dress up or down, for example. And as a rule the information is not stored or collected with other information about the same person.

On the other end of the spectrum is New York City's "Domain Awareness System," developed by Microsoft. It collects information from many different CCTVs across the city as well as other sources, such as speed cameras and radiation monitors, and possibly in the future of cell phone locators. It stores this information, combines it with other information, and analyzes it. The information originally collected in both situations is the same; it is the great difference in the level of cybernation that makes the second situation much more of a threat to privacy than the first.

Finally, a fourth variable, *accountability*, deserves consideration. This variable measures the extent to which those who collect information have erected barriers to access by unauthorized parties and are subjected to supervision and oversight to ensure that they use the information legally and legitimately. These measures include firewalls, passwords, audit trails, supervisors, inspectors general, and congressional committees.

All accountability measures limit cybernation, not collection. Some entirely prevent agents from gaining access to personal information, others limit storage of information by regularly deleting it or stashing it away where it can only be accessed with additional judicial scrutiny, and still others minimize or de-identify information so that it cannot be analyzed as efficiently. Less cybernation occurs when accountability measures are robust. (Ideally, accountability mechanisms would be built into the design of future technologies.) And where cybernation is limited, fewer privacy violations will occur even if the volume and sensitivity of information collected by a given actor are considerable. Conversely, if databases lack accountability mechanisms, the risk of privacy violations will be high even when the information under consideration is of lower volume and sensitivity, because of the potential to draw inferences through unauthorized secondary usages.

G. Conclusion

"Privacy protection" has long meant according special protection to private spaces such as houses, cars, and containers. We have seen that this association has been criticized, for good reason, as both over- and underprotecting privacy on various grounds. An earlier attempt to fashion privacy as based on other foundations than the barriers of private spaces, in *Katz*, largely failed. This chapter suggests that using the volume of information collected, its sensitivity, and the extent to which it is cybernated may well serve to mark the limits of a personal sphere that individuals carry with them wherever they go, including in public spaces. These markers, replacing the role of walls in the traditional home-centric privacy doctrine, will inform us on whether or not a given item or a collection of information about a person is entitled to a high level of protection from government intrusion.[80]

5

The Privacy Merchants

A. Corporate Surveillance, Tracking, Data Mining, and Profiling

Most informed citizens probably know by now that corporations collect information about them, but they may well be unaware of the extent and scope of the invasions of privacy that are now widespread. Many may be aware of tracking tools referred to as "cookies," which are installed on one's computer by visited websites. They are used to identify the person and to remember his or her preferences. Some people protect themselves from such tracking by employing software that allows them to clear cookies from a computer. However, corporations have recently begun to install "supercookies" that are very difficult to detect, and if removed, secretly reinstall themselves.[1] As one report concluded: "This means that privacy-sensitive consumers who 'toss' their HTTP cookies to prevent tracking or remain anonymous are still being uniquely identified online by advertising companies."[2]

Major cell phone and mobile technology companies offer services that allow lovers, ex-spouses, lawyers, or anyone else to find out where a person is—and track their movements—by using their cell phones' GPS capabilities.[3] A German politician who inquired about location storage information discovered that over a six-month period, his longitude and latitude had been recorded over 35,000 times.[4]

There are two kinds of corporations that keep track of what Internet users buy, read, visit, drink, and who they call, e-mail, and date, among other things. Some merely track users' activity on their sites as part of regular business; recording purchases and viewed products helps them increase sales. This is true for nearly every major online retailer. Other corporations make shadowing Internet users—and keeping very detailed dossiers on them—their main line of business. (I will refer to them as privacy merchants. They sell information to whoever pays the required price.

In 2005, one such company—ChoicePoint—had records on over 220 million people.[5] Professor Christopher Slobogin notes that the amount of information culled by corporate data miners

> can provide the inquirer with a wide array of data about any of us, including basic demographic information, income, net worth, real [sic] property holdings, social security number, current and previous addresses, phone numbers and fax numbers, names of neighbors, driver records, license plate and VIN numbers, bankruptcy and debtor filings, employment, business and criminal records, bank account balances and activity, stock purchases, and credit card activity.[6]

For example, in 2009, a law professor at Fordham University gained minor notoriety when he assigned his class to create a dossier on Justice Antonin Scalia using only the information they could find online. The result was a fifteen-page document "that included the justice's home address and home phone number, his wife's personal e-mail address and the TV shows and food he prefers."[7] Some privacy merchants even keep dossiers on the crimes a person has committed, their divorces, political leanings, and their interests in topics that include religion, the Bible, gambling, and adult entertainment.[8] Other companies amass lists of "victims of sexual assault, and lists of people with sexually transmitted diseases. Lists of people who have Alzheimer's, dementia and AIDS. Lists of the impotent and depressed."[9]

Although several data-mining companies allow individuals to opt out of their databases, people must contact each company individually, and even then information may still linger in some search results or websites. Google, for example, generally does not remove search results if the information contained is truthful and not illegal.[10]

The privacy merchants are limited by laws that Congress (and states) have enacted that carve out subsets of data, particularly medical and financial records, in which the privacy merchants cannot freely trade. However, very little attention has been paid to the fact that information is fungible. Through a process that might be called "privacy violating triangulation" (PVT), one can readily derive much about a person's medical, financial, or other protected private side by using "innocent facts" that are not privileged by law. A piece of seemingly benign information—for instance, the number of days a person failed to show up for work, or whether the person purchased a wig—suggests volumes about one's medical condition. By building a portfolio of many such apparently innocuous facts, one could infer a great deal, effectively violating the realm of privacy surrounding individuals' most sensitive information. Thus, a study of Facebook shows "how the on-line social network data could be used to predict some individual private trait that a user is not willing to disclose (e.g., political or religious affiliation)."[11]

Some individuals may think that they can protect themselves from tracking and dossiers by using pseudonyms and multiple "mailboxes." However, some companies have developed software to match pseudonyms used on message boards and blogs with real names and personal e-mail addresses.[12] The subjects of this tracking—who are unaware that their anonymity has been stripped—include people who use online pseudonyms to discuss sensitive topics such as mental illness.[13] As Eli Pariser reports, "Search for a word like 'depression' on Dictionary.com, and the site installs up to 223 tracking cookies and beacons on your computer so that other websites can target you with antidepressants."[14] Although the privacy of medical records is protected by law, but "visits" to medical websites or chat groups are not afforded the same protection.

Many companies claim that they do not collect names or that they disassociate names from dossiers. However, at least some companies keep a database of names on file. One such company, RapLeaf, states that it does not share its subjects' names with advertisers; but an investigation found that it does link those names to "extraordinarily intimate databases [. . .] by tapping voter-registration files, shopping histories, social-networking activities and real estate records."[15] And although the company indeed refrains from specifically sharing *names* with its clients, it did share personally identifiable information with them, such as unique Facebook account numbers that can be traced back to the account holder's name.[16]

Privacy advocates have sharply objected to the government's use of deep packet inspection (DPI)—a powerful tool used to analyze the contents of communications transmitted over the Internet—in large part because it is much more intrusive than merely tracking who is communicating with whom. (The difference is akin to reading letters versus examining the outside of an envelope to see who sent the letter and to whom it is addressed.) Now, private companies are offering to perform DPI for Internet service providers to facilitate targeted advertising.[17]

In 2010, Facebook became the most-visited website in the United States,[18] and it neared 700 million users in June 2011.[19] Facebook users put great amounts of personal information, including their religious and political views, educational and professional background, interests, as well as photos and videos of themselves, on their individual profiles. Most important, unlike most other websites where individuals employ usernames or pseudonyms, Facebook is designed for people to use their real names. This makes it vastly more valuable to data miners who seek to gather personally identifiable information in order to assemble dossiers on individuals. Furthermore, each individual's profile is linked to the profiles of their "friends," who may have different privacy settings that allow for broader access to data, such as photographs or group membership, that the individual never chose to exhibit on his or her own profile.

Facebook provides customizable privacy tools and some privacy protection, but it has faced consistent criticism that those protections are unreliable and difficult to manipulate.[20] As Facebook has introduced third-party applications such as games to its site, it has faced mounting difficulties in holding to its end of the bargain.

In a July 2010 letter to Representative John Conyers of the U.S. House Judiciary Committee, a Facebook official stated, "The question posed in your letter asks whether Facebook shares users' personal information with third parties without the knowledge of users. The answer is simple and straightforward: we do not. We have designed our system and policies so that user information is never shared without our users' knowledge."[21] It was a few months later, in October 2010, that the *Wall Street Journal* broke the story of extensive user privacy breaches by Facebook.[22] It discovered that popular Facebook applications were "providing access to people's names and, in some cases, their friends' names" to Internet tracking companies.[23] According to the *Journal*, the breach affected "tens of millions" of users—including those who were vigilant in setting their privacy protections—and was in violation of Facebook's stated policies.[24] In the same month, the *New York Times* reported on two studies that found that "in certain circumstances, advertisers—or snoops posing as advertisers [on Facebook]—may be able to learn sensitive profile information, like a person's sexual orientation or religion, even if the person is sharing that information only with a small circle of friends."[25]

In addition, the nearly ubiquitous Facebook "Like" and Twitter "Tweet" buttons on websites "notify Facebook and Twitter that a person visited those sites even when users don't click on the buttons."[26] These widgets have been added to millions of web pages and they appear on more than one-third of the world's top 1,000 websites.[27] The tracking, which is used for targeted advertising, continues until the user specifically logs out of their account, even if the user turns off their computer.[28]

One may argue that the private sector merely uses this information for commercial purposes, while the government may use it to jail people, suppress free speech, and otherwise violate their rights. However, one must note that the *violation of privacy by private agents has some similar effects to violations committed by government agents, effects that lead to discrimination and "chilling" of expression and dissent.* Thus, when gay people who seek to keep their sexual orientation private are "outed" by the media, or banks call in loans of those they find out have cancer, or employers refuse to hire people because they learn about their political or religious views, privacy is violated in a manner about as consequential as if the same violations had been carried out by a government agency.

B. Privacy Merchants in the Service of Big Brother

Even if one disregards the facts already cited, which show that corporate violations of privacy are far-reaching and chilling, one must note that the *information corporations amass is available to the government*. Laws may prevent the government from ordering a private company to conduct surveillance on innocent citizens who are not suspected of any crime or from generating dossiers that the government itself is banned from generating. (In other words, when corporations act as government agents, they may be subject to the same or similar limitations the government must abide by.) However, the government can and does use data already amassed by the privacy merchants. Also, prevailing laws do not prevent private corporations from analyzing online activity with an eye toward the government's needs and shaping their privacy-violating data in ways to make it more attractive to government agencies that purchase their services. Indeed, because the government is such a large and reliable client, corporate data banks have strong financial incentives for anticipating its needs.

The thesis that "what is private does not stay private" is far from hypothetical. As Chris Hoofnagle notes, even though Congress limited the executive branch's amassing of personal information in the 1974 Privacy Act, "those protections have failed to meet Congress' intent because the private sector has done what the government has been prohibited from doing."[29]

According to Daniel Solove, "for quite some time, the government has been increasingly contracting with businesses to acquire databases of personal information. Database firms are willing to supply the information and the government is willing to pay for it."[30] Solove points out that government can "find out details about people's race, income, opinions, political beliefs, health, lifestyle, and purchasing habits from the database companies that keep extensive personal information on millions of Americans."[31] Hoofnagle similarly warns that "private sector commercial data brokers have built massive data centers with personal information custom-tailored to law enforcement agents."[32] ChoicePoint, a major Privacy Merchant, has at least thirty-five contracts with government agencies, including the Department of Justice (through which it provides its databases to the FBI), as well as the DEA, the IRS, and the Bureau of Citizenship and Immigration Services.[33]

Even before the 9/11 attacks, the U.S. Marshals Service alone performed up to forty thousand searches each month using private data banks.[34] The exact number of contracts the government has made with corporate data miners is unknown, because many of the contracts are classified.[35] However, one 2006 government study found that at least fifty-two federal agencies had launched—or were planning to launch at the time of the study—at least 199 data-mining projects that relied on the services and technology of commercial data banks.[36] The lists are "typically sold at a few cents per name" to other corporations, and there are roughly four thousand of these privacy merchants.[37]

What does a government dossier based on commercially compiled data contain? According to Julia Angwin's *Dragnet Nation*, her request for information about herself held by U.S. Customs and Border Protection led to a file that contained "thirty-one pages of detailed international travel reservation information from a database called PNR, which stands for Passenger Name Records. PNRs didn't used to be in government hands. They are commercial records held by airlines. But after the 9/11 attacks, [legislation was passed that] soon became codified as requiring the airlines to give the agency electronic access to the entire airline reservation databases."[38] A more complete list of information about Ms. Angwin held by the government, according to her investigations, included "every address [she] had lived at dating back to college . . . every phone number [she] had ever used . . . the names of nearly all [her] relatives (as well as in-laws) . . . [a] list of nearly three thousand people with whom [she] exchanged e-mail in the past seven years . . . records of about twenty-six thousand Web searches . . . [a] glimpse of [her] shopping habits . . . [and her] internal communications with [her] employer, the *Wall Street Journal*."[39] She states that this information mostly "was held by commercial data brokers,"[40] which is how the government gained access to the information.

An overarching 2004 report from the Government Accountability Office on data mining by the federal government in the early 2000s found that 52 different federal agencies used or planned to use some form of data mining, which included 199 planned or operational data mining programs. Of these, 54 programs involved "efforts to mine data from the private sector." (Meanwhile, 77 involved "efforts to mine data from other federal agencies . . . [including] student loan application data, bank account numbers, credit card information, and taxpayer identification numbers."[41]) Moreover, the trend is to extend this use, as evidenced by a 2011 FBI manual that enabled agents to search for private citizens in commercial databases without prior authorization or even notification.[42] In 2011, Google revealed that the U.S. government made the most requests for Internet users' private data in 2010, and Google complied with 94 percent of these orders.[43]

One may well hold that some government usages of private data banks serve legitimate purposes, even if the databases are loaded with extensive dossiers on most adult Americans instead of only those for which there is some evidence or reason to suspect that they are violating the law. However, one must still note that from here on, whether such data banks are in the FBI headquarters or in some corporate office matters little. At most, they are just a click—and a payment—away.

The next segment of this chapter outlines differing approaches to the protection of privacy in the new world in which the traditional distinction between public and private realms, on which many normative and legal conceptions build, in particular those that concern privacy, are much less important and are becoming still less significant. The new amalgamated social world calls for cross-realm or holistic modes of deliberations and policy making.

C. The Main Alternatives

The following deliberations draw on my sociological training and on normative considerations rather than on any legal preparation. I merely chart the "big picture" because, as will become clear, most if not all the alternatives face major hurdles. It therefore seems premature to spell out any of the alternative approaches before strategies and political forces develop that will make it possible to overcome these hurdles. The alternatives are evaluated not on the basis of what would best protect privacy from privacy merchants, but instead on which measures might be taken given the prevailing context in the United States.

1. Change the Norm: A World without Privacy?

One major response to privacy merchants' expanding reach has been well encapsulated by the Scott McNealy, CEO of Sun Microsystems, who stated, "Privacy is dead, get over it."[44] Facebook's founder, Mark Zuckerberg, argues that the social norms that undergird privacy law are obsolete. That is, instead of finding new ways to protect individuals from corporations, individuals should learn to accept changed—in effect, much lower—levels of privacy. He elaborated, "People have really gotten comfortable not only sharing more information and different kinds, but more openly and with more people [. . .] That social norm is just something that has evolved over time."[45] Zuckerberg continued, "We view it as our role in the system to constantly be innovating and be updating what our system is to reflect what the current social norms are."[46] He thus implies that the privacy merchants are not undermining the norm but rather merely tailoring their wares to fit norm changes that have already taken place.

As I see it, it is true that privacy norms are eroding due to factors other than the corporate drive to monetize private information for profit; this is clearly demonstrated by the fact that people appear on talk shows to reveal much about themselves, which is a form of exhibitionism. However, there can be little doubt that corporations, especially new social media companies led by Facebook, are aiding, abetting, and seeking to legitimate the erosion of privacy.

The *Wall Street Journal* editors have argued that these changes in norms indicate that introducing new laws or regulations to better protect privacy is not called for. L. Gordon Crovitz pointed out that, as of March 2011, more than half of Americans over the age of twelve have Facebook accounts.[47] He proceeded to ask: "If most Americans are happy to have Facebook accounts, knowingly trading personal information for other benefits, why is Washington so focused on new privacy laws? There is little evidence that people want new rules."[48]

Furthermore, Crovitz argues, consumers value the benefits of information gathering, which include better-targeted ads, specific recommendations for customers, and huge troves of data for research (such as in Google Flu Trends, which tracks search terms about illnesses to assist epidemiologists). "People are increasingly at ease with sharing personal data in exchange for other benefits," he argues.[49]

Some public opinion polls show that the American people care a great deal about their privacy. Others suggest that various segments of the public vary in their feelings about this right. For example, according to a 2009 survey, 73 to 86 percent of Americans object to the tracking methods used to personalize their advertisements. Furthermore, the study found that 82 percent of young people, who are generally believed to be apathetic about privacy, had at some point refused to provide information to a company because it was too personal. Eighty-six percent of Americans—84 percent among respondents ages 18 to 24—felt that their permission should be sought before pictures of them were posted online.[50]

Other data reveal a more varied picture. In a 1995 survey, Alan Westin divided the public into three "camps" over privacy concerns. About 25 percent of respondents were "privacy fundamentalists" who valued privacy especially highly; 55 percent were "privacy pragmatists" who adjusted their expectations based on the relative value of information they provided and their trust in specific companies; and 20 percent were "privacy unconcerned," or people who had no problem with giving out personal information.[51]

A 2002 study found that while 70 percent of consumers were concerned about their privacy, 82 percent were willing to give out personal information in exchange for the chance to win a hundred dollars in a sweepstakes.[52] The rise in popularity of location-tracking social networking sites such as Foursquare, Facebook Places, and Gowalla, which offer discounts to users who log visits to various businesses and restaurants, suggests that people are indeed willing to trade information, such as their locations and consumption habits, that was once considered private for certain benefits. According to one survey, the coupon reward systems on these sites were the main incentive for users to join.[53]

One must take into account, however, that it is very likely that those who have relatively little concern about privacy are unaware that their less sensitive information can be used for PVT and that privacy is a right that is not subject to majority rule. Even if only a minority cherishes it, it is still a birthright of all Americans.

2. *The Self-Regulation Option*

The prevailing system in the United States—and the de facto prevailing system in the European Union—relies to a significant degree on self-regulation and individual choice. That is, it relies on the assumption that consumers will choose the services and products of those corporations that protect privacy at the level the consumers seek, that users can set their privacy controls to the level they prefer, and that, as a result, corporations that provide less privacy protection than the public seeks will lose business and be incentivized to enhance their privacy protection. (Additionally, some scholars have argued that marketing in this vein is protected as free speech under the First Amendment, an argument not addressed in this chapter.[54]) These ideas are founded on the standard libertarian argument, as noted by Susanna Kim Ripken: "Respect for individual autonomy, responsibility, and decision-making is deeply entrenched in our culture and law. We believe that people can order their own economic affairs and, given sufficient information, can make their own personal assessments of the risks and benefits of transactions."[55]

None of these assumptions withstand sociological scrutiny. The thesis that consumers are rational actors who make decisions in their best interests and in line with their personal preferences and available information has been disproven beyond reasonable doubt by the studies of behavioral economists.[56] For this very reason, transparency does not work. That is, the suggestion that if corporations simply declare their privacy standards consumers could choose those that suit them is erroneous if not misleading. Privacy statements are written in legalese, in terms few can penetrate; the privacy settings provided are complex, cumbersome, and frequently revised after the users have posted information on the site that they cannot erase.

Furthermore, without regulation, there is no assurance that corporations will adhere to their privacy declarations, or at least to their implied promises.[57] This does not refer necessarily to outright false statements but rather to carefully crafted yet misleading commitments to privacy that end up entrapping the consumer. For instance, after public outcry occurred over the iPhone's hidden location-tracking capability, Apple released a statement denying that they tracked users' locations and saying that they rather maintained "a database of WiFi hot spots and cell phone towers around your current location." As Mark Rotenberg of the Electronic Privacy Information Center (EPIC) pointed out, this database is precisely how the company tracks locations, even if it is not tracking the device itself.[58] A study by DoubleVerify surveyed five billion advertisements and found that an icon explaining the privacy policy was clicked on only 0.002 percent of the time—and even then, after users reviewed the advertisers' information practices, only 1 percent opted out of the targeted advertising.[59] "That's an opt-out rate of just 0.00002%," Crovitz notes. "People seem to have adjusted to this new technology faster than regulators are willing to admit."[60] Crovitz argues that the fact few consumers read these statements shows they do not care; in actuality, data already cited strongly suggests that they do not use them because they find them impenetrable.[61] Another national survey found that 57 percent of adult Americans were under the false impression that if a website merely had a privacy policy, then it would not share their information with other companies.[62] Moreover, *individuals cannot protect themselves from corporations* that employ covert tools such as Flash cookies, supercookies, and widgets.

Large corporations—which do business in all fifty states, as well as overseas—find it in their interests to promote regulation that would provide some modicum of privacy. This is the case because such corporations incur considerable costs when they have to adjust their way of doing business to different state laws and deal differently with various segments of the market, some of which are more regulated than others under the current patchwork of privacy laws.

Therefore, some large corporations that were once opposed to legislation now favor a federal omnibus privacy law that would simplify the patchwork of federal sector-specific laws and preempt state-specific statutes. A Microsoft white paper from 2005 advised, "Federal privacy legislation should pre-empt state laws that impose requirements for the collection, use, disclosure, and storage of personal information."[63] Such a law would likely set standards and ceilings (e.g., caps on damages caused by privacy violations) that states could not exceed. State laws demanding higher privacy standards than a federally mandated norm would be invalidated or at least weakened significantly. Indeed, it seems they would accept only legislation that included preemption. Former eBay CEO Meg Whitman explicitly testified before Congress that "legislation without preemption would make the current situation possibly worse, not better, by creating additional uncertainty and compliance burdens."[64] The ideal legislation for Microsoft and similar entities would provide "baseline privacy protection" over which companies would be encouraged to "compete on the basis of more robust privacy practices"[65]—essentially regulating themselves. According to Microsoft Deputy General Counsel for Erich Anderson's testimony before Congress, a federal law should be crafted only as "an effective *complement* to" self-regulation.[66]

State and sectoral laws have already addressed a number of privacy issues (e.g., setting limits on tracking consumers for targeted advertising[67]) while Congress has been largely inactive in this area.[68] Hence, following this line would, in effect, reduce privacy standards in those states that lifted them and could prevent them from adding protections in the future.[69] Moreover, the corporate proposal does involve some federal legislation rather than merely relying on self-regulation. Indeed, it seems impossible to restrain the privacy merchants without calling in Big Brother.

3. Consent for Secondary Use: Opt In Rather than Opt Out?

A rather different approach holds that individuals who release information about themselves for a specific purpose or transaction, for example, to purchase a book from Amazon, would be understood to still "own" this information. Amazon could use it for other purposes (or sell that information to other parties) only with the explicit consent of the consumer, rather than on the basis of a privacy statement on its web pages or on presumed consent. Other words have been used to refer to the same idea in different contexts; for example, consumers would have to opt in to grant secondary and additional use of private information rather than opt out.[70] In American discourse, the term "owned" is used because information is treated as property and private information as private property. Europe embraces the same idea; however, privacy is treated more as an individual right—as part of the personhood, which is violated when one's private sphere is violated.

In 1995, in an effort to establish minimum protections for Internet user privacy and establish baseline consistency among the data protection laws of EU member states, the European Council issued what is commonly called the "Data Protection Directive." The directive, which scholars have called "aggressive"[71] and "extraordinarily comprehensive,"[72] took effect in October 1998. Based on a legal tradition that "expressly recognizes the fundamental right to the protection of personal data,"[73] the directive is credited with having established the most influential and prominent data protections in the world to date.[74] However, it has proven difficult to ensure compliance in those countries governed by the directive. Although the law set out ambitious goals for the standardization of privacy protection in Europe, it was hampered from the start by significant gaps in member states' compliance and enforcement. According to one observer, "although the EU Data Privacy Directive has been approved by the EU itself, it is not self-implementing. Before taking effect in individual nations, each of the fifteen EU member countries must pass its own implementing legislation. As of the effective date, only five had done so."[75]

The directive requires that personal data be processed "only with the consent of the data subject,"[76] with limited exceptions carved out for national security, law enforcement, and some basic state functions such as taxation.[77] The intentionally broad language of the directive includes but is not limited to such actions as collecting, storing, recording, adapting, retrieving, and erasing data; and "data" itself is defined broadly enough to include not only text, but also photographs, video, and sound. Its restrictions recognize that certain kinds of data are particularly sensitive and vulnerable to abuse; thus, it contains heightened restrictions on processing data that would reveal the subject's personal traits, such as race, ethnicity, religious beliefs, or health background. In most cases, collecting and passing on these kinds of information requires the subject's *written* consent, or the companies cannot proceed.

The law also requires a degree of transparency. Data processors must disclose to their subjects the ways in which they intend to use the data.[78] Finally, in one of the directive's most restrictive and controversial portions, the drafters attempted to address the "borderless" nature of the Internet and the likelihood that user data could be processed in or transmitted to countries that were not subject to the law's protections. To protect against this vulnerability, the directive contains a provision that requires member states to prohibit the transfer of data to countries that have not adopted an "adequate level of protection" for personal data.[79] However as we have seen, implementing these protections has proven difficult, and enforcement across Europe has, at best, been inconsistent.

According to a 2011 report from the Center for Democracy and Technology, "although it is comprehensive in many ways, the [European] Data Protection Directive has significant weaknesses. Erratic enforcement and uneven implementation have left consumers and industry confused as to how the Directive's principles apply to emerging practices."[80]

In 2011, various EU authorities called for new, stronger privacy protection measures, especially in response to Facebook; however, so far these calls have not been translated into new laws, regulations, or enforcement mechanisms.

Limiting involuntary secondary usages of private information is much more popular in Europe than in the United States, as evidenced by the fact that the directive was enacted relatively early in the Internet's lifespan, while a comprehensive American approach has yet to be articulated. However, *the differences between the American and European approaches are much less pronounced than they may first seem.* This is the case because Europeans do allow involuntary secondary usages for a variety of purposes, which include national security, preventing criminal activity, journalistic freedom of speech, and personal use (for instance, an address book);[81] because the United States has limited a variety of secondary usages of what might be called "sensitive information;"[82] and because of what is called a "compliance gap"—that is, a gap between what is mandated by European laws and the extent to which governments enforce these laws.[83] The European Union's privacy protections suffer from this gap.

The ban on involuntary secondary usages burdens consumers, who have limited capacity to evaluate various privacy statements and corporate assurances that statements are indeed heeded. They are unaware of the risks of PVT. Business lobbies tend to strenuously oppose this approach, which makes it very unlikely to be enacted in the United States or heeded in Europe. And differences in laws and enforcement levels among countries, across whose borders the same information readily flows, greatly limit the value of this way of protecting privacy from private invasions.

4. Ban Public Use of Private Information?

Those who adhere to the traditional distinction between the public and private realm and to the precept that the main danger to privacy comes from Big Brother may suggest that banning the government from using private data banks is the way to proceed. The 1974 Privacy Act already states that the government may not *maintain* personal data records for citizens who are not the subjects of investigations;[84] it would be relatively simple to add that they also may not *use* records that already exist in the private sector. Still, these clarifications would not be necessary if the privacy merchants were limited to trading only in less sensitive information, and they would be of little use if the privacy merchants were not so limited. If the law permitted the use of sensitive information, it would, in effect, assume that it should be acceptable for data banks to be used for profit but not to enhance public health, security, or other components of the common good. (Security these days often brings to mind measures taken to prevent terrorist attacks. A considerable number of civil liberty advocates hold that these dangers have been exaggerated and that rights have therefore been unduly curtailed. However, one should note that security also encompasses criminal justice systems, which have utilized data banks to curb criminals.[85])

5. Increased Public Regulation of Sensitive Information?

A limited approach to curbing the privacy merchants would entail expanding the American patchwork of sectoral laws that limit privacy violations in one specific area or another. As Gina Stevens catalogues, "Federal laws and regulations extend protection to consumer credit reports, electronic communications, federal agency records, education records, bank records, cable subscriber information, video rental records, motor vehicle records, health information, telecommunications subscriber information, children's online information, and customer financial information."[86] One could add more areas to this long but seemingly arbitrary list.

The patchwork of laws can be viewed as being based on a rationale that treats differently three main areas—private information gleaned from public records (e.g., information about homeownership), relatively sensitive information (e.g., medical and financial information), and information that is in effect deemed less sensitive (e.g., most information about consumer choices). One can see the patchwork as being largely based on the level of sensitivity of the information. Public records, therefore, are open for dissemination online because this information was not private in the first place; less sensitive information is considered to need little protection because its use by third parties causes no or little harm; and sensitive information is protected. If one finds that some area is not well-protected, the argument runs, one can add another "patch" of legislation to cover it.

The patchwork approach has two serious defects, one that is oft-cited and one that is less often noted. It is widely recognized that the patchwork lags woefully behind technological developments in the private sector. Thus, legislation that attempts to cover uncovered areas is often "proposed" and "drafted" without ever being enacted. For example, as one proposed bill called for a federal requirement of a "Do Not Track" option for online advertising. Another suggested bill would deal with the relatively new technology of geolocation and mobile privacy.[87] The Federal Trade Commission is reportedly working on a regulatory framework governing social networking sites in the wake of high-profile FTC complaints against Google Buzz and Twitter. The FTC also plans to target smartphones, which is a market that regulation has thus far left virtually untouched.[88] However, none of these laws were enacted and they lag considerably behind technological developments employed by the privacy merchants, and, given the current antiregulatory climate, they are unlikely to be enacted in the foreseeable future.

Less often noted is that the distinction between "sensitive" and "less sensitive" information is much less obvious than it seems and is likely to further weaken in the near future. Even if sensitive information such as medical or financial records becomes better protected online, less sensitive—and therefore, less protected—information can reveal volumes of sensitive information thanks to PVT. As Marcy Peek points out, "The Internet has allowed commercial decision-makers to manipulate technology in such a way as to identify persons according to a multitude of variables and categories."[89] Each page Internet users visit and each ad they click on tracks their unique IP address to create a detailed portrait of their offline persona. Peek explains, "Through various means such as cookies, Web bugs, and personal data input such as zip codes, corporate marketers can obtain a person's demographic and other information and 'tag' an individual on the basis of such information." The individual is then categorized and ranked against other users. The result is "Weblining," an online version of the offline discriminatory practice of "redlining" individuals by denying or increasing the cost of services based on their demographic. After the Fair Housing Act of 1968 prohibited redlining, which used a mortgage applicant's neighborhood to discriminate along racial lines, banks used instead other markers of race as a basis for racial discriminations, relying on the social clubs people joined or churches they attended, for example. In other words, items of information that were not sensitive were used to divine other information that was meant to be private. Easy access to this type of nonsensitive information streamlines this practice.

As early as 2000, *Business Week* highlighted a PVT service, offered by data broker company Acxiom, called InfoBase Ethnicity System, which matched names against information about housing, education, and income in order to identify the unpublicized ethnicity of an individual or group.[90] More recently, a computer consultant named Tom Owad wrote a simple piece of software allowing him to download public wish lists that Amazon customers post to catalog products they plan to buy. He downloaded over 250,000 wish lists in one day, used Yahoo's People Search to identify addresses and phone numbers, and published a detailed map that showed the locations of people interested in certain books or themes. Owad explained, "It used to be you had to get a warrant to monitor a person or group of people. Today, it is increasingly easy to monitor ideas. And then track them back to people."[91] Most people who put simple items of information about their preferences on their Facebook profiles are unlikely to know that they can be used to divine their personality traits with 90 percent accuracy, as if they had taken personality tests.[92]

All of this suggests that laws that ban the use of sensitive information but do not require any action on the part of the millions of effected citizens—the way medical, financial, and select other records are now protected—could be reinforced by banning PVT of protected information. That is, the wall that separates more and less sensitive types of information could be shored up. (Granted, the debate about what information is sensitive and what information is not would continue.) The law could ban the privacy merchants from using information about consumer purchases (and other such "less" sensitive information) to divine one's medical condition (and other such "more" sensitive information).

Given the current pro-business, antiregulatory climate in Congress, the Supreme Court, and, it seems, among the voters, enactment of such laws in the United States may seem very unlikely. The prospect of such legislation improves if one notes that it would mainly curb those few corporations that make selling private information their main line of business. Other corporations that merely keep profiles of their own customers' preferences would not be affected, although their ability to sell this information to other parties might be limited in order to reduce the risk of PVT, and corporations' ability to advertise would be set back because they would not be allowed to use sensitive information in their targeting. Nevertheless, if such laws against PVT could be enacted, they would help shore up privacy to reasonable levels in the future, and without them, I expect PVT to otherwise be much extended. It is better to ban this approach before it catches on widely then try to eradicate it once is it has become widespread.

D. Conclusion

Corporations, especially those that make trading in private information their main line of business—the privacy merchants—are major violators of privacy, and their reach is rapidly expanding. Given that the information these corporations amass and process is also available to the government, it is no longer possible to protect privacy only by curbing the state. Suggesting that norms have changed and that people are now more willing to give up their privacy may be true, but only up to a point. The extent to which private aspects of one's medical and even financial condition are revealed is unlikely to be widely accepted as a social good. And violations of the privacy of dissenters and, more generally, privacy violations that intrude on one's political and social views (e.g., tracking what people read) have chilling effects, whether or not the majority of the public understands the looming implications of the unbounded profiling of most Americans. Self-regulation cannot come to the rescue, because the success of self-regulation rests on the assumption that individuals can sort out what corporations are doing behind the veils of their privacy statements, which is an unrealistic assumption. Banning the use of less sensitive information (particularly information about purchases) for the purposes of divining more sensitive information (e.g., medical information)—that is, outlawing privacy violating triangulation—may serve, if combined with laws that "patch" current legislation, to cover new technological developments (e.g., social media). If such dual progress is possible, there will be much less reason to prevent the government from drawing on the data banks maintained by the privacy merchants, because the government would be limited to less sensitive information, and PVT of innocent Americans would be banned. Without such progress, one must assume that what is private is also public in two senses of these words: First, that one's privacy, which includes sensitive matters, is rapidly being corroded by the private sector and second, that whatever the private sector learns is also available to the government.

6

The Private Sector: A Reluctant Partner in Cybersecurity

It may seem obvious that the private sector should be keen to protect its computers and networks from cyber attacks by criminals and foreign agents. After all, hacking has caused considerable losses of trade secrets and other proprietary information. Moreover, evidence suggests that cyber attacks can take a kinetic form, which can harm the equipment and facilities—such as the national electrical grid—of those attacked. However, as will be seen shortly, the private sector is far from rushing to protect itself from such attacks. The reasons for this reluctance range from the understandably pragmatic to the ideological. Meanwhile, in spite of major implications of this reluctance for homeland security, both the Bush and the Obama administrations limited themselves to cajoling the private sector to embrace much stronger cybersecurity measures rather than mandating their introduction.

A. Threat Levels

Private sector firms suffer considerable damage from cybersecurity breaches. A report from the Center for Strategic and International Studies finds that the costs to the global economy—which encompass losses of intellectual property, outright cybercrime, unauthorized access to confidential business and stock information, the costs of recovering from cyber attacks, and the value of reputational damages—of malicious cyber activity are "probably . . . [as much as] $400 billion"—or even $1 trillion per year. The United States alone is estimated to suffer up to $120 billion in economic losses per year.[1] In 2012, one metallurgical corporation reportedly "lost technology to China's hackers that cost $1 billion and 20 years to develop."[2] In some cases, companies have been driven entirely out of business by Chinese hackers' persistent cyber espionage.[3]

One report estimates that 508,000 American jobs have been lost due to cyber crime.[4] General Keith Alexander, until recently the director of the National Security Administration and commander of the U.S. Cyber Command, has estimated that economic espionage, including the kind practiced by Chinese and Russian hackers, represents "the greatest transfer of wealth in history."[5]

No industry is immune: cybersecurity firm Mandiant estimated in 2006 that cyber attacks tied to China's People's Liberation Army (PLA) alone targeted twenty separate, major industries including telecommunications, energy, and aerospace.[6] Even Google—arguably one of the most sophisticated companies in the world with regard to computer networks—fell victim to a complex hack that originated in China, during which the hackers "appropriated some of Google's search engine source codes, a vital piece of intellectual property."[7]

These estimates of losses do not include the legal costs of data breaches and those resulting from consumer confidence; moreover, companies are often forced to pay fines when their cybersecurity measures fail to protect consumer information. Heartland Payment Systems, for example, was slapped with $150 million in fines and legal costs that stemmed from a 2007 cybersecurity breach in which more than 100 million credit and debit card numbers were illegally obtained by hackers.[8] One research institute estimated that malicious attacks cost American firms $277 per customer or user whose information was put in jeopardy by a company's cybersecurity failures.[9] Nevertheless, many corporations resist introducing many of the cybersecurity measures recommended by the U.S. government.

B. Reasons for Weak Private Sector Response

The private sector's reluctance to adopt strong cybersecurity measures is driven by a combination of principles and practical concerns. Four of the most frequently articulated arguments against government mandated private sector cybersecurity standards follow.

First, significant segments of the private sector consider proposed requirements to introduce cybersecurity measures to be an additional form of government regulation. The Business Software Alliance opposes placing "undue regulatory burdens on industry,"[10] and the U.S. Chamber of Commerce opposes "legislation establishing regulatory-based cybersecurity standards."[11] The Heritage Foundation opposed the same bill because it would "create a cumbersome regulatory process." These and other corporate leaders and economically conservative commentators adhere to the laissez-faire and libertarian principles that private enterprise has a right to be left alone by the government and that the private sector is capable of independently determining how much and what kind of cybersecurity it needs.

However, as James A. Lewis, a highly regarded cybersecurity expert at the Center for Strategic and International Studies, points out, "The market *has failed* to secure cyberspace. A ten-year experiment in faith-based cybersecurity has proven this beyond question."[12] That is, ten years after the industry's conversation about private sector cybersecurity began, corporations continued to be inundated with cybersecurity breaches. Christopher Cox, former chairperson of the Security and Exchange Commission, put it more bluntly: "Voluntary regulation [of cybersecurity] does not work."[13]

Because corporations are considered rational actors, one might well expect that they would voluntarily take measures to protect their trade secrets and hence profits. The reasons they often do not are varied. For example, CEOs have been shown to focus on short-term costs and benefits, to the detriment of longer-term effects. The consequences of stolen trade secrets often take years to unfold because competitors need time to use the information they gained to build and market their own products. Moreover, humans tend to be poor at assessing the probabilistic costs of their actions.[14] Therefore, it is unsurprising that CEOs and other executives seem to underestimate even the short-term consequences of failing to shore up cybersecurity. This problem is compounded by executives' inexperience with technology. "Most [board members and executives] have gray hair," one banker and media executive said. "It's like having someone who has never paid any attention to their health talk to a doctor."[15] One expert on cybersecurity, meanwhile, writes, "Cyber-security resembles environmental law in that both fields are primarily concerned with negative externalities. Just as firms tend to under-invest in pollution controls because some costs of their emissions are borne by those who are downwind, they also tend to underinvest in cyber-defenses because some costs of intrusions are externalized onto others."[16] Whatever the reasons, *The Wall Street Journal* writes that in the first six months of 2014 alone "1,517 U.S.-traded firms . . . have cited hacking as a business risk in filings," and that "federal officials and others say many companies remain ignorant of, and unprepared for, Internet intruders."[17]

Second, other opponents of government cybersecurity regulations claim that government mandates will actually hamper cybersecurity and other innovations in the private sector. In 2012, the U.S. Chamber of Commerce called on Senate Republicans to filibuster a bill that would have established cybersecurity standards for private sector critical infrastructure, on the grounds that the bill could actually "hamper companies trying to defend against cyber intrusions."[18] The argument seems to be that establishing clear standards for companies would impede their flexibility by forcing them to introduce cumbersome or inefficient cybersecurity measures.

Third, private sector representatives have suggested that cybersecurity regulations would impose substantial costs, which the private sector would be incapable of meeting profitably. A company would need to spend millions in order to develop effective cybersecurity systems.[19] Given that about 82,000 strains of malware were created daily in 2013, it would take large sums of money to "stay ahead of the curve."[20] Furthermore, "businesses consider it unfair and inappropriate for the government to impose on private industries security requirements that businesses consider a public-sector responsibility. Such requirements are viewed as 'unfunded mandates.'"[21] That is, corporate leaders argue that the provision of security is the job of the government; thus, they hold that if the government requires others to do part of the job by adding security measures above and beyond those they would already independently introduce, the corporations should be compensated for the related costs. However, these claims are hard to justify when one considers the sheer bulk of many private sector corporations' budgets: Target, the object of a notorious December 2013 breach, had a $1.6 million cybersecurity system in place, true, but their revenues that year topped $72 billion—making their investment in cybersecurity roughly 0.0002 percent of their revenue.[22]

Fourth, the private sector has expressed concern that regulations mandating that corporations report cybersecurity breaches to the federal government and share news of cyber threats with their industry peers would cause them damaging publicity or lead to lawsuits alleging liability for damages to private citizens. One law office that provides corporate counsel wrote that Target's "potential total costs could reach over $1 billion" following a major cybersecurity breach in December 2013. Another source estimates that the cost of Target's failure could top $18 billion once lost revenues due to negative publicity are factored in.[23] When retailer Neiman Marcus suffered a similar security breach a few weeks later, it—and three other retailers—waited a month to notify customers, presumably in an effort to minimize negative publicity.[24]

In April 2014, the U.S. Senate introduced a bill that would incentivize private sector sharing of cybersecurity data by providing liability protection against lawsuits.[25] Senator Dianne Feinstein, chair of the Senate Intelligence Committee, stated that the bill "allows companies to monitor their computer networks for cyber-attacks, promotes sharing of cyber threat information and provides liability protection for companies who share that information."[26] However, this bill has not been adopted.

Moreover, not everyone agrees that the protection of corporations from liability will properly incentivize the private sector to adopt cybersecurity measures. Senator Jay Rockefeller has argued that offering "safe harbors" against liability for damages to third parties caused by breaches of cybersecurity in exchange for company compliance with President Obama's new framework would not lead companies to develop dynamic, effective cybersecurity measures. Instead, "such an approach would likely have the opposite effect. . . . Giving companies unprecedented liability protections based on cybersecurity standards that they themselves have developed would increase the likelihood that the American taxpayers will one day find themselves on the hook for corporate bailouts of unknown scope following a cyber disaster."[27]

C. A Reluctant Federal Government

In face of strong private sector opposition, the federal government has largely resorted to cajoling the private sector to implement cybersecurity measures and has eschewed mandatory regulation. Stewart Baker, who served as Assistant Secretary for Policy at the Department of Homeland Security, has described the fate of cybersecurity proposals advocated by Richard Clarke, the first White House cybersecurity czar. According to Baker, the proposal "sidled up toward new mandates for industry, would have formed a security research fund that would have drawn on contributions from technology companies, and would have increased pressure on Internet companies to provide security technology with their products. However, these requirements were viewed as too onerous for business by many within the Bush administration, and ultimately anything that could offend industry, anything that hinted at government mandates, was stripped out."[28] One bill proposed by Congress initially "called for mandatory minimum security standards" for the private sector, but the Chamber of Commerce and other corporate representatives opposed the regulations. To salvage the bill's chances of passing, it was rewritten to advocate voluntary standards; nonetheless, the bill failed.[29] And President Obama, in a 2009 address regarding cybersecurity policy, explicitly stated, "My administration will not dictate security standards for private companies."

Instead, the federal government has recently taken a number of preliminary steps to encourage the private sector to adopt more stringent cybersecurity measures. In August 2013, it identified a number of possible incentives that could be used to entice the private sector to adopt cybersecurity best practices, including "cybersecurity insurance, federal grants, and legal protections for companies that invest additional money in cybersecurity efforts."[30] The government also offered guidance to sixteen critical infrastructure sectors about how to shield themselves from cyber attacks, but did not mandate compliance with its recommendations.[31] The General

Services Administration, in conjunction with the Department of Defense, recommended that private sector entities be required to comply with "baseline" cybersecurity principles at all levels of the supply chain as a condition of being awarded contracts with the federal government.[32] However, this recommendation has not been adopted. Several pieces of legislation have been proposed in Congress to either sanction private sector entities that fail "to adopt 'reasonable' data security practices" or to grant the Federal Trade Commission authorization to craft cybersecurity regulations for the private sector.[33] However, like other proposed legislations, these drafted bills have not yet become law. Cybersecurity in the private sector, as this section has demonstrated, remains far from satisfactory.

D. Implications for Homeland Security

One might hold that if the private sector fails to protect itself from cyber attacks, it will suffer the consequences and eventually mend its ways. The same line of thinking suggests that the government should focus on protecting its computers and networks, especially those that belong to the Departments of Defense and Homeland Security, the Central Intelligence Agency, and the Federal Bureau of Investigation. This is, in effect, the position that the Bush and Obama administrations have followed. However, this approach ignores that considerable amounts of defense and homeland security work are carried out by the private sector.

For fiscal year 2013, the federal government awarded a total of $460 billion in contracts, much of which seems to have gone to defense contractors.[34] In 2010, the Department of Defense spent about $400 billion of its $700 billion annual budget on private contractors that provided vehicles, armor, weapons, transportation, logistical support, and many other goods and services, which ranged from aircraft carriers and nuclear submarines to hand grenades and Meals Ready to Eat (MREs). The federal government also outsources much of the work of intelligence collection and analysis to private sector contractors. About "one in four intelligence workers has been a private contractor, and 70 percent or more of the intelligence community's secret budget has gone to private firms," according to a *Washington Post* report.[35] And private security firms such as Blackwater—which has since been renamed Xe Services and, later, Academi—were contracted to protect diplomats,[36] offer counterterrorism training, and supplement U.S. military forces in Iraq and elsewhere.[37]

Thus, inadequate cybersecurity at private firms allows adversarial governments and nongovernmental actors to acquire information that could greatly harm U.S. defense and homeland security. To cite a recent example, on May 19, 2014, Attorney General Eric Holder Jr. announced charges against five members of the People's Liberation Army's Shanghai cyberunit and alleged that the hackers infiltrated the computer networks of several American corporations.[38] Among these were Allegheny Technologies, which provides "materials and components" to a diverse group of clients including defense contractors; and Alcoa, which manufactures a range of materials used in defense.[39] In the past, General Dynamics, Boeing, Lockheed Martin, Raytheon, and Northrop Grumman—the United States' leading defense contractors[40]—have all fallen victim to hackers. And a cyber-espionage operation against Lockheed Martin in 2007 made it possible for China to steal design details of the F-35 Lightning II, which were subsequently used to develop China's J-20 stealth fighter plane.[41]

Moreover the private sector is responsible for supplying and maintaining much of the technology, which includes information technology, used by the government. The computers and software used by the Department of Defense—and other federal agencies—are themselves designed, manufactured, and often serviced by the private sector. Prior to the 1990s, the Pentagon used in-house programmers to design secure software tailored to the military's needs. However, the military has since increasingly shifted to off-the-shelf commercial software as a means of cutting costs and satisfying Congress, which seems to be influenced by private sector lobbying.[42] These technologies are vulnerable not only because they are produced in the private sector, but also because the private sector often sources its equipment and components overseas—which includes China.

Third, the private sector is responsible for the maintenance of much of the United States' critical infrastructure, including energy, telecommunications, transportation, health services, and banking and finances. Without the private sector's willing adoption of stronger cybersecurity measures, these critical services remain vulnerable to kinetic cyber attacks. On June 6, 2014, the Financial Stability Oversight Council released a report that shows that the financial industry is vulnerable to cyber attacks. It held that "cyber incidents that disrupt, degrade, or impact the integrity and availability of critical financial infrastructure . . . [could] threaten the stability of the financial system."[43] Another June 2014 report from the Government Accountability Office cautioned that "maritime security plans required by law and regulation generally [do] not identify or address potential cyber-related threats." Thus, private "maritime stakeholders" at U.S. ports, which handle more than $1.3 trillion in goods per year, remain vulnerable to cyber attacks, which could shut down business communications, disable physical security systems, and more.[44]

In short, the difference between the public and private sectors is much smaller than is often assumed in public discourse.[45] There can be no reliable cybersecurity in the public realm unless there is also heightened cybersecurity in the private realm. The security chain is only as strong as its weakest link—and the private sector's link is simultaneously poorly forged and critically important to U.S. defense and security.

What can be done? The private sector, especially those firms that manufacture defense items such as submarines and aircraft carriers, as well as those that provide hardware and software to the government, would be much more attentive to cybersecurity needs if the federal government were to disqualify from receiving government contracts any corporations that are not in full compliance with government cybersecurity standards. President Obama's 2013 Cybersecurity Executive Order has called for this step, and the White House has directed a joint working group to "develop an implementation plan for these recommendations."[46] However, this strong corrective assumes a different political climate, in which Congress, which is rather responsive to corporate lobbying, would allow the administration to set standards and develop blacklists. At the moment, such blacklists are not even drafted for corporations that are found to engage in corruption. One government agency might cease to grant a corporation contracts, but there is no list of corrupt corporations that other agencies can consult. The publication of articles like this one and increased public outcry on the subject might help change the political climate and advance cybersecurity.

7

Liberal Communitarian Approach to Privacy and Security[1]

A. Balancing Privacy and Security

1. The Liberal Communitarian Approach

Liberal communitarian philosophy (developed by the author[2]) assumes that nations face several fully legitimate normative and legal claims and that these claims can be neither maximized nor fully reconciled, as there is an inevitable tension among them. It follows that society must work out some balance among the conflicting claims rather than assume that one will always trump the others. This chapter applies this approach to the balance between security and privacy.[3]

In contrast to this balancing approach, contemporary liberals tend to emphasize individual rights and autonomy over societal formulations of the common good.[4] At the opposite end of the spectrum, authoritarian communitarians (mainly in East Asia[5]) privilege the common good a priori, and pay mind to rights mainly to the extent that they serve the rulers' aims.

As discussed in Chapter 1, the Fourth Amendment is an eminently liberal communitarian text. When it comes to give-and-take over what qualifies as legitimate public policy, liberal communitarianism starts from the assumption that the public's right to privacy must be balanced with the concern for national security (and public health, among other common goods), rather than from the position that any breach of privacy contravenes an inviolable basic right.

2. The Advocacy Model

Deliberations about public policy as carried out by elected officials, in think tanks, and in public discourse in the contemporary United States often follow a model that differs sharply from the liberal communitarian one, which emulates the advocacy model found in American courts. According to this model, interested parties are divided into antagonistic, ideological camps, with each side—and there are only two—presenting its respective interpretation of the facts in the way that will most strongly support its brief. Following the notion that one ought to "zealously" defend one's client, each side feels free to make emotive points, provide stretched interpretations and selective facts, and advance particularistic normative arguments favorable to its case. The implicit assumption is that the proper judgment (if not "the truth") will arise out of the clash of two extreme advocacy positions. American judges (unlike, for instance, French ones) act as neutral referees, and the jury is kept mum during the proceedings.

In public discourse, the advocacy model is reflected in the increasingly polarized debates between liberals and conservatives over numerous issues including the role of government, gun control, abortion rights, and even climate change.[6] Liberal communitarianism and other intermediary positions are often barely heard over the noise from the resulting clash.

In comparing the advocacy and the liberal communitarian approaches to public discourse, one notes that intermediary or third positions (not necessarily compromises) find little room in the former. Moreover, the advocacy approach does not take into account the basic tenets of the balancing approach of the Constitution, especially the Fourth Amendment. Typical pro-privacy arguments run as follows: There is a right to privacy that is important both in its own right and as a necessary means for realizing various other values such as democracy, creativity, and the flourishing of the self. The government is violating this right by this or that act; thus, the government should be made to desist. The implicit assumption is that the whole normative and legal realm is the domain of the right and any consideration of other values, such as security, constitutes an "intrusion." When Nadine Strossen was asked when she served as the president of the American Civil Liberties Union (ACLU) if she ever encountered any security measure of which she approved, she first responded with a firm "no" and then corrected herself and approved of fortifying the doors of commercial airliners that separate the pilot's cockpit from the cabin holding the passengers.[7] Similarly, the ACLU objected even to the use of handheld computers at Transportation Security Administration (TSA) checkpoints—describing them as "a violation of the core democratic principle that the government should not be permitted to violate a person's privacy, unless it has a reason to believe that he or she is involved in wrongdoing"—despite the fact that these computers were using the same data as all the other computers and simply reduced the distance agents had to travel to review the data. That is, they added a bit of convenience rather than constituting a new intrusion.[8]

However, the Fourth Amendment and the liberal communitarian approach it reflects divide searches between those that are reasonable and those that are not, *and hence reasonable searches do not constitute an intrusion and are not a violation of privacy*. That is, the normative and legal realm is divided between segments in which security should take precedence and those in which privacy should. The discourse should be about where the boundary lies. It is hence misleading to argue as if the whole domain was that of privacy and any attention to security entails a diminution of privacy. The "turf" is divided between these two concerns from the get-go. (It is hence just as untenable to argue that the realm is one of security only and that any concern for privacy ipso facto entails a diminution of security.)

3. Anti-Balance Arguments

Because the idea of balance is at the essence of the approach here followed—and because it has been directly challenged—I offer a brief defense of the concept. Some critics contend that one should not think in terms of "balance" when weighing the values of privacy and security. For example, Marc Rothenberg writes

> When we confronted the issue of privacy ... we could not say that we needed to balance privacy and security. Both interests are substantial. . . often times in discussions where people said, "Well, privacy is important but so is the First Amendment;" "Privacy is important but so is open government;" "Privacy is important but so is this other thing." And on many of these issues we came to realize that if you look closely there may be a way to pursue both interests simultaneously.[9]

David Medine, the chairperson of the Privacy and Civil Liberties Oversight Board, made this point strongly when he stated that "the 9/11 commission and President Obama have said—and I certainly believe—that we can have both strong security and strong protections on privacy and civil liberty, and our job is to try to maximize both."[10]

One wonders if one can maximize *any* value, even when it is not in conflict with some other value, in the real world, which is full of constraints. One further notes that much of ethics concerns itself not with delineating right from wrong, but rather with exploring the tension between various goods—for instance, trade-offs between equality and freedom. True, there are conditions in which both security and privacy can be enhanced; for example, when a regime collapses and a measure of law and order is restored after a period of chaos and lawlessness. However, under most conditions some balancing is needed because both values cannot be maximized. Thus, numerous court cases weigh which side—privacy or the public interest—should take precedence in the given situation and conditions.

4. Within History

The balance between privacy and security that the liberal communitarian paradigm seeks must be constantly adjusted as historical circumstances change (e.g., following the 2001 attacks on the U.S. homeland) and following technological developments (e.g., improvements in facial recognition technology). Thus, a society ought to afford more leeway to security measures if there are valid reasons for thinking that the threat to the public has significantly increased, and give less leeway once the threat has subsided. This chapter next turns to examining the criteria that can serve to help sort out where the balance lies in a particular historical situation.

B. The Four Criteria: Finding the Balance

The liberal communitarian approach draws on four criteria to identify a proper balance between the competing values of security and privacy for a given nation in a given time period.[11] First, a liberal democratic government will limit privacy only if it faces a well-documented and large-scale threat to national security, not merely a hypothetical threat or one limited to a few individuals or localities. The main reason this threshold must be cleared is that modifying legal precepts—and with them the ethical, social, and public philosophies that underlie them—endangers their legitimacy. Changes, therefore, should not be undertaken unless there is strong evidence that either national security or privacy has been significantly undermined.

The 9/11 attacks constituted a significant change to historical conditions by revealing the serious threat posed by nonstate actors determined to strike within the borders of the United States. Because there have been no significant new attacks within the country since 2001, there is a growing tendency to call for a rebalancing, to oppose enhanced security measures (e.g., surveillance by the NSA and special judicial proceedings for suspected terrorists), and to call for more attention to privacy concerns (e.g., by relaxing TSA search standards and restricting the use of surveillance technologies such as drones). However, although the United States has done much to disrupt al Qaeda and other such groups, the threat of terrorism still seems considerable. There remain many hundreds of thousands of people around the world who deeply hate the United States and what it stands for, consider it to be the "Great Satan," wish it harm, and believe that using violence against it constitutes an act of martyrdom. It seems reasonable to assume that some of these individuals will act on their beliefs. At the same time, al Qaeda has regrouped and established new affiliates in Africa,[12] the Arabian Peninsula,[13] and in other parts of the world.[14]

Worse, there is a significant danger that these hostile groups might get their hands on a weapon capable of inflicting far more damage than the planes that brought down the Twin Towers—which is to say, a nuclear weapon. Both Russia and Pakistan have less-than-fully secured nuclear arms within their borders.[15] The situation in the latter nation seems to pose a particular threat, as the government has so far been either unable or unwilling to combat terrorists within its borders and has experienced at least six serious terrorist attempts to penetrate its nuclear facilities.[16]

In 2009, Najibullah Zazi—a Denver cab driver who was trained in explosives by al Qaeda—was caught constructing bombs that he planned to detonate in the New York City subways.[17] The NSA intercepted an e-mail between Zazi and an al Qaeda operative that tipped the government off to the plot and prevent it from being carried out,[18] apparently only days before Zazi and his accomplices planned to carry out the attack.[19] At the same time, a similar plot to bomb the New York Stock Exchange was also foiled by the government's surveillance.[20] Overall, U.S. intelligence officials claim that PRISM (an NSA surveillance program, revealed by the Snowden leaks, that collects the Internet communications of non–U.S. nationals) and the collection of phone company metadata disrupted fifty-four terrorist plots, one-fifth of which were to be carried out within the borders of the United States.[21] This number does not include the plots that were foiled by using more traditional methods or those that were successfully carried out, such as the Boston Marathon bombing. To conclude, it is impossible to reliably measure the scope of the terrorist threat, even for those who have full access to all available intelligence. However, given the evidence just cited, it seems that the time has not yet come to rebalance by reducing security measures.

To turn to the second criterion, once it has been established that national security needs shoring up, one had best seek to establish *whether this goal can be achieved without introducing new limits on privacy*. For instance, it would satisfy this balancing criterion to store data so that it would be available on very short notice if needed to track the movements and whereabouts of a particular individual, but encrypt and secure data, and making it accessible only with a court order—a procedure reportedly followed by those overseeing and carrying out the NSA program that holds American phone records.[22]

Third, to the extent that privacy-curbing measures must be introduced, they should be *as nonintrusive as possible*. For example, in 2013, the TSA gave up its use of body scanners that revealed almost nude images and began using instead scanners that produce "cartoon-like" images, on which the scanners mark the places where hidden objects are detected.[23] In this way, the TSA was able to carry out the same thorough search in a way that was far less intrusive than full-body pat downs or scanning that revealed every contour of the traveler's body.

Fourth, measures that *ameliorate undesirable side effects* of necessary privacy-diminishing measures are to be preferred over those that ignore these effects. Thus, to the extent that those engaged in counterterrorism searchers are instructed to ignore misdemeanors such as minor drug offenses or vandalism, this criterion is met.

C. Narrowing the Gap

1. Generalized Search Is Legal and Legitimate

The privacy model most often employed by privacy advocates is that of probable cause and individualized search. These advocates argue that, before law enforcement officials search anyone, it should be required—and indeed is required, according to the Constitution—that they present to a court of law evidence demonstrating that strong reason exists (enough to convince a judge) to believe that the particular person is likely to be a terrorist. Only then, according to these advocates, can said person be subjected to surveillance.[24]

The courts, however, have long established that when there is both a clear public interest and the privacy intrusion is small, "general searches" (i.e., of masses of people, without individualized causes) are legal and necessary, thus employing, in effect, a similar line of analysis to the liberal communitarian one outlined earlier. This principle has been applied to airport screening,[25] sobriety checkpoints,[26] drug tests of those whose jobs involve public safety,[27] and the screening of mail and Internet communications. This endorsement of general searches has been supplemented by other rulings that have legitimated the government's power to conduct generalized searches.

General searches were further legitimized by Section 215 of the Patriot Act and the National Security letters authorized by the same. This legislation allows the government to conduct surveillance without first identifying an individual as a suspected terrorist and also grants it the authority to search through third-party databases without notifying suspects—as long as the information is "relevant" to a terrorism investigation.[28]

2. Computers Are Blind, Deaf, and Dumb

The incontrovertible fact that privacy and security pose conflicting demands and hence must be balanced does not mean that one cannot find ways to reduce the conflict between these two core values. One major way is to draw a sharp line between what is stored in and processed by computers—and what is revealed to human agents. Computers, per se, do not violate privacy. They do not gossip. They see no evil, hear no evil, and speak no evil. They can (vastly) facilitate privacy violations—but only as perpetrated by human agents. (Indeed, with respect to much of the data collected by the NSA, "they park stuff in storage in the hopes they will eventually have time to get to it or that they'll find something that they need to go back and look for in the masses of data . . . most of it sits and is never looked at by anyone."[29]) Hence, those who are concerned with finding a reasonable balance between security and privacy should focus on the interface between computers and human agents. That is, we should ensure that once the computers flag particular individuals, this information is revealed only to law enforcement authorities and used by them in legal and accountable ways.

Thus, computers can pull out all those who purchased a one-way ticket, paid with cash, and got the ticket at the last moment. It is far from clear, at least to this sociologist, that finding such patterns can suffice to identify terrorists. However, such searches could lead to closer computerized scrutiny (e.g., to see if those who drew attention have also made calls to areas in which terrorists train, have traveled to those same areas, or have visited al Qaeda websites) and, if suspicious activity is found, the computers could then alert a human agent.

D. Trust but Verify

1. Curb Abuses

Critics have strong reason to hold that, if the government is granted the power to collect information about the private lives of individuals, the government will abuse it. Among possible abuses are the use of data to find and prosecute people of opposing political views, which some have called the Nixon effect;[30] to stigmatize people whose conduct violates established norms but not the law, such as those who have adulterous affairs, abortions, or unusual sexual preferences, which one might call the "Scarlet Letter" effect; to keep information that, in the past, would have been slowly forgotten, thereby allowing people to develop new identities, such as a person whose "conviction of graffiti vandalism at age 19 will still be there at age 29 when [they're] a solid citizen trying to get a job and raise a family"[31]; and to go after crimes other than terrorist acts.

There is no question that, in the past, all of these abuses have taken place. One should also note that they are not one and the same kind. The

Nixon and Scarlet Letter effects are clearly troubling, and one must discuss how to curb and deter them. The status of a newly minted right by privacy advocates—the right to be forgotten—is much less clear, because evidence shows that erasing the past much more often leads to people who abuse children, failures to revoke the medical licenses of alcoholic and addict doctors who have killed patients, and con artists to abuse the elderly.[32]

The question of using personal information to find criminals rather than terrorists raises a serious question of balance. On the one hand, there is reason to hold that the extraordinary powers granted to the government to counter terrorism, given the special threat, should not be used for other purposes. On the other, in a society in which over 35 percent of homicide cases remain unsolved, with that number rising to nearly 60 percent for cases of rape and almost 90 percent for instances of burglary and motor vehicle theft, some extension of powers to enhance public safety might be justified.[33] Sorting out this particular balance between privacy and public safety other than counterterrorism is beyond the purview of this chapter but deserves much more attention that it has been granted so far.

The discussion next turns to the question of what measures can be taken to further ensure that counterterrorism powers will not be abused in any of the ways they have been in the past. That is, instead of arguing that there is no need to rebalance security and privacy in order to minimize future terrorist attacks—the challenge now is, given the assumption that a rebalancing is called for, what measures can be added to those in place to ensure that the enhanced powers will be employed only for legitimate purposes?

The reason the challenge is worded in terms of which measures should be "added" rather than which should be "employed," is that many are already in place. The executive branch has layers upon layers of supervisors, who are the first line of accountability. In addition, there are Inspectors General and Privacy Officers who often serve as quite forceful critics of the practices of concern here.[34] Congress has various committees charged with oversight, and there is also the investigative branch of the Government Accountability Office.[35] The courts, too, play an important role in checking and balancing abuses of government power. The media also frequently acts as a major guardian against abuses. Investigative bodies such as the Pike and Church committees—as well as the 9/11 Commission—also serve to review and vet the government's claims and behavior. In the past, all these institutions served to reveal abuses when they occurred and acted to curb them, albeit often only after considerable delay. Further, the fact that abuses occurred at all suggests that there is reason to further enhance scrutiny of the government and to establish additional precautionary measures.

Accountability versus Transparency

In searching for measures to enhance scrutiny, one must make a sharp distinction between two major ways of proceeding. (1) Enhanced transparency and (2) increased accountability (and oversight).

Enhanced transparency refers to an increase in the information about counterterrorism measures provided to the media and the general public, as well as to all members of Congress rather than to a select few with security clearance who serve on specialized committees. Following the revelations of the NSA programs in 2013, there was considerable demand for such disclosures and for increased transparency. The president emphasized that the programs were transparent,[36] with aides stating that they were going to try to be even more so,[37] and additional information was released by the government[38] on top of the continued stream of leaks. At the same time, over a quarter of the Senate has urged the White House to be more transparent about its surveillance practices.[39]

Although, as I argue later in this chapter, increases in transparency are often not the best way to proceed when compared to improvements in accountability, some potential ways to enhance transparency should be introduced. For example, the government should release summaries of the effects of its security measures without going into details that might help terrorists.

The second approach is to increase the power of and add layers to institutional accountability and oversight mechanisms. Although both might be called for, there are strong reasons to rely more on enhanced accountability and oversight than on much enhanced transparency. The distinction reflects the well-known difference between direct democracy (which is the idea behind transparency—the people will know all the details and judge the merit of the programs) and representative democracy (which assumes that a good part of the judgment will be made by elected representatives, and the public will judge them in turn).

Significantly higher levels of transparency present two kinds of serious problems. The first is well known and plagues all efforts for direct democracy. There are sharp limits to the capacity of the public, which is busy making a living and leading a social life, to learn the details of any government program and evaluate it—especially given that, in the end, they cannot vote any program up or down, but have only one "holistic" vote for representatives and all that they favor and oppose. Second, high transparency is, on the face of it, incompatible with keeping secret that which must be kept secret. Moreover, when the government responds to calls for more scrutiny with the release of more information—so as to demonstrate that the secret acts did, in fact, improve security and did not unduly violate privacy—these releases encounter several difficulties. Each piece of information released potentially helps the adversaries. This is, in effect, the way intelligence work is often done—by piecing together details released by various sources. Thus, the publication of information about which past operations of terrorists the government aborted could allow those groups to find out which of their plots failed because of American government interventions and which failed because of technical flaws, the weakness of their chosen agents, or some other reason. Also, it is nearly impossible to spell out how these cases unfolded without giving away details about sources and methods; that is, unless the government releases misleading details. Sooner or later, though, some whistleblower would likely expose the ploy, undermining the whole enterprise, which was meant to build trust in government. Thus, one intelligence official reports that the leaks regarding the NSA snooping programs have already led to terrorist groups "changing their communications behavior based on these disclosures," meaning that we might "miss tidbits that could be useful in stopping the next plot."[40]

Moreover, however much information about specific cases the government releases, skeptics are sure to find details that need further clarification and documentation. (This is the reason public relations experts urge those whose misdeeds are under public scrutiny to "tell all" right from the start, which is a strategy that may serve well politicians who cheat on their spouses, but would not serve those who deal with combating terrorism.) Thus, following the uproar over PRISM, technology companies sought to "reassure users" by releasing reports on the frequency of government data requests. The result, as reported by *The New York Times*, was that "rather than provide clarity, the companies' disclosures have left many questions unanswered."[41] When NSA Director General Keith Alexander released details about how the agency's surveillance programs had thwarted terrorist plots, the media immediately asked for more.[42] Moreover, there is no way for the media to determine whether the released cases are typical or were chosen because they reflect well on the government.

By contrast, a representative democracy approach suggests that one ought to search for ways to enhance the accountability and oversight power of various institutions including Congressional committees, the Foreign Intelligence Surveillance Act (FISA) appeal courts, the Government Accountability Office (GAO), various inspectors general, and privacy officers.

A report on the operation of the Terrorist Finance Tracking Program (TFTP) provides a powerful example. A project developed by the U.S. Treasury, the TFTP collects large amounts of data from a financial messaging system, called Swift, that records data on financial transfers that were conducted. The TFTP used this information to uncover terrorist networks and to prevent multiple attacks.[43] Importantly, the TFTP was subjected to significant oversight, with only narrowly focused searches and analyses of the data being permitted, and two different groups of independent auditors ensuring that those restrictions were being strictly adhered to.[44] Moreover, any time a government analyst wanted to query the system, they would have to submit a reason for their request, which could then be approved or denied by a Swift representative.[45]

Briefing many more members of Congress may well not be the best way to proceed, as most members of Congress do not have the security clearance that the members and key staffers of the intelligence committees of Congress possess, and many are known to be notorious leakers themselves. Moreover, the public's trust in Congress is at a historical low point.

Instead, the media and the public would benefit from a regular review conducted by an independent civilian review board. Such a board would be composed of individuals like those who served on the 9/11 Commission: bipartisan, highly respected by the public, able to work together, not running for office, and possessing the necessary security clearance. While not everyone agreed with that commission's conclusions, the members were still well-respected and largely trusted, and many of their recommendations were eventually implemented.

The new board would issue reports, perhaps annually, that would state whether the government collected information for political reasons or security concerns, whether they collected information in the pursuit of minor crimes rather than terrorists, and generally whether they did so for legitimate and legal goals. However, instead of revealing detailed case studies, the civilian review board would provide statistics. For example, if it reported that there were a large number of cases in which serious threats were averted, such as the planned attack on New York City's subway, the public would learn that the threats to national security warranted increased efforts to enforce anti-leak legislation. If, on the other hand, the board reported that many cases involve fairly minor threats, this would tilt the consensus the other way.[46] (If the current Civil Liberties and Privacy Protection board would be properly staffed, funded, and its powers increased, it might serve such a function).

3. Can We Trust the Government?

A common claim among civil libertarians is that even if little harm is presently being inflicted by government surveillance programs, the infrastructure is in place for a less-benevolent leader to violate the people's rights and set us on the path to tyranny. For example, it has been argued that PRISM "will amount to a 'turnkey' system that, in the wrong hands, could transform the country into a totalitarian state virtually overnight. Every person who values personal freedom, human rights and the rule of law must recoil against such a possibility, regardless of their political preference."[47] A few things might be said in response.

First, all of the data that the government is collecting is already being archived (at least for short periods—as discussed earlier) by private corporations and other entities. It is not the case that PRISM or other such programs entail the collection of new data that was not previously available. Second, if one is truly concerned that a tyrant might take over the United States, one obviously faces a much greater and all-encompassing threat than a diminution of privacy, and the response would have to be similarly expansive. One could join civic bodies that seek to shore up democracies, or work with various reform movements and public education drives, or with groups that prepare to retreat to the mountains, store ammunition and essential foods, and plan to fight the tyrannical forces. But it makes no sense to oppose limited measures to enhance security on these grounds.

8

The Right to Be Forgotten

A. Second Chances: A Generic Opportunity

A young man in upstate New York drinks too much and gets a little rowdy, picks a fight, smashes up the bar, and is arrested. When he gets into trouble again a short time later, the judge sends him to jail for a week. After his release, he gets fired and cannot find a new job because he has a record. The local newspaper carries a story about his misconduct. The merchants on Main Street refuse to sell him anything on credit. The young women gossip about him and refuse to date him. One day, he has had enough. He packs his meager belongings, leaves without a good-bye, and moves to a small town in Oregon. Here, he gains a new start. Nobody knows about his rowdy past, and he has learned his lesson. He drinks less, avoids fights, works in a lumberyard, and soon marries a nice local woman, has three kids, and lives happily ever after. Cue the choir of angels singing in the background.

The idea that people deserve a second chance is an important American value. Perhaps it grows out of America's history as a nation of immigrants who moved to the United States to start new lives. And as the American West was settled, many Easterners and Midwesterners found a place there for a second beginning. More profoundly, the belief in a new beginning is a tenet of Christianity, which allows sinners to repent and be fully redeemed, to be reborn. In a similar vein, the secular, progressive, optimistic, therapeutic culture of today's America rejects the notion that there are inherently bad people. As individuals, Americans seek insights into their failings so they can learn to overcome them and achieve a new start. From a sociological perspective, people are thrown off course by their social conditions—because they are poor, for instance, and subject to discrimination. But these conditions can be altered, and then these people will be able to lead good lives. Under the right conditions, criminals can pay their debt to society and be rehabilitated, sex offenders can be reformed, and others who have flunked out can pass another test. Just give them a second chance.

Today, a wide variety of public figures call for giving everyone a second chance. Texas governor and former presidential candidate Rick Perry said, "The idea that we lock people up, throw them away, and never give them a chance of redemption is not what America is about [. . .] Being able to give someone a second chance is very important."[1] New York Representative Charles Rangel is "a firm believer that upon release, ex-offenders should be afforded a second chance to become productive citizens by providing rehabilitation and education that will help them join the workforce."[2] Former Secretary of State Hillary Clinton frequently asserts that "everyone deserves a second chance, a third chance to keep going and to make something of themselves [. . .] That was one of the most important lessons of my life." Famous singer and former drug addict El DeBarge called for "the world to know that everybody deserves a second chance."[3] Rabbi Bernard Barsky asked, "How could a Jewish community not be committed to giving ex-felons a second chance? Our entire faith is based on stories of second chances."[4] And even church leader the Reverend Glenn Grayson, whose eighteen-year-old son was shot and killed, said that "if [God] can give us a second chance, [. . .] there are things you have to atone for, but you deserve a second chance."[5]

The Internet poses a great technological challenge to social forgiveness. By indexing digital versions of local public records, the Internet acts as a bright light that casts people's shadows much further than ever before: criminal or otherwise debilitating records now follow people wherever they go. True, arrest records, criminal sentences, bankruptcy filings, and even divorce records were accessible to the public long before being digitized. Some were listed in blotters kept in police stations, others in courthouses; anyone who wished to take the trouble could go there and read them. But most people did not. Above all, there was no way for people in distant communities to find these damning facts without going to inordinate lengths.

Following the advent of the cyber age, online databases have dramatically increased the size of the audience that has access to public information and the ease with which it can be examined. Several companies have started compiling criminal records and making them available to everyone in the country and, indeed, the world. For instance, PeopleFinders, a company based in Sacramento, California, recently introduced CriminalSearches.com, a free service to access public criminal records, which draws data from local courthouses. Similar services provide access to many other types of public records that range from birth records to divorces. According to the National Association of Criminal Defense Lawyers, this "growing obsession with background checking and commercial exploitation of arrest and conviction records makes it all but impossible for someone with a criminal record to leave the past behind."[6] This is particularly apparent in the United

States due to its level of technological development and strong protections of free speech.

These developments disturb privacy advocates and anyone who is keen to ensure that people have the opportunity for a new start. Beth Givens, director of the Privacy Rights Clearinghouse, says that Internet databases cause a "loss of 'social forgiveness.'" For instance, a person's "conviction of graffiti vandalism at age 19 will still be there at age 29 when [he's] a solid citizen trying to get a job and raise a family"—and the conviction will be there for anyone to see.[7] Furthermore, as companies "rely on background checks to screen workers, [they] risk imposing unfair barriers to rehabilitated criminals," wrote reporters Ann Zimmerman and Kortney Stringer in *The Wall Street Journal*. Eric Posner argues that "privacy allows us to experiment, make mistakes, and start afresh if we mess up . . . [it] is this potential for rehabilitation, for second chances, that is under assault from Google."[8] In short, as journalist Brad Stone wrote in *The New York Times*, by allowing database producers to remove "the obstacles to getting criminal information," Americans are losing "a valuable, ignorance-fueled civil peace." Moreover, many arrestees "who have never faced charges, or have had charges dropped, find that a lingering arrest record can ruin their chance to secure employment, loans and housing."[9]

In response to this dilemma, some have advocated a "right to be forgotten," which entails allowing a person to delete or otherwise remove from public view information relating to them on the Internet. One of the leading intellectual advocates of online "forgiving and forgetting" is Viktor Mayer-Schönberger, a professor of Internet Governance and Regulation at Oxford University. In his 2009 book *Wired: The Virtue of Forgetting in the Digital Age*, Mayer-Schönberger notes that Europeans have greater concern for privacy than have Americans; this characteristic dates back to World War II, when Nazi Germany used the Netherlands' comprehensive population registry to facilitate the Holocaust, as well as to the East German surveillance state during the cold war. Yet he argues that privacy fares even worse in the digital age than under the Stasi, because online storage and transfer is far more efficient than paper records. According to him, society has traditionally accepted "that human beings evolve over time, that we have the capacity to learn from past experiences and adjust our behavior," with the fallibility of human memory and limits of record-keeping techniques allowing "societal forgetting." However, the Internet, which may "forever tether us to all our past actions," threatens to make it "impossible, in practice, to escape them," with the result that, "without some form of forgetting, forgiving becomes a difficult undertaking." For example, Mayer-Schönberger notes that, for a woman who had spent time in prison a decade ago, having her mug shot posted online effectively renewed her punishment, as her neighbors began to scorn her: "Digital memory, in reminding us of who she was more than 10 years ago, denied her the chance to evolve and change." As a result, he advocates greater capacity for individuals to purge their personal information from the web.

But is the Internet age really destroying second chances, making us less forgiving, and hindering the possibility for rehabilitation and even redemption? The sad fact is that most convicted criminals in the predigital age did not use the second chance that their obscurity gave them, nor did they use their third or fourth chances. Convincing information shows that most criminal offenders—especially those that committed violent crimes—are not rehabilitated; they commit new crimes. Many commit numerous crimes before they are caught again. Thus, while obscurity may well help give a second chance to a small percentage of criminals, it helps a large percentage of them strike again.

Take the case of James Webb (not the U.S. Senator from Virginia of the same name). He had served twenty years in prison for raping six women when, on August 16, 1995, he was released on parole. Rather than look for a new start, he raped another woman the day after he was released. He raped three more women in the next few months. He was re-arrested in December 1995, after he committed the fourth rape. Or consider the case of James Richardson, a New York resident who served twenty years of a life term for raping and murdering a ten-year-old girl. After he was paroled in 1992, he committed three bank robberies before being reincarcerated. Both cases happened before the advent of databanks of criminal convictions.

These two are typical cases. In its most recent study on recidivism in the United States, the Justice Department's Bureau of Justice Statistics tracked a large sample of the 405,000 prisoners released in thirty states in 2005.[10] It found that within five years of their release, 68 percent of them were re-arrested for a new offense. These results were essentially unchanged from a similar survey of prisoners released in 1994.[11] In short, most people who commit crimes are more likely to commit crimes in the future than to make good use of a second chance. This was true long before the digitization of criminal data and the loss of obscurity. Moreover, just because only two-thirds of the prisoners were re-arrested does not mean that the other third did not commit any crimes. Many crimes are never solved and their perpetrators never caught. Studies found that the majority of rapists and child molesters are convicted more than once for a sexual assault—and commit numerous offenses before they are caught again. On average, these offenders admit to having committed *two to five times* as many sex crimes than were officially documented. That is, not only did they fail to use their second chances to start a new life, they used obscurity to their advantage.

In short, the image of a young person who goes astray and who would return to the straight and narrow life if he were only given a second chance does not fit most offenders. Indeed, prisons are considered colleges for crime; they harden those sentenced to spend time in them and make them *more* disposed to future criminal behavior upon release. Social scientists differ about whom to blame for the limited success of rehabilitation. Some fault "the system," or poor social conditions, or lack of job training. Others place more blame on the character of those involved. In any case, obscurity hardly serves to overcome strong factors that agitate against rehabilitation.

Medical malpractice is a good example. Online databases display the records of physicians who do not live up to the Hippocratic oath. The National Practitioner Data Bank allows state licensing boards, hospitals, and other health-care entities to find out whether a doctor's license has been revoked recently in another state or if the doctor has been disciplined. Doctors' licenses are generally revoked only if they commit very serious offenses, such as repeated gross negligence, criminal felonies, or practicing while under the influence of drugs or alcohol.

If these databases had been used as intended in the late 1990s and early 2000s, they could have tracked Pamela L. Johnson, a physician who was forced to leave Duke University Medical Center after many of her patients suffered from unusual complications. In response, Johnson moved to New Mexico and lied about her professional history in order to obtain a medical license there and continue practicing. After three patients in New Mexico filed lawsuits alleging that she was negligent or had botched surgical procedures, she moved again and set up shop in Michigan.

Similarly, Joseph S. Hayes, a medical doctor licensed in Tennessee, was convicted of drug abuse and assault, including choking a patient, which resulted in the revocation of his Tennessee license in 1991. But his license was reinstated in 1993. When he was charged with fondling a female patient in 1999, he simply moved to South Carolina to continue practicing medicine. Likewise, Michael Skolnik died in Colorado in 2001 after what has been reported to be unnecessary brain surgery, which led his mother to become an advocate for medical transparency. The surgeon involved had recently moved from Georgia, where he had lost a malpractice suit of which no record existed in Colorado databases.[12] Similar cases involve many scores of other doctors, especially those who acted while under the influence of controlled substances or alcohol. (The exploits of one of the most notorious of these doctors are laid out in *Charlatan*, by Pope Brock.) Yet the National Practitioner Data Bank is not open to members of the general public, who may only request data that does not identify any particular individual or organization.[13] Even this limited access was temporarily cut off in 2011 by the Department of Health and Human Services at the request of a Kansas doctor with a history of malpractice suits.[14] Thanks to the rise of the Internet, the public has some chance, through a web search or through a detailed search of state licensing board websites, of uncovering information that has leaked into the public sphere, but the lack of a more reliable or accessible option gives some poorly performing doctors their own right to be forgotten—to the detriment of the public.

Beyond the fact that Internet databases do little harm to those who are not likely to reform themselves, the widespread dissemination of information about wrongdoers has real benefits for potential victims. Hospitals hire few doctors these days without first checking them through digitized data sources. Before you hire an accountant, such data makes it possible to discover whether he or she has a record of embezzlement. A community can find out if a new school nurse is a sex offender. Employers may direct ex-offenders to other jobs, or they may still hire them but provide extra oversight, or just decide that they are willing to take the risk. But they do so well-informed—and thus warned—rather than ignorant of the sad facts.

Registration and notification laws for sex offenders provide a good case in point. The Washington State Institute for Public Policy conducted a study in 2005 that evaluated the effectiveness of the state's community notification laws. In 1990, Washington passed the Community Protection Act, a law that requires sex offenders to register with their county sheriff and authorizes law enforcement to release information to the public. The study found that by 1999 the recidivism rate among felony sex offenders in the state had dropped 70 percent from its pre-1990 level, in part due to communities' awareness of the sex offenders in their neighborhoods. In addition, offenders subject to community notification were arrested for new crimes much more quickly than offenders who were released without notification.

The advocates for second chances and an opportunity to start anew without being dogged by one's record tend to call for a generic right. That is, they favor the same basic right for killers and political extremists, rapists and those who were merely arrested but not convicted. This is the case for both normative and practical reasons. Normatively, there is a moral case to be made for giving *everyone* a chance to redeem themselves. A practical reason is that when information only existed on paper, as most of it did until 1980 or so, information about all these different categories of people was difficult to access and distribute. However, such a generic right to be forgotten fails the liberal communitarian test, because it causes a great deal of harm to the common good and only limited benefit to personal good.[15] A person truly out to redeem himself had best start by acknowledging his wrongdoing, expressing true remorse, making amends, and showing that he has restructured his life, not by attempting to erase his past.[16]

B. A Hedged Right to Be Forgotten

What is needed is a mixture of technological and legal means to ensure a hedged right to be forgotten that is differentiated according to the scope of the harm done by the initial act, the extent to which the person has rehabilitated himself, and the scope of privacy that will be granted.

For example, where the inefficiency of paper records once ensured that information would not travel far, the digitized world now requires restrictions if certain kinds of information are to be kept isolated. Formerly, in smaller communities, if a person was arrested his neighbors would learn whether he had been exonerated or convicted. The community might even have had a sense of whether a person who was released had in fact committed the crime, or whether the arrest was unjustified. These days, it is possible to access an arrest record across the globe, but it may be difficult to find out if the arrest was justified. Either arrest records should not be made public (although they might be made available to police in other jurisdictions), or they should be accompanied by information about the outcome of the case.

In addition, a criminal record could be sealed both locally and in online databases after a set period of time, for example after seven years, if the person has not committed any new crime. Considerable precedent for such a move exists. For instance, information about juvenile offenders and presentations to grand juries are often sealed.

One other major concern is that lawbreakers who have paid their debt to society will face hiring and housing discrimination. Protections against such discrimination are already in place, but others could be added. For instance, employers cannot, as a general rule, legally maintain a policy of refusing to hire people merely because they are ex-cons, whether the employer gets this information from a police blotter or a computer.

Internet databases should be held accountable for the information they provide. If they rely on public records, then they should be required to keep up with the changes in these records. They should also provide mechanisms for filing complaints if the online data are erroneous, and they should make proper corrections in a timely fashion, the way those who keep tabs on credit records are expected to do.

These are a few examples of measures that provide obscurity equivalents in the digital age. Still, it is important to remember the importance of gossip fueled by public records. As a rule, people care deeply about the approval of others. In most communities, being arrested is a major source of humiliation, and people will go to great pains to avoid ending up in jail. In such cases, the social system does not work if the information is not publicly available. This holds true for the digitized world, where the need for a much wider-ranging "informal social communication," as sociologists call gossip, applies not merely to criminals, sexual predators, and disgraced physicians. It holds for people who trade on eBay, sell used books on Amazon, or distribute loans from e-banks. These people are also eager to maintain their reputations—not just locally but globally. Stripping cyberspace of measures to punish those who deceive and cheat will severely set back the utility of the Internet for travel, trade, investment, and much more.

This need is served in part by user-generated feedback and ratings, which inform others who may do business via the Internet—much like traditional community gossip would. The ability of people to obscure their past in pre-Internet days made it all too easy for charlatans, quacks, and criminal offenders to hurt more people by simply switching locations. The new, digitized transparency is one major means of facilitating deals between people who do not know each other. With enough effort, its undesirable side effects can be curbed, and people can still gain a second chance. It may also be useful to provide people with greater control over their online presence more broadly, although difficult to implement in a balanced way.

The European Union's evolving privacy legislation is making a major move in this direction. Announced in 2012 and taking effect in 2014, the EU's data protection rules explicitly incorporate the "right to be forgotten." According to Jeffrey Rosen, this legislation has its intellectual roots "in French law, which recognizes le droit à l'oubli—or the 'right of oblivion'—allowing a convicted criminal who has served his time and been rehabilitated to object to the publication of the facts of his conviction and incarceration."[17] At the time of its announcement, commentators disputed the implication of this ruling. Where the EU Justice Commissioner Viviane Reding asserted that this right to be forgotten was merely a limited right for people "to withdraw their consent to the processing of the personal data they have given out themselves,"[18] Jeffrey Rosen warned that it represented "the biggest threat to free speech on the Internet in the coming decade."[19] On the other hand, John Hendel asserted that the right "shouldn't worry proponents of free speech," but only those "companies whose profits rely on mined, invasive data abuses."[20]

The practical implications of this law began to emerge in 2014, when the European Court of Justice, the highest appeals court in matters of EU-wide law, ruled on a case in which a Spanish citizen demanded that a Spanish newspaper remove an outdated story relating to his previous indebtedness, as well as that Google remove the relevant search results.[21] The EU court upheld the Spanish Data Protection Agency's decision, which allowed the newspaper to leave the story posted, but forced Google to take down links to the story from the results of searches *that related to the citizen's name* (as opposed to *all* searches). More broadly, the EU court reaffirmed the broader "right to be forgotten," interpreted as the individual right to ask "search engines to remove links with personal information about them" that is "inaccurate, inadequate, irrelevant, or excessive"—but only under "certain conditions." The court stated this right was "not absolute," but rather "to be balanced against other fundamental rights, such as the freedom of expression and of the media" based on a "case-by-case assessment."

At this point, it is too early to say what effect the EU's "right to be forgotten" will have on the balance among privacy, free speech, and security. While the decision clearly affirms that a person may remove material that he or she posted directly, it remains to be seen to what extent the right will apply to material the person posted that then has been copied by others, or to material that was created by others but relates to the person, who finds it offensive. Given the vagueness and subjectivity of terms such as "inadequate, irrelevant, or excessive," it is plausible that the third type of information applies as well, with negative implications for free speech and even public safety. For example, a Croatian pianist requested in October 2014, in line with the EU law, that *The Washington Post* remove a negative review of one of his performances, which "has marred the first page of his Google results for years."[22]

It is also important to note that the first line of decision for balancing privacy and other values in such cases is not the EU court system, but Google, a company that lobbies for free speech and limited regulation in the United States, and which, as with copyright infringement, has accepted the role of censor only reluctantly. The EU mandate poses a "real, if manageable" burden for Google, which received more than half a million takedown requests in the first half-year following the decision, and complied with about half.[23] Thus, Google accepted a request "to remove five-year-old stories about exoneration in a child porn case," but refused a "request from a public official to remove a news article about child pornography accusations," as well as "to remove a 2013 link to a report of an acquittal in a criminal case, on the ground [sic] that it was very recent." As long as Google takes such a conservative approach to takedown requests, one may expect the right to be forgotten to pose relatively little danger to public safety or free speech—however, as Jeffrey Toobin points out, the proliferation of such laws may lead search companies "to tailor their search results in order to offend the fewest countries" as the costs of compliance (or risks of noncompliance) increase the burden on them.

As for the risk to public safety, under its current practice, Google has asserted that it will "also weigh whether or not there's a public interest in the information remaining in our search results—for example, if it relates to financial scams, professional malpractice, criminal convictions or your public conduct as a government official (elected or unelected) . . . [whether] it relate[s] to a criminal charge that resulted in a later conviction or was dismissed."[24] For its part, in November 2014 the EU data protection authorities "adopted guidelines on the implementation of the judgment of the European Court of Justice (ECJ) on the right to be forgotten."[25]

In short, it is far from clear what exactly the newly minted EU right to be forgotten entails, but it clearly provides a key example of a hedged right rather than a generic one. Whether one would hedge differently is less important, that realizing from the onset that a generic right fails the liberal communitarian test, because of the great harm to the common good—while the hedged one can be recalibrated to meet the test and to take into account changing historical conditions and new technological developments.

9

Balancing National Security and Individual Rights

This chapter deals with the issues that followed from the disclosures in 2013 about the National Security Administration's (NSA) two surveillance programs. One, known as Bulk Collection of Telephone Metadata, collects, stores, and analyzes the records of a significant portion of the phone calls made and received in the United States (from here on, this program will be referred to as phone surveillance). The other, known as PRISM, collects private electronic communications from a number of online providers such as Google and Facebook and is focused on non-Americans.[1] This chapter focuses on the specific issues raised by these two programs, although both programs have attributes and raise issues that are also relevant to other national security programs. I draw on a liberal communitarian approach in its assessment of the issues at hand. Section A of this chapter discusses this approach. Section B responds to critics of the programs who hold that such surveillance is neither needed nor effective. Section C examines the specific grounds on which phone surveillance has been criticized and justified. Section D lays out a similar analysis regarding the PRISM program. Section E examines the alternative ways both surveillance programs may be better controlled, on the grounds that the more the government conducts surveillance the more it needs to be watched. Section F discusses whether accountability measures (such as civic oversight bodies) or transparency requirements would better address surveillance abuses that do occur. Finally, section G is a discussion about the potential dangers these programs would pose if the U.S. government were to be overtaken by a McCarthy-like figure or even a tyrant.

A. A Liberal Communitarian Approach

The liberal communitarian philosophy (as developed by the author[2]) assumes that nations face several fully legitimate normative and legal claims and that these claims can be neither maximized nor fully reconciled, as there is an inevitable tension among them. It follows that we must work out some balance among the conflicting claims rather than assuming that one will always trump the others. This chapter applies this approach to the balance between national security and individual rights, particularly the right to privacy, in the context of recent surveillance revelations. These include the U.S. government's phone metadata surveillance, which collects information such as caller ID, times, and duration of U.S. phone calls, but not what was said,as well as the PRISM program, which collects the Internet communications of foreign nationals.[3]

In contrast to applying this balancing approach, libertarians, civil libertarians, and a fair number of contemporary liberals tend to emphasize individual rights and autonomy over considerations of the common good.[4] At the opposite end of the spectrum are authoritarian communitarians (mainly in East Asia[5]) who privilege the common good a priori and pay mind to rights mainly to the extent that they serve the rulers' aims.[6] In this sense, liberal communitarianism occupies the middle of the spectrum between libertarianism and authoritarianism, and draws mainly on social pressures rather than state coercion.

The text of the Fourth Amendment provides a strong expression of the liberal communitarian philosophy. It states: "The right of the people to be secure in their persons, houses, papers, and effects, against unreasonable searches and seizures, shall not be violated." By banning only *unreasonable* searches and seizures, it recognizes by extension that there are reasonable ones, namely those that serve the common good.

Public intellectuals, elected officials, and segments of the media tend to adopt a one-sided advocacy position whereby they champion one of the two core values of society, arguing that some individual right—e.g., privacy or the right to freedom of speech or assembly—is being violated and that the laws or actions responsible should be halted. They often argue that "it is against the law, hence it is wrong," or that the court ruling or law on which a particular surveillance program is based violates a core value, such as our right to privacy, and hence should be rejected. They do not ask whether the other core value, national security, might justify some scaling back of these rights, and do not recognize that the balance between the core values has often been recalibrated over the decades. To remind the reader, there was no federal right to privacy until the mid-1960s,[7] and until 1919 the Supreme Court failed to endorse a single legal claim that the government had violated the (now semi-sacred) right to free speech guaranteed by the First Amendment—and even then it did so only in a dissenting opinion.[8]

In contrast to the one-sidedness of advocates, the courts, which often use the term "public interest"[9] rather than "the common good," regularly weigh both core values.[10] In several cases, they concluded that the threat to the public interest justified some redefinition or even curbing of rights; in others, they found that the threat level did not justify such infringement. For example, in *New York Times Co. v. United States* the court ruled that, by attempting to suppress the Pentagon Papers, the government failed to meet the "heavy burden of showing justification for the imposition of [prior judicial] restraint," even though such restraint might be justified if the court believed that the release of the information would "surely result in direct, immediate, and irreparable damage to our Nation or its people."[11] By contrast, a court held in *United States v. Hartwell* that, although screenings by the U.S. Transportation Security Administration (TSA) violated privacy, they were nonetheless permissible because "preventing terrorist attacks on airplanes [was] of paramount importance" and, thus, the screenings "advance[d] the public interest" to the point where some violation of privacy was justified.[12] This chapter follows the balanced approach taken by the courts rather than the one-sided advocacy of libertarians and authoritarians.

B. Basic Challenges and Responses

Critics of both surveillance programs argue that terrorism has subsided and hence these programs are not needed.[13] For instance, many statements about the NSA surveillance programs start by arguing that these programs infringe on this or that right and hence are unconstitutional and should be canceled.[14] Even after extensive pleading by the president, the Republican Speaker of the House, and senior members of those congressional committees familiar with the programs, the House of Representatives came within twelve votes (205 to 217) of completely defunding the phone records collection program.[15] Others stated that in establishing many of the antiterrorist measures enacted since 9/11, including the NSA programs in question, Congress was "reckless," as the powers granted have proven "unnecessary and overbroad."[16] Others argue that terrorists can be handled with existing legal authorities and procedures, like other criminals. This position is taken by Karen J. Greenberg,[17] the Director of the Center on National Security, the ACLU's Anthony D. Romero,[18] and Attorney General Eric Holder.[19] Europe also widely holds this view.[20] Still others argue that these surveillance programs are ineffectual and that the phone surveillance program has no proven benefits.

1. Threat Assessments

Those who hold that terrorism has much subsided can draw on President Obama's statements to prove their point. The president announced in May

2013 that "the core of al Qaeda in Afghanistan and Pakistan is on the path to defeat. Their remaining operatives spend more time thinking about their own safety than plotting against us."[21] He echoed this sentiment in August when he stated that "core al Qaeda is on its heels, has been decimated."[22] Administration officials have been similarly optimistic regarding the diminished terror threat,[23] and Obama "pivoted" U.S. foreign policy away from a focus on the Middle East in favor of a focus on East Asia.[24] However, since then, a steady stream of reports has suggested that much remains to be done in facing terrorism, that al Qaeda is rebuilding its strength, and that the pivot to East Asia may well have been premature.

Al Qaeda is regrouping under the banner of "al Qaeda in the Arabian Peninsula" (AQAP). Ayman al-Zawahiri has taken over Osama bin Laden's vacated position. AQAP has expanded from 200–300 members in 2009 to more than a thousand today.[25] This group was behind the "most specific and credible threat" since the 9/11 attacks, a threat that led to the closure of dozens of American embassies across the Middle East,[26] and it managed to capture and control significant territory in Yemen.[27] AQAP also claimed responsibility for the January 2015 Paris attacks, which killed 17 people, including employees at the satirical Charlie Hebdo newspaper.

Al Qaeda affiliates are growing in strength and spreading into additional countries.[28] Al Qaeda increasingly relies on a decentralized network of collaborating terrorist affiliates.[29] Affiliates include groups in Africa (a network that spans Algeria, Mali, Niger, Mauritania, and Libya),[30] the Caucasus, Syria, and Somalia.[31] Taken together, "al-Qaeda [sic] franchises and fellow travelers now control more territory and can call on more fighters, than at any time since Osama bin Laden created the organization 25 years ago."[32] In 2013, al Qaeda in Iraq started a bombing campaign that killed more than three hundred people in three months.[33] The group has transformed Iraq into a staging point for incursions into the Syrian civil war.[34]

At the same time, Syria and Iraq are turning into a haven and breeding ground for terrorists. Experts report that Syria is now "an even more powerful variant of what Afghanistan was more than 30 years ago."[35] The Islamic State of Iraq and the Levant, or ISIS, which was rejected as too extremist even by al Qaeda's leadership, has consolidated its hold over territory in Syria, seized swathes of Iraq, and beheaded American and British citizens. Given its high level of discipline, funding, territory, weapons, and manpower, and especially its recruitment of thousands[36] of American and European nationals who could return to carry out terror attacks at home without having to apply for visas, U.S. officials have branded ISIS an "imminent threat to every interest we have" and launched airstrikes to check its advance.[37] The al Qaeda-affiliated Nusra Front also remains one of the strongest Syrian rebel militias.[38] Western intelligence officials are thus worried that Syria has become "one of the biggest terrorist threats in the world today."[39]

Al Qaeda has also staged a series of major prison breaks. In Iraq, militants used a combination of aggressive mortar fire, suicide bombers, and an assault force to free hundreds of prisoners from two separate prisons.[40] More than one thousand prisoners, including some terrorist suspects, escaped from a Libyan prison,[41] and in Pakistan more than 250 inmates were freed by some 150 militants.[42] In total, more than two thousand prisoners, many al Qaeda-trained militants, were freed in the raids.[43]

In September 2013 al Shabaab—an al Qaeda-linked terrorist organization based in Somalia—carried out a massive, well-planned, sophisticated attack in Nairobi, Kenya. In a three-day standoff in a shopping mall, the group killed more than sixty-five people and left almost two hundred others injured.[44] In February 2015, al-Shabaab released a video threatening attacks on U.S. and European malls.[45] Al Qaeda and its subsidiaries showed that they are agile and adaptable, as was revealed in their use of ink cartridges as bombs and of "implanted" explosives that airport scanners could not detect.

Finally, terrorists have been trying to get their hands on nuclear weapons. Both Russia and Pakistan have less-than-fully secured nuclear arms within their borders,[46] and Pakistan has experienced at least six serious terrorist attempts to penetrate its nuclear facilities.[47]

If the disutility of a particular event is very high, some carefully designed security measures are justified even if the probability that the event will occur is very low. This point requires some elaboration. People tend to assume that if it is very unlikely that one will face a given risk, then it is rational to ignore it. It makes little sense to carry an umbrella if the likelihood that it will rain is one in a thousand, let alone one in ten thousand. One reason (other than the charge of racial profiling) that the New York court ruled that the police procedure of stop-and-frisk should be discontinued was that the procedure resulted in the apprehension of few wrongdoers.[48] Indeed, the main justification for stop-and-frisk is that it gets guns off the streets, but illegal guns were seized in only 0.15 percent of all stop-and-frisk searches.[49] However, this rule of thumb ignores the magnitude of a risk. The larger the risk—even if the probability that it will occur remains unchanged and very low—the more security measures it justifies.

In short, given the level of risk that terrorists pose in general, especially if they acquire so-called weapons of mass destruction (WMDs) one way or another, this risk justifies some enhancements to security measures in accordance with a core element of the liberal communitarian balance. This is especially true if the security measures are minimally intrusive or not intrusive at all—that is, if they do not diminish the other core element, individual rights.

2. Terrorists Cannot Be Handled Like Criminals

Critics of many security measures argue that terrorists could be handled like other criminals and that no special counterterrorism programs are needed.[50] There are, however, strong counterarguments that suggest that terrorists should be treated as a distinct category of criminal. First and foremost, dealing with terrorists requires a focus on *preventing* attacks before they occur. This point is particularly evident in light of the concern that terrorists may acquire WMDs. In bringing terrorists to trial after they have turned part of a major city into a radioactive desert, which would occur even if the terrorists merely used a dirty bomb, whatever deterrent benefit punishment might have[51] is vastly outweighed by the magnitude of the harm already done.[52] In any case, there is little reason to think that those willing to commit suicide during an attack can be deterred at all; such people have little to lose. None of the nineteen people who attacked the U.S. homeland in 2001, terrorized a nation, and left a deep mark on the American psyche can be brought to trial. Even terrorists who are not bent on committing suicide attacks are often "true believers" who are willing to proceed despite whatever punishments the legal system might throw at them.[53] Law enforcement assumes that punishment after the fact deters future crimes (the intent is not to eliminate them but to keep them at a socially acceptable level).[54] This premise does not hold when it comes to acts of terror or bringing justice to terrorists, because the first priority of counterterrorism is to thwart their designs rather than to try in vain to capture and prosecute terrorists in the aftermath of an attack that often is much more damaging than most criminal acts.

Affording terror suspects the right to legal counsel prior to undergoing interrogation imposes a severe cost: information that can no longer be acquired through questioning. One may suggest that a terrorist could refuse to talk, even if not granted this privilege. However, adhering to the regular law enforcement procedures would require that, if a terrorist asks for a legal counsel, the authorities must no longer talk to him, offer deals, or give incentives, let alone apply pressure. Given that terrorists often act in groups and pose more harm than most criminals, the notion of legally binding investigators such that they cannot adequately question a terrorist who has been caught—at least, until an attorney is found— tilts too far from protecting the common good.[55] One may say there is already a "public safety" exception that applies to emergency situations. When dealing with transnational terrorists, this should be the rule, not the exception.[56]

In addition, the criminal procedures of open arrest records, charging suspects within forty-eight hours under most circumstances, and the guarantee of a speedy trial all undermine the fight against terrorism. Counterterrorism requires time to decipher the terrorists' records, to prevent other attacks that might be underway, and to capture other members of the cell before they realize that one of their members has been apprehended. Also, security demands that authorities do not reveal their means and methods; therefore, one often cannot allow terrorists to face their accusers. (Imagine having to bring in a CIA agent or Muslim collaborator that the United States succeeded in placing high in al Qaeda's command in order to have him testify in open court in the United States.)

Furthermore, a law enforcement–based approach to surveillance that requires individualized suspicion is not an effective means of preventing terrorism. As John Yoo points out, "detecting al-Qaeda members who have no previous criminal record in the United States, and who are undeterred by the possibility of criminal sanctions, requires the use of more sweeping methods," such as those adopted by the NSA.[57] Next, the nature of the evidence likely to be presented in a terrorist trial is problematic. Much of it is classified and highly sensitive, which puts the government in the position of having to choose between jeopardizing national security in order to gain a conviction or letting terrorists off easy, if not completely, lest they give away vital sources and methods. When Mounir el-Motassadeq, a member of the Hamburg cell that included four 9/11 hijackers, was brought to trial in Germany for abetting mass murder, his conviction was successfully appealed and a judge ordered his immediate release because without being able to verify the statements made by the prisoners there was not "sufficient proof in either direction."[58]

To avoid all these traps, the government, when forced to deal with terrorists through civilian courts, often turns to plea bargaining. It is estimated that over 80 percent of the guilty terrorist convictions achieved in civilian courts since 2001 have been the result of plea bargains.[59] Although guaranteeing a guilty verdict, plea deals result in light sentences.[60]

In short, there seem to be strong arguments that curbing terrorism justifies additional and, above all, different security measures than those employed in going after criminals. These arguments do not justify any particular security measure or surveillance program, but rather, support the category of extraordinary public safety measures to which they belong. Thus, arguments put forward in this chapter in support of NSA surveillance do not necessarily support surveillance conducted for other reasons, such as counternarcotics law enforcement missions by the Drug Enforcement Administration or the FBI.[61] An examination of the two specific programs under consideration, the phone surveillance program and PRISM, follows.

3. *The Programs Are Not Effective*

A common claim against the NSA programs under discussion, and against other national security programs, is that they are not effective.[62] This is a particularly potent argument for those who oppose these measures because if the programs are ineffectual, presumably nobody will seek to support them no matter how little they infringe upon rights. By contrast, if the programs are proven to be effective, then at least some may begin to wonder if the associated gain in security does not justify some recalibration of rights.

The government argues that PRISM and the collection of phone company metadata disrupted fifty-four terrorist plots, one-fifth of which were to be carried out within the borders of the United States.[63] However, critics have questioned these statistics, expressing skepticism about the reliability of government officials' testimony[64] and the adequacy of the thwarted plots as a metric of efficacy.[65] Section F addresses the question of how to ensure the validity of these and other government claims.

Critics especially wonder about phone surveillance.[66] Some point out that the program was not the "primary" tool in averting any terrorist attacks,[67] and "would very likely fail a full cost-benefit analysis handily even only minimally taking into consideration privacy and civil liberties concerns."[68] However, this criticism can be leveled against any program or instrument used by law enforcement authorities or national security agencies. Surely police cruisers or FBI files or even the U.S. Air Force are often but instruments that in conjunction with others bring about the required outcomes.

There are obviously scores of situations in which phone records would be of obvious help, even if the records alone would not be sufficient to prevent an attack or to find those who committed acts of terror.[69] When the authorities caught one of the two Tsarnaev brothers (the pair responsible for the Boston Marathon bombing), there was reason to suspect that they were cooperating with others and that they planned more attacks, specifically in New York City. It does not take a PhD in counterterrorism to realize that under those circumstances it was very useful to know who the Tsarnaev brothers were previously in contact with by phone. The same holds for efforts to find out if the Tsarnaev brothers acted on their own or were supplied, guided, or financed by overseas sponsors and, if so, by whom.

One telling piece of evidence regarding the effectiveness of electronic surveillance programs is the fact that they hobbled bin Laden. He found out that he was unable to use any modern communication device to run his terror organizations, which had branches on three continents.[70] He was reduced to using the same means of communication people used five thousand years ago—a messenger, which is a very slow, low volume, cumbersome, and unreliable means of communication and command, and which in effect prevented bin Laden from serving as an effective commander-in-chief of al Qaeda. Moreover, once the CIA deduced that using a messenger was the only way left for him to communicate, tracking the messenger led to bin Laden's downfall.[71] Additional reports that there was a sharp decline in al Qaeda's electronic communications following the revelation that the United States had intercepted the communications of Ayman al-Zawahri also proved that the NSA programs forced terrorists to limit their communications.

In short, we have seen that terrorism still poses a serious threat to national security; that terrorists cannot be handled like other criminals, and distinct measures must employed to handle them; and that surveillance programs like PRISM and the phone surveillance program significantly contribute to curbing terrorism. In short these programs do enhance one core element of the liberal communitarian balance. Section C addresses the extent to which they undermine the other core element.

C. Phone Surveillance of Americans

The NSA's phone surveillance program involves the bulk collection of metadata from major telephone providers. These records, which are collected from at least three major phone companies,[72] include the numbers dialed by Americans and the duration of each call, but not the content of the calls.[73] (This is distinct from the bulk collection of billions of cell phone locations globally, which was revealed in December 2013 and which collects data on U.S. cell phones only incidentally.)[74] Experts have said that the phone surveillance program violates individual rights on several different grounds.

1. Third-Party Doctrine

The collection of phone records has been justified on the basis of the third-party doctrine. It holds that once a person voluntarily discloses a fact to another party, he or she forfeits all Fourth Amendment protection when it comes to the disclosed information.[75] Relevant cases include *United States v. Miller* (1976), in which the Supreme Court ruled that bank depositors forfeit their reasonable expectation of privacy when they hand over personal information to a bank. Moreover, sharing such information with a third party necessarily entails the risk that the third party might voluntarily turn over the information to the government.[76] And in *Smith v. Maryland* (1979) the Court held that the voluntary disclosure of information to telephone companies entailed the forfeiture of a reasonable expectation of privacy when it came to telephone records.[77] According to the Office of the Director of National Intelligence General Counsel Robert Litt, "as a result, the government can get this information without a warrant, consistent with the Fourth Amendment."[78]

Though the third-party doctrine is the accepted law of the land, it is controversial,[79] and thus it will not serve as the basis for the defense that follows of government surveillance. My main reason for moving away from the third-party doctrine is that in the cyber age much of our private lives are lived in a cyber world of cloud computing operated by third parties like Google and Facebook. As a result, a massive amount of information that once resided in the private sphere is now in the hands of third parties. If one accepts the third-party doctrine as the basis for a defense of government surveillance, one leaves very little in terms of what is considered reasonably private information protected from search.[80]

In short, we had best determine whether phone surveillance can be justified on grounds other than the third-party doctrine, because if the third-party doctrine must be employed, one may well conclude that the privacy sacrifices this doctrine legitimates are too high a price to pay for whatever security gains these programs offer. (This may not be the case if one considers what might be called a "half third-party doctrine," which excludes sensitive information such as medical and financial information.)

2. "Traffic" versus Content Analysis

Many critics of the phone records collection program refer to it explicitly or implicitly as if the government were listening to American phone calls and hence violating the privacy of millions of people. For example, Glenn Greenwald claims that "the NSA frequently eavesdrops on Americans' calls and reads their emails without any individualized warrants—exactly that which NSA defenders, including Obama, are trying to make Americans believe does not take place."[81] Similarly, Conor Friedersdorf suggests that to believe the NSA *isn't* listening to our calls requires "trusting that the NSA is telling us the truth. But they've lied to us repeatedly."[82] Among the public, a nearly two-to-one majority (63 percent) of Americans believe that the government is collecting the content of Americans' phone calls and e-mails—and 27 percent state that they believe the government is listening to their phone calls or reading their e-mails.[83]

However, given the massive amount of communications content that is generated every day, it would be impossible for the NSA to examine even a small portion of that content unless its employees numbered in the millions. According to one source, "It would take 400 million people to listen and read" through all global communications traffic.[84] As NSA Director Keith Alexander put it, "If you think that we would listen to everybody's telephone calls and read everybody's emails to connect the dots, how do you do that? And the answer is, that's not logical."[85]

Actually, the program collects phone *records* that show who called what other numbers, the times the calls were placed, and their duration—but no more. (Note that even the various leakers did not claim that the content of phone calls was collected.) This is akin to collecting the envelope as opposed reading the actual correspondence enclosed—a practice that is, in fact, regularly carried out in bulk by the U.S. Postal Service (USPS). Indeed, the USPS "photographs the exterior of every piece of paper mail that is processed in the United States" and saves the recorded data for an unknown amount of time.[86]

The government reports that it collects and stores these records in order to have rapid access when it is needed and to stitch together various data; for some reason it neglects to mention that the phone companies keep the records only for only short periods of time[87] while security concerns require longer storage,[88] which necessitates the program.

In short, given the security that comes with the gains engendered by ready access to this information and the fact that the intrusiveness of storing this information is low, phone surveillance, like mail surveillance, passes this part of the liberal communitarian test. It is justified on prudential, pragmatic, and technical grounds, as well as legal ones.

3. General Search and Individualized Suspicion

Privacy advocates often argue that before the government searches anyone it should be required—indeed it is required, according to the Constitution—to present to a court of law evidence demonstrating that there exists strong reason (enough to convince a judge) to believe that the particular person is likely to be a criminal or a terrorist. Only then, according to these advocates, should said person be subjected to surveillance.[89] The phone surveillance program violates this rule on the face of it because it collects the records of millions of people for whom no particularized suspicion has been articulated. Thus, the ACLU filed a lawsuit seeking to halt the program on the grounds that the surveillance carried out was "warrantless and unreasonable."[90]

However, the courts have long established (employing, in effect, a rather similar line of analysis to the liberal communitarian one outlined earlier) that when there is both a clear public interest and the privacy intrusion is small, "administrative searches"—searches that are executed without a warrant or probable cause—are legal and necessary.[91]

One important subset of administrative searches is the "dragnet" search, in which some agent of the government "searches or seizes every person, place, or thing in a specific location or involved in a specific activity based only on a showing of a generalized government interest."[92] They include checkpoints where drivers are stopped for the purposes of investigating a crime,[93] sobriety checkpoints,[94] and airport screenings.[95]

In *Camara v. Municipal Court* the Court held that routine government inspections of homes to ensure they were in compliance with the housing code were permissible, despite the fact that the searches covered every house in a particular area without any sort of particularized suspicion.[96]

In *Michigan Department of State Police v. Sitz*, the Court approved of a sobriety checkpoint at which every vehicle was stopped (drivers demonstrating visible signs of impairment were pulled aside for further screening), on the grounds that the state has a strong interest in curbing drunk driving and that the degree of intrusion involved in a brief traffic stop is minor.[97] The Court held that, given the short duration of the stop and the minimal intensity of the search, the fact that the stops furthered the interests of the state rendered the searches reasonable under the Fourth Amendment.[98]

In *Illinois v. Lidster*, the Court held that a traffic stop for the purposes of investigating a recent hit-and-run accident was permissible, because the Court found a favorable balance between "the gravity of the public concerns served by the seizure, the degree to which the seizure advances the public interest, and the severity of the interference with individual liberty."[99]

And in *United States v. Hartwell*, the Third Circuit Court of Appeals held that TSA screenings, despite lacking individualized suspicion and being conducted without warrants, are permissible because they further a key state interest in a way that is tailored to furthering that interest while also being minimally invasive. According to the court, "preventing terrorist attacks on airplanes is of paramount importance," and thus, given the empirical evidence, screening checkpoints "advance the public interest" in a way that no measure relying upon individualized suspicion could.[100] At the same time, the court held that, in addition to protecting the public, the searches were "minimally intrusive" because the procedures used "were well-tailored to protect personal privacy, escalating in invasiveness only after a lower level of screening disclosed a reason to conduct a more probing search. The search began when Hartwell simply passed through a magnetometer and had his bag x-rayed, two screenings that involved no physical touching."[101] (TSA screening was also upheld on similar grounds in previous rulings, most notably *United States v. Davis*[102] and *United States v. Pulido-Baquerizo*.[103])

General searches were further legitimized by Section 215 of the Patriot Act and the national security letters that the law authorizes. This legislation allows the government to conduct surveillance without first identifying an individual as a suspected terrorist and also grants the government the authority to search through third-party databases without notifying suspects as long as the "information is relevant to a terrorism investigation."[104]

Specifically, Section 215 of the Patriot Act stripped the business records provision provided in the Foreign Intelligence Surveillance Act (FISA; 1978) of the requirement that any requests for such records must involve "specific and articulable facts" if these records pertain to "a foreign power or an agent of a foreign power."[105] However, it provides communications providers with an option for judicial review whereby they might contest the legality of a records request and any associated nondisclosure orders.[106] Section 215 has been cited in a ruling by a Foreign Intelligence Surveillance court as upholding the legality of the NSA's phone records collection program.[107] Section 215 also prohibits the collection of records for an investigation based solely on the basis of a protected First Amendment activity. A U.S. person cannot be the subject of NSA surveillance simply because of what that person says or believes.[108] No evidence has been presented, even following all the leaks, that this section has been violated by the NSA, in contrast to reports that the IRS has targeted Tea Party groups.

Most important and often ignored by critics is the fact that the phone surveillance program does follow the Fourth Amendment rule of particularized search. Although the government collects and stores phone records, an individual's calls cannot legally be scrutinized until it has been established that there are "facts giving rise to a reasonable articulable suspicion" that the number to be searched is associated with a foreign terrorist organization.[109] The basis for that suspicion has to be documented in writing and approved by one of twenty-two highly vetted NSA officers.[110] Far from granting many such searches, in 2012, fewer than three hundred proposed searches met the "reasonable, articulable suspicion" standard.[111]

In November 2014, the USA Freedom Act, which proposed to amend Second 215 and end the bulk collection of metadata of phone calls made by U.S. citizens, was narrowly voted down in the Senate.[112] Moreover, even if Congress allows Section 215 to expire in June 2015, the government may still maintain its authority to collect phone records through an exception in the Patriot Act.[113]

In short, given that phone surveillance does not violate the Constitution or statutory law and that its intrusiveness is low, it should be tolerated. (The term "tolerated" is used to remind the reader that one need not be enamored of such programs in order to consider them necessary and legitimate.) Given this cardinal observation, the question comes down to whether collecting and storing records in computers amounts to a search, general or otherwise—a point next discussed.

4. Computers Don't Search

A major, indeed critical, feature of the phone surveillance program, ignored by many critics, is that it merely stores the records and that particularized suspicion and a court order is required to access and examine the records of any individual. It is hence important to note that computers do not violate privacy, although they vastly increase the risk that privacy might be violated. (How to best address and mitigate that risk is discussed in Section F.)

Computers do not gossip. They see no evil, hear no evil, and speak no evil. They do not engage in pillow talk, leak information to the press, or sell information to the Cubans, Chinese, or anyone else. Hence, those who are concerned with finding a reasonable balance between security and privacy should focus on the interface between computers and human agents. That is, they ought to seek to ensure that once the computers flag particular individuals this information is revealed only to law enforcement authorities and used by them in legal and accountable ways. For this reason, the revelation in July 2014 that most intercepted communications do not belong to legally targeted foreigners and instead belong to U.S. citizens or residents is of little concern as long as actual analysis of the communications focuses narrowly on counterterrorism and U.S. communications are minimized according to law.[114]

In short, privacy advocates would have good reason for concern if the massive collection of records were to include content and if records of who called whom were to be made available to all comers or even to various law enforcement agencies. However, if these records are merely collected and stored so that they will be readily available once a court order is granted for an individualized search—most of the issue is moot beyond the question of how to ensure that access to the computers themselves is under tight surveillance.

5. Keep in Private Hands?

Critics argue that, rather than collect and store phone records in bulk, the government should wait until it has particularized suspicion and a court order and *then* collect the relevant records of that person from the phone companies.[115] However, both prudential and principled reasons favor the government position on this point. Most important, phone companies are not currently required to keep these records, and they keep them for only a short period of time.[116] That is, if the government does not store these records, the records very often will not be available. This alone justifies the collection program.

One may argue that we could have our privacy cake and gain all the security we need if, instead of collecting the records, the phone companies could be required to keep them, for, say, seven years. But this idea raises three problems. First, terrorists and, more generally, criminals use a large variety of phones, including landlines and cell phones, that are managed by different phone companies. (Indeed, some carry multiple cell phones and switch phones as needed to avoid identification.) If the government needs to rapidly trace the calls of a terrorist who has been apprehended it would have to approach different companies, put together different databases, and input the information into its computers, all in short order. Anyone who has combined large databases from several different sources can attest to the fact that such combinations are time-consuming and challenging. There are strong reasons to have these combinations take place before searches actually need to be carried out. (In addition, these large databases are necessary to find patterns.)

Second, if phone companies were to keep the records for as long as the government might need them and were to make them available whenever the government requests them, the difference between such an arrangement and the status quo would be largely cosmetic. Indeed, I have shown elsewhere that, while privacy advocates strongly oppose the possibility of the government maintaining dossiers with detailed and private information about most Americans—including those who have not been charged with any crime—these advocates seem much less agitated when such databases are kept by private companies. Too often these advocates ignore that these private databases are merely a click (and a check) away from government agencies (including the Department of Justice, the IRS, and U.S. Citizenship and Immigration Service), which have scores of contracts to this effect.[117]

This is far from a hypothetical idea. Currently, private corporations keep very detailed dossiers on most Americans, hundreds of millions of them. These include information on "income, net worth, real property holdings, social security number [sic], current and previous addresses, phone numbers and fax numbers, names of neighbors, driver records, license plate and VIN numbers, bankruptcy and debtor filings, employment, business and criminal records, bank account balances and activity, stock purchases, and credit card activity."[118] And they make them available to the government for a fee, without any court order or review.[119] We are conditioned to hold that private sector and privacy go hand in hand, while the public sphere is closely associated with the violation of privacy. Actually, in the cyber age, these boundaries have been blurred. If the government has ready access to private data banks, they do not—by definition—provide extra privacy protection, and if the data banks are not readily accessible, they hinder counterterrorism drives.

One may say that the phone companies could review the government requests and, thus, serve as a sort of privacy-protecting screen. However, on what basis could a phone company lawyer deny government access in the face of government claims that protecting national security requires such access? Should the government reveal to company lawyers, who would lack security clearance and the relevant experience and training when it comes to such matters, the reasons it is interested in a particular set of records? Should phone companies set up their own FISA-like courts to second-guess the government? The answer seems clear: the companies are not in a position to second-guess the government.

The issue of accessibility is becoming more important as the government struggles to keep pace with encryption technology. In the wake of the NSA leaks, U.S. tech firms have faced a backlash not only from privacy advocates[120] but from foreign governments and businesses concerned about U.S. surveillance.[121] In response, tech companies are strengthening their data security measures.[122] Particularly troubling to the effort to balance privacy and security is the plan by some companies to encrypt their data, and their refusals to grant backdoors to the NSA. Indeed, Apple's iPhone 6 has encryption capabilities that Apple itself cannot bypass, even if instructed to do so by a judge once it was established that the user is a terrorist.[123] I leave it to the lawyers to figure out if such encryption qualifies as obstruction of justice, but it surely violates the conception that reasonable searches should be allowed.

In short, the key question related to having the records kept in private hands is whether they would be easily accessible to the government in case of a pressing national security need. If this were the case, it would be only cosmetically different from having the government store the records; if not, the government's ability to fight terrorism would be hindered. Not only is guaranteed access to the records needed, sometimes on short notice, and technical reasons exist for allowing the government to keep the records— one should recognize that keeping these records in private hands adds little to privacy protection.

Taking into account all these considerations, it seems that the phone surveillance program's "correction" to the liberal communitarian balance between individual rights—especially privacy—and national security is limited and not excessively intrusive, abides by the constitution and prevailing law, is structured in a reasonable manner, and contributes to national security protection. Whether it is subject to the level of oversight and accountability necessary to ensure that it will not be abused to spy on people because of their political views, to wantonly ensnare innocent people, or to engage in any other variety of misuse is less clear. This question deserves separate treatment.

D. PRISM

The PRISM program acquires electronic communications (including e-mails, chat logs, videos, VoIP, file transfers, and social networking details) from American-based technology firms, including Microsoft, Apple, Google, Yahoo, and Facebook.[124] The program targets non-U.S. persons located outside the United States. PRISM can be used for various national intelligence purposes, such as keeping under surveillance the military communications of nations hostile to the United States. Here, only PRISM's use as a counterterrorism measure is under review.

The program is authorized by Section 702 of the FISA Amendments Act (FAA) of 2008.[125] Under Section 702, the U.S. government does not unilaterally obtain information on foreign targets from the servers of U.S. ISPs. All information collected is for counterterrorism purposes and is gathered with the knowledge of the ISP. These actions are authorized by written directives from the U.S. Attorney General and the Director of National Intelligence, which are approved by FISC for a period of one year and can subsequently be renewed. The NSA thus does not need an individualized court order to gather intelligence on suspected overseas intelligence targets.[126] Subsequent leaks of other content-collecting programs include the bulk collection of "almost 200 million text messages a day," (with purely domestic communications removed)[127] as well as MUSCULAR, a program that bypasses web firms' security to collect data without their consent (as opposed to PRISM, which is done in cooperation with the firms).[128]

In addition to facilitating the government's surveillance of the live communications and stored data of foreign targets operating outside the United States, PRISM also collects the electronic data of select Americans who communicate with foreign targets.[129]

1. The Legal Basis for PRISM's Surveillance of Foreign Nationals Abroad

Collecting the phone records of Americans is a concern for many American critics; the collection of information about foreigners received much less attention. The question though stands: what are the rights of non-Americans under constitutional, domestic, and international law?

a. Under the U.S. Constitution

As with the phone records collection program, critics have charged the government with a violation of Fourth Amendment rights in the case of PRISM. NSA officials have asserted that non-U.S. persons do not enjoy Fourth Amendment protections.[130] This reasoning is backed by the courts. In *United States v. Verdugo-Urquidez*, the court held that the "Fourth Amendment does not apply to the search and seizure by U.S. agents of property owned by a nonresident alien and located in a foreign country," on the grounds that "the people" protected by the Constitution's Fourth Amendment "refers to a class of persons who are part of a national community or who have otherwise developed sufficient connection with this country to be considered part of that community."[131] The majority did not offer a clear definition of "sufficient connection" but maintained that the Fourth Amendment did not apply to property located abroad that belonged to a foreign national with no residential connection to the United States.[132]

As former Attorney General William Barr put it, "our conventional criminal justice system is designed to apply to people within our political community, but it doesn't make sense to extend those rights to foreign enemies who are trying to slaughter us. These people are just like the Nazi saboteurs."[133] On what ground can terrorists, who are willing to kill and die to undermine the values that undergird the American system of justice, claim to enjoy the very rights and privileges they seek to destroy?[134]

In contrast, the dissenting justices, Brennan and Marshall, challenged the majority's interpretation and contended that the respondent, Verdugo-Urquidez, had developed a sufficient connection with this country because "our Government, by investigating him and attempting to hold him accountable under U.S. criminal laws, has treated him as a member of our community for purposes of enforcing our laws. He has become, quite literally, one of the governed."[135] In short, Brennan and Marshall argued that the government's authority to criminalize, investigate, and prosecute both domestic and foreign conduct originates in the Constitution. As such, the actions the government takes in enforcing that authority is similarly subject to constitutional constraints. The two justices further affirmed that in light of the increasingly globalized reach of American law enforcement and the government's efforts to "hold foreign nationals criminally liable under federal laws for conduct committed entirely beyond the territorial limits of the United States that nevertheless has effects in this country," the extension of constitutional protections to foreign nationals was particularly critical.[136]

The majority, however, maintained that such an interpretation would have a detrimental impact on not just law enforcement's but also the military's activities abroad, as non-Americans with no substantive links to the United

States would flood American courts with lawsuits for damages related to Fourth Amendment violations in foreign countries. Furthermore, they argued, the executive and legislative branches would be "plunged into a sea of uncertainty as to what might be reasonable in the way of searches and seizures conducted abroad."[137]

These divergent views on the extraterritorial application of the Constitution can be traced to the distinct theories invoked in defense of these clashing interpretations of the Fourth Amendment. Social contract theory, on one hand, contends that "the people" in the Constitution refers to a voluntary party to the social contract (i.e., citizens or "a class of persons who are part of a national community or who have otherwise developed sufficient connection with this country to be considered part of that community").[138] By contrast, natural rights theory views the Constitution as a constraint on the American government's activities everywhere—as limits on the actor rather than rights given to a specific kind of victim.[139] At present, the prevailing legal consensus supports the former theory, and foreign nationals abroad are consequently excluded from the protection of the Constitution's Fourth Amendment.

b. Domestic Law

Section 702 of FISA enacted in 2008 authorizes the PRISM program to collect, without a warrant, the electronic communications of foreign targets reasonably believed to be both non- U.S. citizens and outside the United States.[140] Furthermore, according to the FISA Amendments Act, any foreign national outside the United States can be targeted for surveillance as long as the government's objective is to collect foreign intelligence.[141] FISA broadly defines "foreign intelligence collection" as "information with respect to a foreign power or foreign territory that relates to *the conduct of the foreign affairs of the United States.*"[142]

In accordance with FISA, the Attorney General and Director of National Intelligence can issue one-year blanket authorizations for the surveillance of non-citizens who are reasonably believed to be outside the United States.[143] Along with this authorization, the Attorney General also provides the FISC with a "written certification containing certain statutorily required elements."[144] The court reviews the certification as well as the targeting and minimization procedures mandated by FISA regulations.[145] If the judge determines that the targeting and minimization procedures adequately restrict the acquisition, retention, and dissemination of private information related to U.S. persons and are consistent with the requirements of the FISA subsections and the Fourth Amendment, the judge enters an order approving the certification.[146] If, on the other hand, the court decides that the 702 application does not meet the aforementioned requirements, the judge issues "an order directing the government to, at the government's election and to the extent required by the Court's order, either correct any deficiency identified by the court's order not later than 30 days after the date on which the Court issues the order, or cease, or not begin, the implementation of the authorization for which the certification was submitted."[147]

Ergo, PRISM meets not only the constitutional requirements as they are widely understood, but is also in accordance with the relevant laws concerning FISA and related matters.

c. International Law

Article 12 of the Universal Declaration of Human Rights, to which the United States is a signatory, affirms that "no one shall be subjected to arbitrary interference with his privacy, family, home or correspondence, nor to attacks upon his honor and reputation. Everyone has the right to the protection of the law against such interference or attacks."[148] The International Covenant on Civil and Political Rights (ICCPR), which was ratified by the United States in March 1976, reaffirms this principle in nearly identical terms. International law has recognized the right to privacy as a fundamental human right. The Universal Declaration of Human Rights (UDHR), which Professor Richard Lillich describes as the "Magna Carta of contemporary international human rights law,"[149] is widely accepted as customary international law.

One must nevertheless take into account that the UDHR is not legally binding, and signatories are consequently not legally responsible for violations of the declaration's provisions. Furthermore, although the U.S. Congress ratified the ICCPR, it did so with an "unprecedented number of reservations, understandings, and declarations"—effectively "rendering the treaty powerless under domestic law."[150]

Most important, because spying has been practiced since the beginning of history and is very frequently and regularly practiced by one nation against others, disregarding the privacy rights of foreign nationals is widely tacitly accepted as part of "normal," albeit not normative, international life.[151] It is considered uncouth to submit friendly nations to surveillance, but it is not considered a serious violation of the prevailing standards of international relations. PRISM fits into a world that is rife with many more serious violations of the UDHR.

d. Executive Order

Some hold that the focus of public debate on Section 215 of the Patriot Act is misguided given the greater surveillance powers "authorized under Executive Order 12333" under the Reagan administration.[152] This executive order is not subject to judicial or congressional oversight,[153] and it "authorizes collection of the content of communications, not just metadata." The order does not authorize the specific targeting of U.S. persons without a court order, but it authorizes retention of their communications when collected inadvertently, "does not require that the affected U.S. persons be suspected of wrongdoing[,] and places no limits on the volume of communications by U.S. persons that may be collected and retained." This order is not the legal basis of either of the two programs under discussion, and thus lies outside the scope of this discussion, but if the account given by the *Washington Post*'s John Napier Tye is accurate, it is a serious matter that deserves a separate analysis.[154] According to Tye, it was on the basis of 11233 order that the White House counsel's office instructed him to remove from a speech the assertion that Americans have "the opportunity to change" the "scope of signals intelligence activities" through the "democratic process." This raises serious questions about congressional and judicial oversight over the executive branch and thus about the separation of powers, which was much debated throughout 2014 due to President Obama's own use of executive orders and recess appointments to bypass Congressional deadlock.[155]

2. Americans Abroad

FISA bans monitoring the Internet activity of American citizens abroad by mandating that activities authorized under Section 702 "not intentionally target a U.S. person reasonably believed to be located outside the United States."[156] In addition to noting that the NSA's surveillance activities are subject to oversight by the FISC, the executive branch, and Congress, Director of National Intelligence James Clapper stated that the program must not be used to "intentionally target any U.S. citizen, any other U.S. person, or anyone located within the United States."[157]

These statements sound much more absolute than they should. One notes that people are hardly required to show their passports when they "travel" in cyberspace. It is far from obvious what their target's nationality is when the NSA is watching someone overseas. The NSA uses the following procedure to deal with this attribution problem. The process of acquiring data on a foreign target begins when an NSA analyst "tasks" the PRISM system with acquiring information about a new surveillance target.[158] The request to add a new target is subsequently reviewed by a supervisor who must endorse the analyst's "reasonable belief," which is defined as 51 percent confidence, that the specified target is a foreign national who is overseas at the time of collection.[159]

NSA analysts examine the following three categories of information to make the above determination:

> They examine the lead information they have received regarding the potential target or the facility that has generated interest in conducting surveillance to determine what lead information discloses about the person's location. For example, has the target stated that he is located outside the United States? With whom has the target had direct contact, and what do we know about the location of such persons? [. . .] They conduct research in NSA databases, available reports, and collateral information to determine whether the NSA knows the location of the person, or knows information that would provide evidence concerning that location. For example, the NSA will review their own databases as well as databases of other intelligence and law enforcement agencies to determine if the person's location is already known. [. . .] They conduct technical analyses of the facility or facilities to determine or verify information about the person's location. For example, the NSA may examine Internet content repositories for records of previous Internet activity that may indicate the location of the target.

In addition, the NSA maintains records of telephone numbers and electronic accounts, addresses, and identifiers that the NSA has reason to believe are being used by U.S. persons. Before targeting an individual for surveillance, a telephone number or electronic communications account is checked against these records in order to ascertain whether the NSA has reason to believe the target is a U.S. person.[160] However, "in the absence of specific information regarding whether a target is a U.S. person, a person reasonably believed to be located outside the United States or whose location is not known will be presumed to a be non-U.S. person unless such person can be positively identified as a U.S. person, or the nature or circumstances of the person's communications give rise to a reasonable belief that such person is a U.S. person."[161]

Critics contend that these standards and procedures are far from rigorous and do not satisfactorily ensure that targeted persons are not American citizens or residents.[162] Numbers are difficult to come by because the intelligence community maintains that it is "not reasonably possible to identify the number of people located in the United States whose communications may have been reviewed under the authority" of the FISA Amendments Act that authorizes PRISM.[163] John D. Bates, the chief judge of the FISC, has noted that, given the scale of the NSA's data collection, "the court cannot know for certain the exact number" of wholly domestic communications collected under the act.[164]

Critics cite an NSA internal audit dated May 2012, which found 2,776 incidents in the preceding twelve months of unauthorized collection, storage, access to, or distribution of protected communications. Most of these incidents were unintended, and many involved failures of due diligence or violations of operating procedures. However, "the most serious incidents included a violation of a court order and unauthorized use of data about more than 3,000 Americans and green-card holders."[165]

Other reports show that these violations make up just a tiny fraction of 250 million communications that are collected by the NSA each year;[166] practically all were inadvertent, mostly technical mistakes, such as syntax errors when making database queries[167] or the programming error that interchanged the Washington, DC area code (202) with the international dialing code for Egypt (20)[168]; measures were taken to reduce error rate[169]; willful violations of privacy led to termination of the offending employees[170]; and the NSA was responsive to internal audits and deferred to court guidance—which shows oversight works.[171]

Moreover, if an NSA analyst incidentally obtains information that involves a U.S. person, he or she has to follow "minimization" protocols. If the communication has no foreign intelligence value, he or she cannot share or disseminate it unless it is evidence of a crime. Even if a conversation has foreign intelligence value, that information can only be disseminated to someone with an appropriate need to know the information pursuant to his or her mission.[172]

The NSA put it as follows: "We're a human-run agency operating in a complex environment with a number of different regulatory regimes, so at times we find ourselves on the wrong side of the line . . . [If you] look at [the] number [of violations] in absolute terms that looks big, and when you look at it in relative terms, it looks a little different."[173]

The Supreme Court has not ruled on the applicability of the Fourth Amendment to U.S. citizens abroad, but in April 2000 a federal district judge decided in *United States v. Bin Laden* that an exception to the warrant requirement for Americans abroad existed for foreign intelligence searches.[174] Citing "the president's constitutional power over foreign affairs, the policy costs of imposing a warrant requirement, and the absence of a warrant procedure"—as well as the fact that FISA explicitly specifies that it limits the president's authority to collect foreign intelligence only within the borders of the United States—the judge held that the warrantless phone surveillance and search of the home of an American citizen living in Kenya (who was in communication with al Qaeda) was permissible.[175] The judge, however, additionally required that there be probable cause to suspect that the defendant was an agent of a foreign power and that the searches or seizures were first authorized by the president or attorney general for the foreign intelligence exception to be applicable.

3. Cross-Border Communications

The government's initial position has been that PRISM is not targeting Americans or those known to reside within the borders of the United States.[176] In addition, the NSA cannot target a foreign communication with the intention of back tracking to a person in the United States.[177]

However, critics of the PRISM program, such as Senator Ron Wyden (D-OR), have argued that a loophole in Section 702 allows the government to conduct "backdoor" or warrantless searches of Americans' communications.[178] Specifically, critics argue that the incidental collection of data belonging to Americans who communicate with foreign nationals abroad further increases the potential pool of Americans being electronically monitored by the government. When the NSA collects information on a foreign target "means, at minimum, that everyone in the suspect's inbox or outbox is swept in." Furthermore, "intelligence analysts are typically taught to chain through contacts two 'hops' out from their target, which increases 'incidental collection' exponentially."[179] And the 2008 amendment to FISA removed the warrant requirement for any communication involving a foreign target — even if the communication involved an American sender or recipient.[180]

Much of the legal reasoning that justifies the collection of phone records (e.g., the general acceptance of "checkpoint searches" as being in accordance with the Fourth Amendment), can also be used to justify PRISM's incidental collection of communications between Americans and those across the border. In addition, the fact that these communications occur at the cyber-equivalent of a border also could be used to justify this kind of search. The Supreme Court has held that "searches made at the border, pursuant to the longstanding right of the sovereign to protect itself by stopping and examining persons and property crossing into this country, are reasonable simply by virtue of the fact that they occur at the border."[181] The Court has similarly maintained that such searches without probable cause are reasonable not just at the physical borders, but at the "functional equivalents" of the border as well.[182] These searches are all justified by the fact that the United States has an overriding interest, and authority, to protect its "territorial integrity" as well as preserve national security.[183] More broadly, the exception is based on the government's "sovereign right to protect itself from terrorist activities, unlawful migration, and contraband."[184] Whether PRISM should be applied to dealing with acts other than terrorism is a very weighty normative and legal issue that calls for a separate treatment that is beyond the scope of this chapter.

The review so far suggests that PRISM is a legal and reasonable program. This assumes that it is employed as depicted by the government. How to ensure that this is the case and that the program will be properly contained and held accountable in the future is next explored.

E. New Revelations

In the wake of media reports about PRISM and the NSA's telephone metadata program, additional reports based on the Snowden leaks and other sources have revealed still more about the NSA's programs. While significant, these new revelations have not altered the basic facts about NSA surveillance that the initial leaks of summer 2013 revealed: that it consists of broad foreign surveillance, including significant inadvertent collection of information belonging to U.S. persons, and that the government minimizes this inadvertently collected data but retains the ability to use it under certain circumstances. The most novel revelation has been that the NSA discovers, hoards, and uses (rather than discloses) computer security vulnerabilities,[185] but such activity, even if problematic from a public policy or cost-benefit analysis standpoint, clearly falls within the NSA's mandate of espionage and surveillance rather than virus protection.

A troubling revelation is found in reports that the NSA collected "almost 3 billion pieces of intelligence on U.S. citizens in February 2013 alone" as estimated by the NSA data analysis tool known as Boundless Informant.[186] While this was relatively little compared to countries like Iran (14 billion pieces of intelligence) and the total (97 billion pieces of intelligence) over that period, it remains large in an absolute sense for collection that is deemed "inadvertent," and it belies previous public statements by the NSA that it is unable to estimate how much collection of information about Americans takes place.

Other revelations are similar in kind. The collection, month-long storage, and access of "'100 percent' of a foreign country's telephone calls" using the MYSTIC and RETRO tools,[187] the bulk collection of "almost 200 million text messages"[188] and "nearly 5 billion" cell phone location records daily[189] and 250 million e-mail and instant message address books yearly[190]—the large scale of these activities is perhaps surprising, but they are the types of endeavors that would be expected t of the NSA in the cyber age. As for the NSA's XKeyScore tool, details of which were recently leaked and which is reported to allow "analysts to search with no prior authorization through vast databases containing emails, online chats and the browsing histories of millions of individuals," the NSA argues that "there are multiple technical, manual and supervisory checks and balances within the system to prevent deliberate misuse" and that "every search by an NSA analyst is fully auditable, to ensure that they are proper and within the law."[191]

F. Accountability vs. Transparency

1. Serious Charges

So far, this chapter has assumed that the two surveillance programs' main features are those that have been reported and has not speculated as to whether the government is actually collecting the content of phone calls in addition to metadata. One can have some confidence in the information because it largely emanates not from the government, but rather from leakers who have proven themselves quite willing to reveal the government's flaws and misdeeds. The evidence so far suggests that the government basically follows the procedures indicated, and, moreover, even liberal critics have had to admit that there are no specific cases in which an innocent person was actually harmed by these programs. As the *New Yorker*'s Hendrik Hertzberg has observed, "In the roughly seven years the programs have been in place in roughly their present form, no citizen's freedom of speech, expression, or association has been abridged by them in any identifiable way. No political critic of the Administration has been harassed or blackmailed as a consequence of them. They have not put the lives of tens of millions of Americans under 'surveillance' as that word is commonly understood."[192]

Two very serious specific charges have been leveled against the NSA. One concerns reports that the NSA often failed to comply with the laws that are supposed to govern its operations.[193] "For several years, the National Security Agency unlawfully gathered tens of thousands of e-mails and other electronic communications between Americans" via "upstream" collections, which is a program authorized by Section 702 of FISA. This program is distinct from both PRISM and the phone surveillance program.[194] However, such violations bring into question the extent to which the NSA can be trusted to heed the law. Along similar lines and in contrast to statements by President Obama and other public figures that the NSA has never abused its powers, such abuse has occurred on a small scale.[195] In addition to the aforementioned violations of procedure, which were mostly unintentional, the chairman of the House Intelligence Committee has stated that "approximately a dozen" cases of "willful violations" have been uncovered over the last decade involving "improper behavior on the part of individual [NSA] employees,"[196] most of which involved surveillance of love interests. In response to this controversy, Senator Dianne Feinstein (D-CA), chair of the Senate Intelligence Community, argued that while "any case of non-compliance is unacceptable [. . .] the NSA takes significant care to prevent any abuses and that there is a substantial oversight system in place."[197] And the former deputy director of the CIA likewise asserted that there "has been no systematic abuse, there has been no political abuse, it has been minor, very minor."[198]

To prevent further loss of public trust, it is important that the NSA uphold its promise to "identify problems at the earliest possible moment, implement mitigation measures wherever possible, and drive the numbers down."[199] This is particularly true given that, according to the head of the FISC, that court relies "upon the accuracy of the information that is provided [by the NSA]" and "does not have the capacity to investigate issues of noncompliance."[200]

The second serious charge is that the NSA has misled the public and watchdogs regarding the extent and nature of its program. An FISC judge charged the government with providing misleading statements, noting that "the government has now advised the court that the volume and nature of the information it has been collecting is fundamentally different from what the court had been led to believe."[201] In a particularly sharply worded footnote, the judge, John Bates, stated, "The court is troubled that the government's revelations regarding NSA's acquisition of Internet transactions mark the third instance in less than three years in which the government has disclosed a substantial misrepresentation regarding the scope of a major collection program."[202]

Similarly, Judge Reggie B. Walton accused the NSA of having repeatedly provided the FISC with misinformation with respect to how the telephone metadata was being used.[203] Walton wrote that the "government has compounded its noncompliance with the court's orders by repeatedly submitting inaccurate descriptions of the alert list process" and that it "has finally come to light that the F.I.S.C.'s authorizations of this vast collection program have been premised on a flawed depiction of how the N.S.A. uses the phone call data."[204] Given these findings, one can either hold that these programs ought to be canceled, which is the position taken by a considerable number of members of Congress on both the right and the left,[205] or one can conclude that the NSA needs to be more closely monitored. The preceding discussion suggests that, given that threat level and the need for enhanced security measures, one at least should closely test the thesis that a better monitored NSA could be brought to fully function within the law before one considers canceling either the phone surveillance or PRISM programs. One can accord the government license to conduct surveillance of the population commensurate with the degree to which its surveillance programs are *themselves* subject to surveillance. This approach is next explored.

There are two major ways to implement such "guarding of the guardians": increasing transparency and increasing accountability. While I cannot stress enough that both have a contribution to make, I shall attempt to show that enhanced accountability should be relied on much more than enhanced transparency. (I will also suggest a particular means for strengthening accountability.)

2. The Limits of Enhancing Transparency

Enhanced transparency entails releasing more information about details of the surveillance programs to the media and hence to the public, as well as to members of Congress in general (rather than only to a select few with security clearance who serve on specialized committees). Following the revelations of the NSA programs in 2013, there was very considerable demand for such disclosures, that is, for increased transparency.[206] The president's aides stated that they were going to try to be even more transparent,[207] and the government released additional information[208] on top of the continued stream of leaks. Over a quarter of the Senate signed a letter urging the White House to be more transparent about its surveillance practices.[209]

There are some potential ways that transparency could be enhanced. For example, the government might release summaries of the FISA rulings that justify its programs without going into specifics of the facts on which these cases are based and that concern the government's knowledge about specific suspects. The government has begun, since the revelations in 2013, to make moves toward such transparency. A judge on the nation's intelligence court directed the government to review the possibility of publicly releasing some of the court's presently classified opinions regarding the NSA's phone records collection program.[210] The Office of the Director of National Intelligence has developed a web page at which it makes public formerly classified material that helps to explain the way the programs in question function.[211] Director James Clapper also stated that his office would release additional information regarding the number of secret court orders and national security letters sent out each year in the process of collecting data, as well as the number of people such searches affected.[212]

High transparency, however, is on the face of it incompatible with keeping secret that which must be kept secret. Moreover, when the government responds to calls for more scrutiny by releasing more information—so as to demonstrate that the secret acts did, in fact, improve security and did not unduly violate privacy—these releases encounter several difficulties. First, each piece of information released potentially helps the adversaries. This is, in effect, the way intelligence work is often done: by piecing together details released by various sources. Thus, the publication of information about which past terrorist operations the government aborted could allow those groups to find out which of their plots failed because of U.S.

government, technical flaws, the weakness of their chosen agents, or some other reason.²¹³ Second, it is next to impossible to spell out how these cases unfolded without giving away details about sources and methods. (That is, unless the government releases misleading details. But sooner or later some whistleblower would likely expose the ploy, which would undermine the whole enterprise, which was meant to build trust in government.) Thus, one intelligence official reports that the leaks regarding the NSA snooping programs have already led to terrorist groups "changing their communications behavior based on these disclosures," which means that we might "miss tidbits that could be useful in stopping the next plot."²¹⁴

Moreover, regardless of the amount of information about specific cases the government releases, skeptics are sure to find details that need further clarification and documentation. (This is the reason public relations experts urge those whose misdeeds are under public scrutiny to "tell all" right from the start. This strategy may serve well politicians who cheat on their spouses, but it would not serve those who combat terrorism.) Thus, following the uproar over PRISM, technology companies sought to "reassure users" by releasing reports on the frequency of government data requests. The result, as reported in *The New York Times*, was that "rather than provide clarity, the companies' disclosures have left many questions unanswered."²¹⁵ When NSA Director General Keith Alexander released details about how the agency's surveillance programs had thwarted terrorist plots, the media immediately asked for more.²¹⁶ Moreover, there is no way for the media to determine whether the released cases are typical or whether they have been chosen because they reflect well on the government.

3. Increasing Accountability

A considerable number of suggestions have been made regarding how greater oversight could be implemented to hold the government to account. These include the following:

- A panel of high-level, independent experts who could review the technologies being used by the NSA and provide recommendations regarding how to balance privacy and security²¹⁷
- FISA could include a "privacy advocate" who would add an adversarial element to requests made by the courts.²¹⁸ Legislation to this effect has been introduced by two members of the House who propose creating an "Office of the Constitutional Advocate," which would be led by an advocate appointed by the judicial branch.²¹⁹ Skeptics of the proposition to empower FISA point to the fact that much NSA

surveillance, particularly that taking authority from executive order, "lies entirely outside of FISC review," and as such "is only subject to the NSA's internal 'checks and balances.'"[220]
- Annual reports by Inspectors General regarding the activities of the NSA[221]
- Stronger laws protecting whistleblowers; a category that should be limited to those who go through established channels rather than leak information to the public and the press.[222]
- Subjecting the NSA to closer oversight by various Congressional committees.[223] One should note, however, the danger of overcorrecting for the current problems. Famously, the Department of Homeland Security is subject to so many committees that its senior staff spends a very large portion of their time testifying before Congress and preparing for such appearances.
- Reforming how FISA court judges are selected to ensure greater independence from government and creating multiple judge panels that might allow for dissents.[224]
- Senator Dianne Feinstein has suggested that the government should keep records for only two or three years rather than for the present five-year retention period.[225] However, there is no apparent evidence that such a short period is sufficient. Sleeper cells often stay inactive for ten years or longer. A case in point is the Russian spy ring that was broken up in 2010.[226]
- Implement audit trails to ensure that only the proper authorities have access to any given piece of information.[227]

A report on the operation of the Terrorist Finance Tracking Program (TFTP) provides a powerful example. A project developed by the U.S. Treasury, the TFTP collects large amounts of data from a financial messaging system (called Swift) that records data on financial transfers. The TFTP used this information to uncover terrorist networks and to prevent multiple attacks.[228] Importantly, the TFTP was subjected to significant oversight—only narrowly focused searches and analysis of the data were permitted, and two different groups of independent auditors ensured that those restrictions were being strictly adhered to.[229] Moreover, any time a government analyst wanted to query the system, they had to submit a reason for their query that could then be approved or denied by a Swift representative.[230] (It is not obvious that this arrangement is scalable to the NSA level. Queries by analysts are already reviewed by managers at NSA. Select queries are subject to a "two person" rule.)

Other suggestions involve Congress; for example, some have suggested increasing the number of members of Congress who are being briefed or changing the committees that are charged with overseeing the NSA. Each and all of these measures deserve close study. Some of these moves are clearly necessary to further ensure that the NSA abides by all the applicable laws and regulations and to assure the public that it does. Given the current level of distrust of the government in general, one must wonder if even all these measures taken together would suffice or if some extraordinary steps need to be taken; the next section explores this.

4. Civic Oversight

Consideration should be given to introducing a greater role for civic bodies that are not part of the government but that help oversight; a regular review conducted by an independent civilian review board is one example. Such a board would be composed of the kind of people who served on the 9/11 Commission: bipartisan, highly respected by the public, able to work together, not running for office, and possessing the necessary security clearance. While not everyone agreed with that commission's conclusions, they were still well-respected and largely trusted, and many of their recommendations were eventually implemented. (Critics of this proposal may suggest that these missions are already carried out by the Civil Liberties Board and the President's Intelligence Advisory Board [PIAB].)

However, these bodies have not been given the power they need for important segments of the public—the parts that have legitimate concerns, rather than the parts that automatically distrust all government does and states—to feel confident that accountability is adequate.

The new board would issue reports that would state whether or not the government collected information for political reasons (as opposed to security concerns), in the pursuit of minor criminals (as opposed to terrorists), or for legitimate and legal goals. However, instead of revealing detailed case studies, the civilian review board would provide statistics. For example, if the board were to report that there were a large number of cases in which serious threats, such as the planned attack on New York City's subway system, were averted, the public would learn that the threats to national security warranted increased efforts to enforce antileak legislation. If, on the other hand, the board reported that many cases involved fairly minor threats, this would tilt the consensus the other way.[231] (If the current Civil Liberties and Privacy Protection Board were to be properly staffed, funded, and granted more power, it might serve such a function).

The board should ensure that the government is adequately kept in check while also ensuring that the system of accountability does not tilt too far in the opposite direction by placing too many restraints on the NSA. One does not, for example, want to impose procedures like those that prevented the FBI from setting up a sting operation to capture Tamerlan Tsarnaev, one of the Boston Marathon bombers. According to U.S. officials, a sting operation can only be undertaken if there is "evidence that someone is already contemplating violence"—an evidentiary threshold that Tsarnaev's activities did not pass before he bombed the Boston Marathon and that prevented the FBI from sharing relevant information about the terrorist brothers with the Boston police department.[232] The liberal communitarian balance can be lost both by moving in the direction of too much security and by imposing too many limitations on security. Indeed, oversteering in one direction often leads to overcorrections in the opposite one.

The Privacy and Civil Liberties Oversight Board, an independent, bipartisan executive branch agency established in line with the Implementing Recommendations of the 9/11 Commission Act of 2007, can play such a role. So far, the board has released two major reports relating to the leaked NSA programs. The first, which was released in January 2014, recommended discontinuing the bulk metadata program on the grounds that its performance to date did not justify its "significant ramifications for privacy and civil liberties."[233] By contrast, the second, which was released in July 2014, recommended maintaining PRISM because it has "proven valuable in the government's efforts to combat terrorism" and contains "reasonably designed" minimization procedures and precautions against "illegitimate purposes," though with minor reforms to safeguard privacy and civil liberties interests.[234] Privacy advocates and others such as the American Library Association, American Civil Liberties Union, and the Center for Constitutional Rights, however, criticized these recommendations as too limited.[235]

G. The Coming Tyrant?

A common claim among civil libertarians is that, even if government surveillance programs are presently inflicting little harm, the infrastructure is in place for a less-benevolent leader to violate the people's rights and set us on the path to tyranny. For example, it has been argued that PRISM "will amount to a 'turnkey' system that, in the wrong hands, could transform the country into a totalitarian state virtually overnight. Every person who values personal freedom, human rights and the rule of law must recoil against such a possibility, regardless of their political preference."[236] Similarly, *The Atlantic*'s Conor Friedersdorf argued that, thanks to PRISM and the collection of phone records, "the people in charge will possess the capacity to be tyrants— to use power oppressively and unjustly—to a degree that Americans in 1960, 1970, 1980, 1990, or 2000 could've scarcely imagined." He further emphasized that "it could happen here, with enough historical amnesia, carelessness, and bad luck."[237] And Senator Rand Paul (R-KY) has been "careful to point out that he is concerned about the possible abuses of some future, Hitler-like president."[238] In less alarmist fashion, Center for Constitutional Rights attorney Shayana Kadidal warns that if "judges, members of Congress and other elected officials [are not] exempted from NSA surveillance," the "chilling effect" of the NSA's access to confidential or embarrassing information on them would threaten to "corrupt the political process." She points to the practices of J. Edgar Hoover during his time as director of the FBI as a cautionary example.[239] A few things might be said in response.

First, all of the data that the government is collecting is already being archived (at least for short periods, as discussed earlier) by private corporations and other entities. It is not the case that PRISM or other such programs entail the collection of new data that was not previously available to the government through a subpoena.

Second, if one is truly concerned that a tyrant might take over the United States, one obviously faces a much greater and all-encompassing threat than a diminution of privacy, and the response has to be similarly expansive. One can join civic bodies that seek to shore up democracies; or work with various reform movements and public education drives; or join groups that prepare to retreat to the mountains, store ammunition and essential foods, and plan to fight the tyrannical forces. But it makes no sense to oppose limited measures to enhance security on these grounds.

Conclusion

Revelations about two surveillance programs—the one that collects the phone records of Americans, and the one that collects digital communications by foreigners overseas—should be assessed by drawing on a liberal communitarian paradigm that seeks a balance between security and privacy (and other individual rights). Such an evaluation shows that we do face a significant terrorist threat, hence the continued need for enhanced security; that this threat cannot be mitigated by dealing with terrorists as criminals; and that the government reports that the programs are effective.

At the same time, the means used to conduct surveillance of Americans are either not intrusive or only minimally intrusive. Records need be collected because otherwise they are not maintained or are not readily accessible. Computers that store these records do not, per se, violate privacy. Before any individual's records can be searched, probable cause must be established. In short, the program seems to qualify on both constitutional and legal grounds. And the program that conducts surveillance of foreigners overseas does not violate American laws insofar as it does not ensnare Americans.

Finally, the extent to which the government should be accorded more surveillance powers should be tied to great surveillance of its surveillance programs. Several suggestions have been made to increase the accountability of the NSA; drawing on a civilian security review board that is independent of the government is the most important of these. Thus, two balances must be maintained: the balance between rights and the common good, and the balance between the need to act and the need to ensure that action is in accordance with our liberal communitarian values.

10

DNA Searches: A Liberal Communitarian Approach[1]

Arguments concerning the conditions under which public authorities may collect, analyze, and retain DNA samples and profiles for the purpose of investigating crimes ("forensic DNA usages") are often couched in terms of a familiar debate between individual rights and the common good. That is, the arguments are framed as a confrontation between those who champion individual rights, especially privacy, and those concerned with the common good, especially public safety and national security. Members of the first camp frequently argue that forensic DNA usages without "individualized suspicion," without specific authorization by the courts, constitute a gross violation of basic rights. Those of the second camp often argue that these searches significantly curb crime, including terrorism, and that the interventions involved are limited.

By contrast, the liberal communitarian approach, which this chapter develops and applies to the issues raised by forensic DNA usages, assumes that all societies face two fully legitimate normative and legal claims—those posed by individual rights and by the common good—and that neither a priori trumps the other. Each society must work out the extent to which it tilts toward one of these two major claims on a given issue. The author has previously explored such a balance between individual rights and the common good as it applies to National Security Agency programs, the Patriot Act, public health laws, publication of state secrets, Megan's laws, national identification cards, and medical privacy.[2] These studies revealed that liberal communitarianism favors a distinct balance between individual rights and the common good for each of these areas of public policy. (For a discussion of this balance as it applies to privacy and security, see Chapter 7.)

This chapter will show that policies concerning forensic DNA usages have a profile all their own. The article first briefly reviews the history of forensic DNA usages, next addresses the criticisms of DNA usage by various advocates of individual rights, and then examines the contributions of this technology to the common good. More attention is devoted to issues raised by rights advocates than to their contributions to the common good, because the latter are much less contested. In conclusion we find that these DNA usages pose a surprisingly distinct liberal communitarian balance.

It cannot be stressed enough that this chapter does not seek nor provide a comprehensive—let alone exhaustive—review of all the issues raised by forensic DNA usages concerning intrusions into individual rights or contributions to the common good. It merely seeks to place these usages in the liberal communitarian context and ask whether—on balance, at this time in history, in the United States—these usages tilt excessively in one direction or the other.

A. The History of Forensic DNA Usages

The first state DNA database used for forensic purposes was established in the United States, in Virginia in 1989,[3] and was followed in 1990 by a pilot program of fourteen state and local laboratories linked by specially designed software called CODIS.[4] This pilot program expanded into an FBI-operated system of state and local DNA profile databases in forty-one states and the District of Columbia beginning in 1991.[5] A National DNA Index System (NDIS) became operational in October 1998. It contains qualifying DNA profiles, or DNA profiles that meet NDIS standards according to federal law, uploaded by participating federal, state, and local forensic laboratories.[6] (Note that state and local jurisdictions may have less stringent rules about which DNA profiles may be included in their DNA databases.) As of July 2014, NDIS included more than eleven million DNA profiles.[7]

Congress has expanded the breadth of the NDIS database over time. When NDIS was established, it was authorized to contain DNA identification records for "persons convicted of crimes" as well as "analyses of DNA samples recovered from crime scenes . . . from unidentified human remains . . . [and] voluntarily contributed from relatives of missing persons." Congress defined a set of crimes that it considered sufficiently serious to warrant collecting DNA samples from those who commit them, including murder, sexual abuse, and kidnapping;[8] these crimes are referred to as "qualifying offenses." Initially, Congress included in NDIS only the DNA profiles of individuals who were then in custody for qualifying offenses at the state level, but eventually it also authorized the inclusion of DNA profiles of individuals who were convicted of and incarcerated for qualifying offenses at the federal level or in the District of Columbia. In 2000, Congress also authorized the inclusion in NDIS of DNA profiles collected from probationers and parolees who had been previously convicted of qualifying offenses, and it retroactively approved the collection of DNA samples from individuals then in custody who had been previously convicted of a qualifying offense. In 2001, it expanded the definition of "qualifying offenses" to include all "crimes of violence" and "acts of terrorism that transcend national boundaries," and in 2004 it further expanded the definition to encompass any federal felony.

The next step in the expansion of forensic DNA usages has been the collection of DNA samples from individuals arrested *on suspicion*, but not yet convicted or even per se charged, of having committed a qualifying offense, prior to a court's establishment of their guilt. As of 2014, twenty-eight states collect DNA samples from arrestees, while such collection was authorized at the federal level with the DNA Fingerprint Act of 2005 and extended through the Katie Sepich Enhanced DNA Collection Act of 2012.[9] In 2013, the U.S. Supreme Court ruled in favor of the constitutionality of DNA sampling and profiling of arrestees in *Maryland v. King*.[10]

While great expansions have been made to the scope of forensic DNA usages, still greater expansions could be made if a universal database that contains DNA profiles collected from all of a country's citizens, residents, and visitors were to be introduced. In 2006 and 2007, British Prime Minister Tony Blair and Lord Justice Stephen Sedley respectively called for the introduction of a universal DNA database in the United Kingdom.[11] However, following public outcry and EU and UK Supreme Court rulings[12] the UK instead passed legislation in 2012 to limit its DNA database to convicts.[13] Others have called for a universal database, but to date, no country has created one. Portugal, which announced it would establish a universal DNA database but abandoned the plan in the face of cost and ethical considerations, came closest.[14] (A private company in Iceland also gained approval to build a universal national health database including DNA—for research rather than crime-fighting purposes, increasing privacy concerns—but ultimately went bankrupt before completing the database.[15])

In addition to DNA profiles generated from samples from people suspected of or convicted of qualifying offenses, NDIS contains DNA profiles generated from DNA samples collected at crime scenes ("evidentiary" profiles and samples, respectively) and from missing persons and their relatives.[16]

B. Individual Rights Concerns

1. Forensic DNA Usages and Sensitive Information

Critics of forensic DNA usages fear that the database will enable access to sensitive information[17] about DNA donors. They are concerned that DNA profiles will reveal to those who have access to these databases details about the person's medical history, genetic background and origins, current medical conditions, familial relationships, and even information about the DNA of other members of their family.[18] George J. Annas, Chair of the Department of Health Law, Bioethics and Human Rights at the Boston University School of Public Health, adds that as technology advances, analysts will be able to discern an individual's complete probabilistic medical "future" by analyzing their DNA.[19]

To address these concerns, one must avoid the trap of conflating DNA samples and DNA profiles. A DNA sample is the material, including blood, saliva, and other tissues, that is collected from an individual and that contains his or her complete set of genetic information ("genome"). A database of complete genomes, unless property supervised and limited in accessibility, would raise the privacy concerns outlined above. DNA profiles, on the other hand, merely document the length of certain fragments ("loci") of DNA that vary greatly from person to person. DNA profiles are derived by analyzing DNA samples. Only a select few, especially variable ("polymorphic") loci, are analyzed and included in the profile.[20] (In the United States, DNA profiles involve thirteen of these loci.) The tiny amount of genetic information included in the profile, sometimes referred to as "junk" DNA, reveals very little about the donor. DNA profiles contain no known information about the donor's "phenotype"—that is, their physical traits, including diseases to which they have, had, or are predisposed.[21] However, the information included is sufficient to identify the donor because the probability of two individuals—except for identical twins—matching all loci is exceptionally small.[22] Indeed, the courts have repeatedly recognized scientific consensus that forensic DNA profiles functionally "reveal nothing more than the offender's identity."[23] An *amicus curiae* brief by a coalition of scientific experts in *Maryland v. King*, which was filed in support neither of the petitioner nor the respondent,[24] summed up the issue as follows:

> The DNA variations used for criminal identification represent common, normal human variation and have, at most, only weak associations with any diseases or physical or behavioral traits. However, they may provide powerful information about the presence (or absence) of genetic relationships with family members, as well as very weak information about geographic or ethnic origins.[25]

The crucial point, which critics should not overlook, is that the DNA databases consist of DNA profiles, not DNA samples. Only a small amount of genetic information is translated into a CODIS-compatible DNA profile and stored in the database. In all but a handful of jurisdictions, the DNA samples from which DNA profiles are derived are retained by the originating laboratory.

Some have argued that, to better protect individuals' privacy, these samples should be destroyed after DNA profiles have been extracted. Britain is destroying its DNA samples while retaining profiles of convicted criminals.[26] The EU Court of Human Rights, while acknowledging the difference between samples and profiles, ruled that both should be destroyed for those not convicted of a crime.[27]

The samples ought to be kept in order to provide for reanalysis as technologies develop, for exoneration, for convicting criminals of additional crimes of which they have originally not been charged, and for ruling on the guilt or innocence of arrestees that have been released but new evidence that implicates them has been established.

Instead of destroying the samples, additional steps should be taken to prevent unauthorized analysis and sharing of DNA samples. All such measures that limit secondary usages of genetic information and that ensure the legality of these usages—as opposed to measures that simply limit the *collection* of such genetic information—are measures that enhance accountability.[28] (The term accountability is used throughout this article to refer to institutionalized arrangements that serve to ensure that the material at hand is used legally, without undue use, access, or disclosure—and that proper oversight and enforcements mechanisms are in place, to generate the incentives to ensure that the various legally set rules and procedures are observed).

Several accountability measures have already been implemented. CODIS matches do not reveal identifying information about a person whose DNA profile is searched, such as name or social security number; instead, each profile is labeled with a specimen identifier, the originating laboratory's identifier, and the initials of the technician who created the profile. The originating laboratories keep the samples and records of the personal information associated with each specimen.[29] If a match is found, the authorities seeking a match have the information necessary to contact the appropriate laboratory, which then releases the identifying information in accordance with applicable federal, state, and local law, often after re-testing the retained DNA sample to verify the match.[30] Thus, a "firewall" of sorts exists between insensitive, searchable profile information and sensitive, personally-identifiable information and samples.

Moreover, the sensitive information contained in retained DNA samples is protected by law. Congress enacted laws that impose heavy penalties for unauthorized disclosure of DNA profile information[31] and other information that could be derived from analyzing DNA samples.[32] The courts have provided for the possibility that advances in genetic technology could necessitate reconsideration of the sensitivity of "junk" DNA,[33] acknowledging that if advances in genetic technology find that "junk" DNA, including that found in DNA profiles, contains meaningful information, this information would be have to be accorded additional protections. Likewise, the Supreme Court's permissive attitude towards police DNA usage may change if that usage changes in character: "If in the future police analyze samples to determine [...] hereditary factors not relevant to identity, that case would present additional privacy concerns not present here."[34]

In this area, as in so many others, attention focuses on "Big Brother," on the government. Americans tend to fear and distrust the government while assuming that the private sector will promote liberty rather than undermine it. However, as we have seen elsewhere,[35] private corporations increasingly act in ways that violate individual rights, in particular privacy. A full review of DNA usages, well beyond the purview of this paper, would have to examine the growing role private companies play in the analysis of DNA and their marketing of this information to other private actors—and to the government.

Finally, abuse of DNA information is much less widespread than critics assume. A 2009 report by the Department of Justice Office of the Inspector General found one rare example of such outright abuse; it reported that a forensic laboratory in Texas had given CODIS access to one individual that the FBI had failed to authorize.[36] Even in this case, the unauthorized access appears to have occurred as a result of oversight rather than malicious attempts to gain genetic information about specific individuals in the database.

In short, critics' concerns about the exposure of sensitive information contained in DNA samples are valid, but they are not relevant to the DNA profiles included in the national databases used by law enforcement authorities. Samples are and ought to be kept in local storage, to allow retesting (if there evidence of error or abuse in the first round of analysis) and to provide for opportunities for more analysis as technologies are further developed. Samples are already reasonably well protected, although more such protection could be improved. There is little evidence that privacy is violated in the ways anticipated by critics; most of the criticisms levied against forensic DNA usages are hypothetical rather than based on evidence.

2. Fishing Expeditions and Dragnets

Another cause for concern relating to forensic DNA usages is that they could encourage unwarranted intrusions by the police into the lives of innocent individuals.[37] "Fishing expeditions," in which the police examine in details the lives of people not suspected of having committed any crime, are a major category of such intrusions. These are opposed by civil libertarians on the ground that all human beings are likely to have committed some kind of offense at one point or another, and hence if fishing expeditions are allowed, very large parts of the populations would find itself in court if not incarcerated, and all would live in constant fear of being convicted. In the terms employed here, fishing expeditions would greatly undermine the liberal communitarian balance, by grossly violating rights.

Such DNA fishing expeditions are rare and should be avoided. They become more of a concern the greater the range of DNA included in the evidentiary databases. These expeditions are less troubling if the databases include only DNA from the scenes of serious crime, such as murder and rape, and very troubling –if they would include DNA collected from litter left by people in public spaces or other misdemeanors.

The second category of criticism targets methods of investigation whereby the police conduct partial match searches, mainly familial searches. In such searches, when DNA collected from a crime scene partially matches a profile in the police database, the individual from the database is excluded from suspicion, but it is more likely that a closely related rather than unrelated person is the source of crime-scene DNA, which leads police to investigate the partially matching individual's family. Such searches have been used relatively often in the United Kingdom, solving several high-profile cases, but to date are less common in the United States.[38] Police argue that such "partial matches" are a useful investigative tool that helps investigators solve difficult cases and deters crimes (because potential criminals fear both they are more likely to be caught, and that their families may come under surveillance[39]), and New York recently passed a new law to allow for such searches despite objection by the ACLU.[40] Critics warn that in addition to exacerbating privacy concerns associated with expanding the DNA database generally, familial searches "effectively include individuals based on genetic association, rather than suspicion or even conviction of crimes,"[41] risk revealing private family associations (such as marital infidelity), and "expose innocent relatives to life-long surveillance and possible surreptitious collection of DNA simply because they are related to someone in the national database."[42] In this sense, restricting access to and disclosure of such personal information is especially important for partial match searches. Critics also allege the partial match searching exacerbates the racial inequities characteristic of forensic DNA usages more generally (see below).[43]

A more general cause for concern is that such partial match searching, can generate false positives, exposing unrelated innocents to unwarranted police intrusion.[44] Consider the case of Raymond Easton.[45] Easton was a forty-eight-year-old man who was arrested for a burglary that was committed two hundred miles from his home on the basis of a partial match between the DNA of the suspect and Easton's DNA that was collected three years prior to the burglary for a minor domestic incident that did not lead to him being charged with a crime. Although Easton suffered from Parkinson's disease and could not drive, the police were convinced of his guilt on the basis of the partial DNA match. Ultimately, the charges against Easton were dropped in light of his corroborated and strong alibi combined with a more rigorous DNA test calling Easton's involvement in the burglary into question. Nonetheless, Easton was exposed to considerable stress during the investigation on the basis of the partial match between his DNA and the perpetrator's. Partial match searches could expose hundreds of people who have not committed the crime to the stresses of being a suspect, which can help to explain why Erin Murphy, Professor of Law specializing in criminal law and forensic evidence at New York University calls such searches "suspicionless, generalized, and arbitrary."[46]

In response to this latter concern, one might note that while the stress of being the subject of a police investigation is considerable and should not be discounted, it is unnecessary to abandon the use of partial match searches to guard against the danger of over-inclusive matches. According to Sonia Suter, the utility of familial searches could be maximized by studying the effectiveness of DNA profiling in actually convicting criminals (particularly whether familial searches add value to and/or impose hidden costs on police investigations); improving and evening out the mixed performance of crime labs, and restricting familial searches to serious crimes and those "most susceptible to resolution through DNA analysis. At the same time, costs can be minimized through a reasonable minimum threshold for "partial" matches, legislative approval and police adoption of technologies and analytical techniques that reduce the likelihood of false positives,[47] nondisclosure by police of family secrets (such as infertility, adoption, or infidelity) revealed by the analysis, and prohibition of surreptitious collection of "abandoned" DNA from innocent family members (as opposed to suspects.)[48] Liberal communitarianism could support such measures, in addition to the establishment of trained oversight and accountability boards to address ethical violations, abuses of privacy, and conflicts that arise between individual rights and the common good. This has already been done in California, where the Familial Search Committee (FSC)—a panel comprised of scientists, officials, and lawyers—"review[s] the progress of cases [involving familial searches] and provide[s] legal and ethical checkpoints at major steps in the investigation."[49] In the famous case of the "Grim Sleeper" serial killer, the FSC was tasked with reviewing all of the information that suggested a database offender was closely related to the donor of forensic DNA samples, and it was only with their authorization that the name of the database offender was released to the Los Angeles Police Department as an investigative lead.[50]

A third category of criticism targets "dragnets," which, with respect to DNA sampling, entail the DNA testing of large numbers of individuals whom authorities have neither probable cause nor reasonable suspicion to believe perpetrated a crime, but who live or work near a crime scene.[51] (That is, unlike random fishing expeditions, dragnets are targeted, if broadly so). Some dragnets included collections of hundreds or even thousands of DNA samples—one 1998 dragnet in Germany took DNA samples from some 16,500 people.[52]

Critics raised a number of concerns about dragnets.[53] First, they point out that "DNA profiles of dragnet volunteers are generally not destroyed after it is determined that the volunteer is innocent, but rather] are often retained in law enforcement databases, as most state laws "do not address the retention or expungement of genetic information obtained from suspects or samples given "voluntarily."[54] To address this concern, DNA samples and profiles of innocents collected through dragnets should be destroyed or sequestered following the conclusion of the investigation.

Second, critics contend that dragnets suffer from cost and effectiveness concerns: Of 292 DNA dragnets in England and Wales since 1995, about 20 percent produced meaningful leads, but only 1 out of the 18 dragnets conducted in the United States since 1990 leading to a viable suspect, a success rate of less than 6 percent.[55] This is not a principled objection; as costs decline, dragnets would seem more justified. Even 6 percent is far from a poor ratio especially if dragnets are limited, as most seem to be, to very serious crimes.

In short, although at first blush the difference between fishing expeditions and dragnets may seem to be small, fishing expeditions constitute a much greater violation of individual rights than dragnets. Even dragnets should be limited merely to seeking to solve major crimes.

3. Abandoned DNA

When police seek a DNA sample from a suspect, and cannot secure that suspect's consent or a warrant for DNA testing, they often obtain a DNA sample surreptitiously, using what legal scholars refer to as "abandoned DNA." In a 2003 case, for example, police posed as a fictitious law firm in order to convince a suspect to send them a letter—from which they then extracted the suspect's DNA.[56] The legal basis for this practice comes from the Supreme Court ruling in California v. Greenwood (1988)[57] that the Fourth Amendment does not prohibit the search of discarded garbage.

Critics argue that the collection of abandoned DNA centers represents "the uncritical surrender of important civil liberties."[58] Elizabeth Joh holds that police that use abandoned DNA bypass "criminal procedure rules that normally apply to searches and seizures" as well as restrictions on adding DNA profiles to CODIS, and she disputes the idea that California v. Greenwood, a ruling about garbage, justifies the practice.[59] And, collecting DNA in this way, critics, believe, violates the expectation of privacy of people who are often unaware that they leave their DNA behind. (This last concern would hold only as long as this police practice, often featured in TV shows, does not become more widely known). Despite the Greenwood ruling, the collection of abandoned DNA has not been unanimously accepted by judicial and legislative authorities. The Oregon Appeals Court excluded abandoned DNA evidence in State v. Galloway and Hoesly[60] (though with a property rather than privacy-based argument), and lower courts in a number of states have established higher standards for state and local police on police use of abandoned property more generally.[61]

In response, one notes that if police were not be entitled to collect abandoned DNA (without a warrant), they would logically also have to be banned from collecting abandoned hair or finger prints, or examine trash, on the same grounds. Such limitations would greatly hamper the police's work and greatly tilt the liberal communitarian balance away from public safety.

4. Racial Profiling

Forensic DNA usages have also been challenged on the grounds that they discriminate against people of color in the United States, especially Black and Latino men. Critics argue that at all stages of DNA usages—arrestee sample collection, convicted offender sample collection, database searches, and partial match searches—people of color are disproportionately affected. This is due to institutional racism in the American criminal justice system, which has many sources, including that the laws are harsher on street crime (more likely to be committed by minorities and those of low income) than white collar crime, despite the fact that the latter imposes greater economic harm;[62] harsher penalties for the use of crack cocaine (more often used by minorities) than for the use of cocaine (more often used by white people); biases build into the composition and attitudes of many local police forces as well as socio economic conditions that predispose some groups to commit more crimes that others.

One aspect of racial profiling relates to the ways DNA samples are collected. In cases where police have a loose physical description of a crime suspect and a DNA sample collected from the crime scene, they may refine their DNA dragnet by requesting DNA samples only from members of the racial group matching that physical description. (An intensive analysis of a DNA sample may even estimate a suspect's race when a physical description is unavailable, although such analysis raises further ethical concerns and its reliability may not meet "legal and scientific standards for trial admissibility."[63]) While such practice may constitute an efficient use of police resources, it is also a form of racial profiling, and has raised controversy as such.[64]

Another aspect of racial profiling relates to the disparities in the data banking of DNA profiles. Howard Cooke pointed to racial disparities in convicted offender DNA databases as early as 1993 and voiced opposition to their use on these grounds.[65]

Michael Purtill asserts that the disproportionate impact along racial and ethnic lines may be severe enough to violate the Equal Protection Clause of the Fourteenth Amendment.[66] Diane C. Barca has identified the disproportionate impact of partial match searches on people of color as a prominent concern advanced by civil libertarians and experts on the subject.

Whatever racial discrimination exists in the criminal justice system (and elsewhere) should indeed be eliminated. To proceed requires major changes to the law, public education, job training, and housing, among other major societal changes. However, the fact that racial discrimination persists does not by itself agitate against forensic DNA usages, because they do not cause discrimination any more than any other police tools. The same basic disparity exists in the number of people of color who are fingerprinted, stopped and frisked, arrested on minor grounds, and so on. Thus, even if an end was made to all DNA usages, racial discrimination would not be significantly diminished. To reiterate, the disproportional profiling of minorities is mainly a result of discrimination but not one of its causes.

True, if critics could show that forensic DNA usages inflicted substantially greater harm than other policing methods, that the burden of DNA usages falls disproportionately on people of color would suggest that DNA usages should be limited. For instance if evidence would validate the argument that the larger number of minority DNA in the databases than that of white people would lead to claims that predispositions to crime are genetically rooted. However no such evidence seems to be available.

Most important, as we shall see, DNA usages provide a surprisingly favorable communitarian balance compared to other law enforcement tools. Moreover, because people of color disproportionately suffer from crime, any measures that would weaken law enforcement, especially measures as substantial as stopping or greatly limiting DNA usages, would harm these communities more significantly than white ones.

Moreover, DNA profiling has the potential to counteract racism in other aspects of the criminal justice system. In July 2014, for example, as part on an ongoing effort to apply DNA testing to rape evidence, a Texas man was exonerated for a 1990 rape. He had spent more than a decade in jail, having pled guilty after "his attorney urged him to accept a plea deal because a jury likely would not side with a black man accused of raping a white teenage girl." Unfortunately, his previous petitions for DNA testing had been denied.[67]

Some have advocated the establishment of a universal DNA database as a way to eliminate racial disparities.[68] Advocates argue that a universal database, also referred to as a national DNA registry, would answer compositional criticisms of existing databases (that is, the perceived unfairness of racial disparities, familial search, and arrestee sampling) by treating everyone equally. At the same time, advocates argue, such a database would deliver major benefits to law enforcement "in deterring potential offenses, in generating investigative leads, and in exonerating the innocent," while removing the need for additional intrusions (such as fishing expeditions or dragnets).

Critics counter that a universal database would alienate the public, constitute an unconstitutional intrusion given the absence of individualized suspicion, and undermine privacy and anonymity of millions of people, at the risk of radically altering the relationship between the citizen and government" to create a nation of suspects.[69] (Such proposals have also been labeled "prohibitively expensive," but this is a decreasingly relevant objection as DNA profiling technology and computer technology lead to declines in cost.[70])

A liberal communitarian response can draw on a "law" formulated by the author in a different context.[71] Namely, one can grant more license to primary data collection (in this case, DNA)—the stronger accountability is. That is, the balance here is not between individual rights and the common good, but between the guards (law enforcement authorities) and their guardians (such as Inspector Generals, Congressional oversight, the courts, the media, and civil rights advocacy groups). Such accountability must be robust, prevent mission creep, and compensate for a mindset among some law enforcement authorities that heavily favors the common good over privacy rights,[72] but the fact that there seems to be very little abuse due to improper use of the data (and much due to insufficient analysis) is encouraging and favors such data bases as their costs decline. Nor should one be stopped by the argument that even if current the DNA information is well guarded, one day a tyrant may come and abuse it. (As a colleague wrote, "no matter what safeguards are put in place today, is there any real assurance they will control next year or next decade?") If the people do not come together to prevent such a development, much more will be lost than

DNA privacy. It makes no sense to refuse to introduce effective plumbing into a house, because a hurricane may come one day and blow it away. One needs to ensure that it is built on solid foundations and that this are continually fortified.

5. Violations of the Fifth Amendment's Right to Freedom from Self-Incrimination

James Gans argues that "DNA request surveillance," that is, "the observation of individuals' fear of a match between their DNA and material connected with a past (or future) crime, by assessing their response to a request to provide a DNA profile voluntarily," violates protections against self-incrimination "because it forces people who are reluctant to undergo DNA profile surveillance to reveal that reluctance to investigators," which "can support an inference that such individuals" are guilty.[73] A different argument put forward in the early days of DNA profiling argued that the technology itself raised Fifth Amendment issues, due to "the unique autobiographical nature" of DNA.[74]

This notion that DNA evidence is qualitatively different than other forms of physical evidence, known as DNA exceptionalism, has been rejected by the overwhelming majority of case law. The courts held the freedom from self-incrimination does not extend to material evidence, as was recognized in *Schmerber v. California* and other subsequent cases.[75] Whether or not a piece of evidence violates the Fifth Amendment turns on whether it is compelled, incriminating, and most of all testimonial in nature.[76] "In order to be considered testimonial," writes Nicholas Soares, a public interest lawyer in Washington, DC, "a compelled communication must force the defendant to reveal the contents of his mind."[77] In other words, the act of producing testimonial evidence is roughly defined as "the disclosure of one's knowledge or beliefs, the contents of which are incriminating."[78] While Nita Farahany convincingly argues that advances in neuroscience threaten to break down the already tenuous dichotomy between "testimonial" and "physical" evidence, a DNA sample in and of itself clearly does not constitute self-incrimination because it reveals nothing of the suspect's mind.[79] Thus, the Court of Appeals for the Tenth Circuit flatly rejected claims that "requiring DNA samples from inmates amounts to compulsory self-incrimination," countering with the assertion that DNA samples are not testimonial in nature.

Moreover, if the notion that collecting a DNA sample violates the right to be free from compelled self-incrimination is taken to its logical conclusion, it would exclude almost all physical evidence. A suspect could refuse to stand in a lineup on the grounds that his face is a vessel for certain biometric information. Another suspect could refuse to provide a breath sample that contains information about her alcohol level. In other words, suspects could refuse to provide material evidence—on the very grounds that it contains the information that might convict them, which is of course the reason to collect evidence in the first place. The consequences of this approach to physical evidence are virtually unlimited—*Schmerber* has been applied by the lower courts to "handwriting exemplars, fingerprints, voice exemplars, dental impressions, urine samples, sobriety tests, gunshot residues, hair samples, and other techniques"[80]—and would broaden the definition of testimonial evidence so expansively that the term becomes meaningless.

C. The Benefits of Forensic DNA Usages

To reiterate, liberal communitarianism concerns itself with the extent to which a public policy entails intrusions on individual rights and the extent to which the same policy contributes to the common good. If the intrusions on individual rights are small, if limits on these intrusions can be readily and effectively enforced—that is, if accountability is high—and the contributions to the common good that stem from these intrusions are substantial, the policy should be tolerated *unless* a policy with a more favorable liberal communitarian profile becomes available. (The courts often employ a similar approach, albeit without using the same terminology.)

To apply this approach to forensic DNA usages, it is insufficient to demonstrate that the intrusions on individual rights caused by DNA usages are much smaller than critics contend and that the law can further curtail them. Instead, the scope of DNA usages' contributions to the common good must also be assessed.

I find it odd that people who will readily sign on to the statement that "it is better that one hundred guilty persons should escape than that one innocent person should suffer" are not willing to let the DNA of one hundred people be tested to catch one serial killer or rapist. True, the rights of those that are tested and found innocent need to be protected, but this can be achieved by more accountability (along the lines suggested by Suter; Greely, et al.; and Ge et al.[81]) and not by less testing. One need not burn down the house in order to roast a pig, as Justice Felix Frankfurter put it in another context.[82]

1. Contributions to the Common Good: Enhancing Public Safety

The current case for increasing forensic DNA usages may at first seem surprising given that public safety in the United States has greatly improved since crime rates peaked in the early 1990s. During the 1990s, the United States reported a 40 percent decline in violent crimes, including homicide,[83] and "between 1993 and 2012 the violent crime rate . . . dropped by 48 percent."[84] The number of murders in the United States in 2011 was 17 percent lower than it was in 2001.[85] Rates of property crime have also decreased; in 2009, the property crime rate per 100,000 inhabitants was 3,036, down from 5,073 in 1990.[86]

However, despite declining overall crime rates, clearance rates—the rates at which crimes are considered "solved for crime reporting purposes"[87]—have fallen steadily for more than half a century. FBI statistics for 2012 found that property crimes were cleared at a rate of 19.0 percent—less than one in five.[88] Moreover, 2011 statistics showed that less than half—47.7 percent—of violent crimes were cleared. However, given the relatively low cost of DNA analysis as explored in previous sections and the low clearance rates indicated, it follows that law enforcement must be further enhanced for the sake of crime victims who seek resolution, to deter future crimes, and to maintain the legitimacy of the criminal justice system. If the "costs" to rights were significantly higher than we found (in the real world and not some hypothetical one) this preceding communitarian balancing calculation would change. Indeed, it is important to note that as clearance rates reach the upper limit, costs are likely to rise sharply, however we are far from the upper limit.

Forensic DNA usages are not a perfect solution: critics argue they are rife with errors, particularly those caused by poor lab work, deliberate misrepresentations, and problems with chain of custody.[89] The potential sources of error in DNA usages begin at the scene of a crime. An evidentiary DNA sample may be degraded, available in extremely limited quantities, or contain the DNA of multiple individuals.[90] In several cases when an evidentiary sample was too small for analysis, analysis was performed anyway, which led to false convictions.[91] Also, all samples from a single case are often analyzed in the same "batch," and it is well-recognized that "inadvertent switching, mixing or cross-contamination of samples can cause false matches."[92] Nearly two thousand cases of potential laboratory error involving DNA evidence have been identified in the United States.[93] One Houston, Texas, crime laboratory, for example, was closed for several years following revelations of systemic laboratory errors and misleading testimony that ultimately culminated in three exonerations and necessitated retesting thousands of cases.[94] Such problems also exist in the United Kingdom, where the Forensic Science Service laboratory has botched 2,500 cases.[95]

However, the reliability of forensic DNA usages becomes a strength rather than weakness when viewed in perspective. Forensic DNA usages are vastly more reliable than other forensic scientific methods and police tools, in particular the use of eyewitnesses and police line ups. According to the National Research Council of the National Academies, "Except for DNA, no method has been shown to be able to consistently and accurately link a piece of evidence to an individual or single source."[96] A 2009 report by the National Academy of Sciences that compared the reliability of various forensic science methods found that DNA analysis was one of the only methods grounded in real scientific theory and analysis, and the only method for which estimating error probability was possible. By contrast, the report found serious flaws with, and a lack of scientific basis for, analyzing and matching fingerprints, tire tracks, footprints, firearms, hairs, written or printed documents, burn and accelerant patterns, bite marks, and some blood patterns.[97] The consequences of flawed analysis can be dire, as when Cameron Todd Willingham, a Texas man, was convicted of murdering his three children by arson (based on faulty burn analysis from arson "experts") and executed.[98] Of the 225 wrongful convictions overturned by DNA testing through 2009 (more on this later), more than half "involved unvalidated or improper forensic science."[99] Although conclusive error rates for forensic science methods are inherently elusive, that DNA analysis is one of the few forensic science methods based on sound science rather than the lay "wisdom" of law enforcement officials suggests it may produce fewer errors than other methods. In particular, the reliability of DNA evidence strongly contrasts with that of eyewitness testimony, which has long been criticized for its reliance on faulty human memory.[100] Eyewitness accounts yield false positives about a third of the time,[101] and 72 percent of convictions overturned through DNA testing were based at least in part on eyewitness testimony.[102]

Evidence shows that increased forensic DNA usages are a very effective tool for enhancing public safety.[103] Several studies have examined the relationship between the application of forensic DNA usages and crime clearance rates. One study—a particularly persuasive, randomized controlled trial—found that when DNA testing[104] was used the percent of burglaries cleared increased by as much as 40 percent compared to control groups.[105] Another study found that DNA database expansion generated great benefits for crime clearance in the categories of sexual assault and robbery with or without a firearm.[106] A systematic review of studies on the effectiveness of DNA evidence in investigating crime "compared to other more traditional forms of investigation" found "generally positive results regarding the utility of DNA testing [. . .] when used to investigate a broad range of crime types." For these reasons, the review concluded that DNA evidence's utility for crime investigations is sound.[107]

Others have attempted to quantify the effectiveness of DNA database searches. The FBI's traditional metrics for measuring the success of NDIS and CODIS are the number of matches produced by searching the database without any prior expectation of finding a match ("cold hits") and the number of investigations aided. These metrics may not provide an accurate assessment of forensic DNA usages' value, however, because hits may be caused by laboratory error, falsely inflated by partial matches, or otherwise unrelated to the actual outcome of a case; and "number of investigations aided" is a term so vague as to be meaningless. One study moved beyond these metrics and found that about 60 percent of cold hits eventually resulted in conviction or other legal action. In other words, the study found that many cold hits are of real, measurable use to an investigation. The numbers are particularly high for the most serious crimes.[108] Another value of forensic DNA usages is their ability to link suspects to crimes long after the crimes have been committed, when eyewitness memories have faded and the victims or suspects may have passed away.[109]

According to the general rule that the more accountability to which a police method is subjected, the more license the authorities should have to collect that information,[110] several measures should be implemented to improve forensic DNA usages. These include mandating additional training for individuals who recover DNA evidence from crime scenes, as well as investment in improving technology for the collection and analysis of DNA samples. Defenders of DNA usages argue that "modern techniques and procedures" greatly mitigate the possibility of human error in forensic laboratories, and improvements in technology and practice will continue to do so.[111] These include physically separating evidentiary samples from reference samples, physically sequestering different steps in the process of DNA analysis from each other,[112] and using improved means of detecting cross-contamination.[113] For its part, the FBI has introduced guidelines on employee expertise and evidence control to which CODIS-participating laboratories must adhere.[114] Such standards are essential for DNA analysis to be an effective law enforcement tool, not only because they improve police work by ensuring the quality and integrity of the data and competency of the laboratory involved, but because they are a necessary element to accountability and public trust.[115] Along these lines, the Forensic Science and Standards Act proposed in 2014, which aims to "strengthen the criminal justice system, by prioritizing scientific research and supporting the development of science-based standards in the forensic disciplines," is a step in the right direction.

Critics further argue that juries are unable to understand complex statistical concepts such as random match probabilities and to apply them accurately; they argue that juries often overestimate the importance of

DNA evidence.[116] Others argue that Americans have an inflated sense of the importance of DNA evidence due to popular culture. However, the same problem holds for many other technical and "complicated" issues, for instance those involving financial transactions. The American justice assumes that the defense will warn the jury about these misperceptions and that good sense will enable the jury to reach the proper conclusion.

Moreover, the government's failure to analyze many pieces of forensic DNA evidence collected from crime scenes or other sources holds down the clearance rate. The U.S. Department of Justice offers a regular report on the number of backlogged evidentiary DNA cases—defined as a case "that had not been closed by a final report within 30 days after receipt of the evidence in the laboratory"[117]—at approximately 120 publicly funded forensic laboratories. In the most recent iteration of this report, it found that only 15,751 of 107,074 total pending cases, or 14.7 percent, at these laboratories had been closed on time as of December 31, 2011.[118] These figures do not include evidentiary samples that for one reason or another are never sent to forensic laboratories for testing despite containing potentially useful evidence; many rape kits, for example, languish in police storage facilities and are never sent for analysis. Estimates of this rape kit backlog nationwide alone range from 180,000 to 400,000 cases.[119] Lack of political will and a dearth of funding—testing one rape kit alone costs upwards of $1,500—have prevented many evidentiary samples from being analyzed to create DNA profiles for inclusion in NDIS, which has undermined the ability of law enforcement officials to link seemingly separate cases by matching evidentiary profiles.

Granted, the following statement is difficult to quantify, but I have a strong impression that much more injustice is engendered by the backlog than by any of the other issues raised by critics. There are thousands upon thousands of victims who do not get their day in court, for whom justice is denied, and thousands of criminals who are spared punishment and left free to commit more crimes as a direct consequence of the backlog (and it seems, to a lesser extent, due to errors and misrepresentations). Nevertheless this issue is not often listed among the criticisms raised about forensic usages of DNA, it seems because this challenge does not have the cache of a major constitutional or ethical issue. It deserves much more attention. Moreover, like other issues raised by misallocation of resources, by distributive justice, it has major moral implications.

This concern alone should be considered as providing a very strong case for extensive DNA usages for forensic purposes.

All this suggests that finding ways to expedite DNA analysis and reduce its costs should be granted a much higher priority in the allocation of funds available for law enforcement than, say, long jail sentences for nonviolent offenders. Indeed, partly thanks to FBI and National Institute of Justice grants, the private sector has in recent years begun to roll out faster technologies for DNA testing, which, with refinement and economies of scale, may well go a long way toward greatly reducing the backlog problem.[120]

2. The Right to be Cleared

Contrary to the view that while forensic DNA usages may benefit the common good, these gains come at the expense of significant violations of individual rights, such usages greatly advanced both elements of the liberal communitarian balance. They serve to advance not just the common good but also to protect individual rights. This is often overlooked when DNA usages help to serve what might be considered an implicit right—to be cleared of police suspicion. This right may be viewed as derivative of the right to a speedy trial, although it of course is a distinct one.

In the United States, there is almost a ritualistic emphasis that the presumption of innocence—"innocent until proven guilty"—forms the basis of the criminal justice system, and that there are hence two kinds of people: the innocent and the convicted. In practice, however, "suspect" forms a third category in addition to "innocent" and "guilty." Numerous people have undergone some kind of legal process that has indicated they were suspected of having committed a crime, for example by being arrested or served a search warrant. These people have diminished rights compared to those considered innocent, though not to the extent of those already convicted of a crime. For example, they may be subject to fingerprinting or detention without charge for a set period of time, while such measures would be considered outrageous when applied to innocent people who are not suspected of anything.

If no "guilty" party is found, suspects often remain under a cloud of suspicion, sometimes for years. For example, in 1979, fifteen-year-old Jeffrey Womack was brought into custody and questioned in relation to the murder of a nine-year-old girl; he invoked his right to an attorney and refused to say anything to the police, and the case against him was eventually dropped due to a lack of evidence. For the next thirty years, members of the community and police officers harassed Womack, believing him to be a killer. Womack knew that for "practically his entire adult life, he would be staked out, followed, rousted, and hounded."[121] Only in 2008, after Jerome Sidney Barrett was charged in the murder[122] thanks to DNA testing,[123] was Womack's name finally cleared.

Cases like that of Womack, which illustrate the harm suffered by those labeled as suspects, illustrate the need for a new right: the right to be cleared of suspicion, a derivative but not identical to the right for a speedy trial. Forensic DNA usage offers a particularly valuable tool with which to pursue such a right.

Had forensic DNA testing been readily available, law enforcement officials could have quickly excluded Womack and others from suspicion, sparing him decades of harassment and allowing them to focus attention on finding the killer. In fact, had a database of offenders' DNA samples existed at the time, police would have been able to match the evidentiary DNA recovered from the victim's body to Barrett quite quickly. Paul Ferrera, director of the Virginia Division of Forensic Science, found that the Virginia laboratory "typically and routinely eliminate[d] approximately 25 percent to 30 percent of the suspects who the police have centered on in their investigation using our DNA analysis."[124]

Whether one considers the right to be cleared of being a suspect as quickly as possible a new right or merely part of the right to a speedy and impartial trial, DNA usages are particularly effective at honoring this right.

3. Exonerating the Innocent Convicted, and Preventing Miscarriages of Justice

Forensic DNA usages have also exonerated a considerable number of individuals who have been falsely convicted of crimes. Most recently, in July 2014, "DNA evidence exonerate[d] a man who spent 26 years in prison in the 1982 killing of a Washington woman."[125] As of 2014, post-conviction DNA testing had exonerated 317 individuals nationwide, including 18 prisoners on death row.[126] On average, those who are exonerated through DNA analysis spend thirteen years in prison before their innocence is established.[127] Given the strong moral commitment to avoid jailing, let alone executing innocent people—captured in the oft-cited dictate that it is better to let a hundred criminals go free than to imprison one innocent—it is clear that the greatest merit of DNA usages is their ability to advance rights in addition to the common good. Beyond the moral perspective, it is clearly in the interests of the criminal justice system and the public to avoid the large payouts that tend to follow the overturning of wrongful convictions, as with the 41-millin-dollar settlement in July 2014 for five men jailed in connection with a 1989 rape and assault in New York City,[128] or the 40-million-dollar settlement in June 2014 for a similar case in Chicago.[129]

Some critics argue that offenders lack sufficient access to the DNA evidence against them post-conviction, which makes it difficult to retest suspect evidence and obtain exonerations where appropriate. Intense debate revolves around the conditions under which convicted offenders should have the right to retest this evidence; one solution is to reduce the cost of DNA testing so that offering retesting to many would be more feasible.

Moreover, clearing innocent suspects and exonerating those wrongly convicted has an important public safety component. A study of individuals exonerated through the use of DNA analysis found that several actual perpetrators committed additional crimes due to the state's conviction of an innocent individual in their stead. "Among the actual perpetrators identified in [the study's] sample, 37 were convicted of a total of 77 other violent crimes during the time that an innocent person served for their crime."[130] Effective forensic DNA usage thus helps prevent such individuals from escaping justice thanks to police error or an innocent's bad luck.

D. Conclusion

This article has examined forensic DNA usages from a liberal communitarian approach, which holds that both individual rights and the common good have the same fundamental normative standing and that neither trumps the other, per se. Thus, there is a need to determine, for each public policy and each police method, whether the prevailing balance between the two ought to be adapted to better serve the common good or expand individual rights. (In many situations, in which these come into conflict.) These adaptations must be repeated over time to maintain a just and effective balance, following changes in historical conditions and technological developments; for example, the 2011 attacks on the American homeland or the rise of the Internet.

By approaching forensic DNA usages in this context, this chapter suggests that the intrusions involved with these DNA usages are smaller than critics often fear because DNA samples that *do* contain sensitive information are not included in the national databases, while the DNA profiles that are included in these databases contain very little genetic information. Next, the article finds that DNA usages contribute very little to racial profiling, because they mainly reflect institutional racism rather than cause it. Racial discrimination should be overcome, but forgoing DNA usages would contribute very little to this goal. Moreover, the courts' conclusions that DNA sample collection and the creation of DNA profiles do not violate the right to be free from self-incrimination seem compelling. If DNA usages were to be banned, most other forensic tools, including the collection of other forms of material evidence, would likewise have to be banned. Additionally, while the intrusions involved are limited and could be quite readily limited further through the implementation of recommendations already spelled out, DNA usages' contributions to the common good are considerable.

One may first conclude, based on the preceding discussion, that given that forensic DNA usages' contributions to the common good are substantial and their intrusions on individual rights small, these usages compare very favorably to many other public policies that have the opposite profile, for instance, the practice of trading medical records (legal in the United States until 2000).[131] Actually, DNA usages have an unusual profile: *They are the source of major gains to both core elements of the liberal communitarian balance.* They do not merely enhance significantly the common good, but they also enhance the right to be cleared of suspicion and above all exonerate hundreds of innocent individuals.

Many public policies, which tilt heavily in one direction or the other, throw off *some* limited benefits to the other core element of the liberal communitarian balance, other than the one they favor. Thus, for instance, free speech, a core individual right, also somewhat improves governance by helping those in power to discover when their policies are misdirected earlier than when speech is suppressed. And enhanced public safety also helps protect individual rights, such as the freedom of assembly. However, forensic DNA usages are very distinct in that that provide *very major* contributions to both elements of the liberal communitarian balance.

DNA usages should therefore be expanded rather than curbed, first of all, by clearing the existing backlog and second by making them more available to those who seek to appeal their convictions.

Notes

Preface

1. Michael Sandel, *Liberalism and the Limits of Justice* (1998); Charles Taylor, "The Liberal-Communitarian Debate," in Nancy L. Rosenblum (ed.) *Liberalism and the Moral Life* (Cambridge: Cambridge University Press, 1989), pp. 159–182.
2. "The Responsive Communitarian Platform," in Amitai Etzioni (ed.), *The Essential Communitarian Reader* (Cambridge: Cambridge University Press, 1998), pp. xxv–xxxix.

Chapter 1

1. Amitai Etzioni, "The Privacy Merchants: What Is to Be Done?" *University of Pennsylvania Journal of Constitutional* Law 14, 4 (March 2012): 929.
2. Peter P. Swire, "Katz Is Dead. Long Live Katz", *Michigan Law Review* 102, 5 (2004): 904, 912. ("The increasing storage of telephone calls is part of the much broader expansion since 1967 of stored records in the hands of third parties. Although there are no Supreme Court cases on most of these categories of stored records, the Miller and Smith line of cases make it quite possible that the government can take all of these records without navigating Fourth Amendment protections.") Some scholars have suggested that Fourth Amendment restrictions should apply to subsequent use, although the analysis is not sufficiently developed in the courts to constitute a meaningful privacy doctrine. Harold J. Krent, *Of Diaries and Data Banks: Use Restrictions Under the Fourth Amendment*, 74 Tex. L. Rev. 49 (1995–1996). ("If the state can obtain the information only through means constituting a search or seizure, then use restrictions should apply, confining the governmental authorities to uses consistent with the [Fourth] Amendment's reasonableness requirement.")
3. NTO, "The Virginia 'Right of Privacy' Statute," *Virginia Law Review* 38 (1952): 117.
4. Samuel D. Warren and Louis D. Brandeis, "The Right of Privacy," *Harvard Law Review* 4 (1890): 193.
5. For an excellent overview of how advances in information and communication technologies have rendered obsolete the privacy laws (and the doctrines on which these laws are based) of the 1980s and 1990s, see Omer Tene, "Privacy: The New Generations," *International Data Privacy Law* 1 (2011): 15–27. For a discussion of how these changes have particularly affected the privacy expectations of the "Facebook generation," see Mary Graw Leary, "Reasonable Expectations of Privacy for Youth in a Digital Age," *Mississippi Law* Journal 80 (2011): 1033.

6. This is of course not a terribly new position—legal scholars have been discussing the implications for privacy and the Fourth Amendment of the Internet since its introduction as publicly available technology. See Lawrence Lessig, *Code and Other Laws of Cyberspace*, (Basic Books, 1999), 222–23 and Laurence H. Tribe, "The Constitution in Cyberspace, Keynote Address at the First Conference on Computers, Freedom, & Privacy" (March 26, 1991) (transcript available at www.sjgames.com/SS/tribe.html).
7. Erin Smith Dennis, "A Mosaic Shield: Maynard, the Fourth Amendment, and Privacy Rights in the Digital Age," *Cardozo Law Review* 33 (2012): 737. See also Orin Kerr, "The Mosaic Theory of the Fourth Amendment," *Michigan Law Review* 111 (2012): 311, 320 ("Under mosaic theory, searches can be defined collectively as a sequence of discrete steps rather than as individualized steps. Identifying Fourth Amendment search requires analyzing police actions over time as a collective 'mosaic' of surveillance."); Madelaine Virgina Ford, "Mosaic Theory and the Fourth Amendment: How Jones Can Save Privacy in the Face of Evolving Technology," *American University Journal of Gender, Social Policy & the Law* 19 (2011): 1351; Bethany L. Dickman, "Untying Knotts: The Application of Mosaic Theory to GPS Surveillance in United States v. Maryland" *American University Law Review* 60 (2011): 731.
8. Kyllo v. United States, 533 U.S. 27 (2001), internal citations omitted.
9. Payton v. New York, 445 U.S. 573, 591–98 (1980).
10. Dow. Chem. Co. v. United States, 749 F.2d 307, 314 (6th Cir. 1984), *aff'd*, 476 U.S. 227 (1986).
11. Catharine A. MacKinnon, "Reflections on Sex Equality Under Law," *Yale Law Journal* 100 (1991): 1281, 1311.
12. Linda C. McClain, "Inviolability and Privacy: The Castle, the Sanctuary, and the Body," *Yale Journal of Law and the Humanities* 7 (1995): 195, 209.
13. Amitai Etzioni, "The Bankruptcy of Liberalism and Conservatism," *Political Science Quarterly* 128 (2013): 39.
14. Christopher Slobogin, "Public Privacy: Camera Surveillance of Public Places and the Right to Anonymity," *Mississippi Law Journal* 72 (2002): 213. Scott E. Sundby, "Everyman's Fourth Amendment: Privacy or Mutual Trust between Government and Citizen?" *Columbia Law Review* 94 (1994): 1751, 1758–89; Bethany L. Dickman, "Untying Knotts: The Application of Mosaic Theory to GPS Surveillance in United States v. Maryland," *American University Law Review* 60 (2011): 731.
15. Christopher Slobogin, "Public Privacy," 213, 264.
16. Ibid., 265.
17. For a critical analysis of the "Information Sharing Paradigm" that has arisen in law enforcement and intelligence community since 9/11, see Peter P. Swire, "Privacy and Information Sharing in the War on Terrorism," *Villanova Law Review* 51 (2006): 260.
18. Alexander Aleinikoff, writing in 1987, argued that the courts had entered the "age of balancing." "Balancing has been a vehicle primarily for weakening earlier categorical doctrines restricting governmental power to search and seize." T. Alexander Aleinikoff, "Constitutional Law in the Age of Balancing," *Yale Law Journal* 96 (1987):

943, 965. Many civil libertarians have argued that post-9/11, Fourth Amendment rights are being systematically eroded in the name of national security. See Jay Stanley, "Reviving the Fourth Amendment and American Privacy," *ACLU* (May 28, 2010), http://www.aclu.org/blog/national-security-technology-and-liberty/reviving-fourth-amendment-and-american-privacy. See also Orin S. Kerr, "An Equilibrium-Adjustment Theory of the Fourth Amendment," *Harvard Law Review* 125 (2011): 476, 478. ("The theory of equilibrium-adjustment posits that the Supreme Court adjusts the scope of Fourth Amendment protection in response to new facts in order to restore the status quo level of protection. When changing technology or social practice expands government power, the Supreme Court tightens Fourth Amendment protection; when it threatens government power, the Supreme Court loosens constitutional protection.")
19. See Amitai Etzioni, *The Limits of Privacy* (New York: Basic Books, 1999).
20. See note 78.
21. "This point is virtually identical to the demand that courts make of government legislation when they are applying heightened scrutiny—that is, strict or intermediate scrutiny—in First Amendment or Equal Protection Clause cases. The court has also hinted at such a proportionality of means requirement, albeit much less clearly, in its Fourth Amendment 'special needs' cases." Marc Blitz, comment to the author, January 17, 2014.
22. American Bar Association, *ABA Standards for Criminal Justice: Law Enforcement Access to Third Party Records Standards*, 3rd ed. (2013), http://www.americanbar.org/content/dam/aba/publications/criminal_justicesee_standards/third_party_access.authcheckdam.pdf.
23. Shaun Spencer raises concerns about legislating privacy protections. *See* Shaun Spencer, "Reasonable Expectations and the Erosion of Privacy," *San Diego Law Review* 39 (2002): 843, 860. ("Given the powerful influence of various lobbies opposed to strong privacy protection, that role may best be described as a sine qua non. That is, unless the public has a strong desire for privacy in a particular area, attempts to pass legislation establishing that area as a private sphere are doomed to fail…To the extent that legislatures base privacy legislation on social values and norms, they necessarily rely on the same changing expectations as the judicial conception of privacy.")
24. Amitai Etzioni, *From Empire to Community: A New Approach to International Relations* (New York: Palgrave Macmillan, 2004): 67–71.
25. Federal Bureau of Investigation, "'Offenses Cleared,' Uniform Crime Report: Crime in the United States 2011" (October 2012).
26. Smith v. Maryland, 442 U.S. 735, 745 (1979).
27. United States v. Miller, 425 U.S. 435 (1976).
28. Couch v. United States, 409 U.S. 322 (1973).
29. Zurcher v. Stanford Daily, 436 U.S. 547 (1978).
30. Fisher v. United States, 425 U.S. 391 (1976).
31. The preceding examples are laid out in Peter P. Swire, "Katz Is Dead. Long Live Katz," *Michigan Law Review* 102, 5 (2004): 908–916.
32. *Privacy Act of 1974, as amended*, Federal Trade Commission, available at http://www.ftc.gov/foia/privacy_act.shtm (accessed April 7, 2013).

33. The Right to Financial Privacy Act of 1978, 12 U.S.C. §§ 3401–3402.
34. Department of Health and Human Services, "Summary of the HIPAA Privacy Rule," , http://www.hhs.gov/ocr/privacy/hipaa/understanding/summary/.
35. The Video Privacy Protection Act of 1988, 18 U.S.C. § 2710.
36. Gina Stevens, "Privacy Protections for Personal Information Online," *Congressional Research Service* (April 6, 2011).
37. Orin S. Kerr, "The Mosaic Theory of the Fourth Amendment," 111 *Michigan Law Review* 3 (December 2012), 333.
38. Matthew D. Lawless, "The Third Party Doctrine Redux: Internet Search Records and the Case for a 'Crazy Quilt' of Fourth Amendment Protection," *UCLA Journal of Law & Technology* 2 (2007): 1.
39. Orin Kerr and Greg Nojeim, "The Data Question: Should the Third-Party Records Doctrine Be Revisited?" *ABA Journal* (August 1, 2012), http://www.abajournal.com/magazine/article/the_data_question_should_the_third-party_records_doctrine_be_revisited/.
40. Daniel Cooper, "Consent in EU Data Protection Law," *European Privacy Association*, http://www.europeanprivacyassociation.eu/public/download/EPA%20Editorial_%20Consent%20in%20EU%20Data%20Protection%20Law.pdf (accessed April 7, 2013).
41. European Commission, *Why Do We Need an EU Data Protection Reform?*, http://ec.europa.eu/justice/data-protection/document/review2012/factsheets/1_en.pdf (accessed April 7, 2013).
42. "New Draft European Data Protection Regime," Law Patent Group, http://mlawgroup.de/news/publications/detail.php?we_objectID=227 (accessed March 6, 2015).
43. Erica Newland, "CDT Comments on EU Data Protection Directive," *Center for Democracy and Technology* (January 20, 2011), https://www.cdt.org/blogs/erica-newland/cdt-comments-eu-data-protection-directive.
44. "Data protection reform: Frequently asked questions," Europa (January 25, 2012) http://europa.eu/rapid/press-release_MEMO-12-41_en.htm?locale=fr.
45. In the wake of *Jones*, Professor Susan Freiwald identified four factors that the courts use to extend Fourth Amendment protection to new surveillance technologies that "make sense." These include whether the target is unaware of the surveillance; it covers items that the people consider private; it is continuous; and it is indiscriminate (covers more information than is necessary for establishing guilt). Susan Freiwald, "The Four Factor Test," *The Selected Works of Susan Freiwald*, http://works.bepress.com/susan_freiwald/11.
46. People often trust assurances that their sensitive information (names and social security number) can be deleted when their data is collected in large databases. In fact, scientists have shown that individuals can be easily "deanonymized." Paul Ohm writes that this misunderstanding has given the public a false sense of security and has led to inadequate privacy protections, laws, and regulations. See Peter Ohm, "Broken Promises of Privacy: Responding to the Surprising Failure of Anonymization," *UCLA Law Review* 57 (2010): 1701. See also Marcia Stepanek, "Weblining," *BusinessWeek* (April 3, 2000),

http://www.businessweek.com/2000/00_14/b3675027.htm; Jennifer Golbeck, Christina Robles, and Karen Turner, "Predicting Personality with Social Media," *Chi Extended Abstracts* (2011): 253–62.
47. Marcy Peek, "Passing Beyond Identity on the Internet: Espionage and Counterespionage in the Internet Age," *Vermont Law Review* 28 (2003): 91, 94 (evaluating ways to resist discriminatory marketing in cyberspace); Marcia Stepanek, "Weblining," *BusinessWeek* (April 3, 2000), http://www.businessweek.com/2000/00_14/b3675027.htm. (A data broker company Acxiom matches names against housing, education, and incomes in order to identify the unpublicized ethnicity of an individual or group.); Nicholas Carr, "Tracking Is an Assault on Liberty, With Real Dangers," *Wall Street Journal* (August 7–8, 2010), p. W1. ("It used to be . . . you had to get a warrant to monitor a person or a group of people. Today, it is increasingly easy to monitor ideas."); Amitai Etzioni, "The Privacy Merchants: What Is to Be Done?" *University of Pennsylvania Journal of Constitutional Law* 14, 4 (2012): 929, 948–50.
48. Kashmir Hill. "How Target Figured Out a Teen Girl Was Pregnant Before Her Father Did," *Forbes* (February 16, 2012), http://www.forbes.com/sites/kashmirhill/2012/02/16/how-target-figured-out-a-teen-girl-was-pregnant-before-her-father-did/.
49. Orin S. Kerr, "The Fourth Amendment and New Technologies: Constitutional Myths and the Case for Caution," *Michigan Law Review* 102 (2004): 801, 871–2.
50. Christopher Slobogin, "Government Data Mining and the Fourth Amendment," *University of Chicago Law Review* 75 (2008): 317, 320.
51. Glenn R. Simpson, "FBI's Reliance on the Private Sector Has Raised Some Privacy Concerns," *The Wall Street Journal*, April 13, 2001, http://www.wsj.com/articles/SB987107477135398077.
52. For further discussion on these matters, see Amitai Etzioni, "The Privacy Merchants," 929; Amitai Etzioni, "The Bankruptcy of Liberalism and Conservatism," *Political Science Quarterly* 128 (2013): 39 (discussing the collapse of the public-private divide).
53. For more discussion, see Amitai Etzioni, "The Bankruptcy of Liberalism and Conservatism," 39.
54. Kerr sees a greater role here for Congress, while Swire sees a greater role for the courts. See Peter P. Swire, "Katz Is Dead. Long Live Katz," 904, 912; and Orin S. Kerr, "The Fourth Amendment and New Technologies: Constitutional Myths and the Case for Caution," *Michigan Law Review* 102 (2004). This chapter is unable to add to these deliberations other than to recognize that both are needed and neither seems able to keep up with changing technologies.
55. Siobhan Gorman, "NSA's Domestic Spying Grows as Agency Sweeps Up Data," *Wall Street Journal* (March 10, 2008).
56. Peter P. Swire, "A Reasonableness Approach to Searches after the Jones GPS Tracking Case," *Stanford Law Review Online* 64 (2012): 57.
57. Gary T. Marx, "Ethics for the New Surveillance," *The Information Society: An International Journal* 14 (1998): 171, 178.

58. Erica Goode and Sheryl Gay Stolberg, "Legal Curbs Said to Hamper A.T.F. in Gun Inquiries," *New York Times* (December 25, 2012).
59. Tamara Keith, "How Congress Quietly Overhauled Its Insider-Trading Law," *NPR*, April 16, 2013), available at http://m.npr.org/news/Politics/177496734.
60. Amitai Etzioni, *The Limits of Privacy* (New York: Basic Books, 1999).
61. Anna C. Henning, "Compulsory DNA Collection: A Fourth Amendment Analysis," *Congressional Research Service* R40077 (2010): 2.
62. Jack Nicas, "TSA to Halt Revealing Body Scans at Airports," *Wall Street Journal* (January 18, 2013).
63. Cynthia Dwork, "Differential Privacy: A Survey of Results," in M. Agrawal et al., eds., *TAMC, LNCS 4978* (2008): 1–19. "Roughly speaking, differential privacy ensures that the removal or addition of a single database item does not (substantially) affect the outcome of any analysis. It follows that no risk is incurred by joining the database, providing a mathematically rigorous means of coping with the fact that distributional information may be disclosive."

Chapter 2

1. Amitai Etzioni, "A Cyber Age Privacy Doctrine: A Liberal Communitarian Approach," *I/S: A Journal of Law and Policy for the Information Society* 10(2), Summer 2014, http://papers.ssrn.com/sol3/papers.cfm?abstract_id=2348117.
2. For example, in the paper age, arrest records were kept by local police departments; if an individual wanted to see if a given person had ever been arrested, they would have to review many different police departments' files.
3. Elisha Fieldstadt and Becky Bratu, "Missing Passport Databases Not Routinely Checked: Interpol," NBC News, March 9, 2014, http://www.nbcnews.com/storyline/missing-jet/missing-passport-databases-not-routinely-checked-interpol-n48261.
4. Josephine Wolff, "Papers, Please," *Slate*, March 11, 2014, www.slate.com/articles/technology/future_tense/2014/03/mh_370_stolen_passports_why_don_t_most_countries_check_interpol_s_sltd_database.html.
5. Fred Cate, Peter Cullen, and Viktor Mayer-Schönberger, "Reinventing Privacy Principles for the Big Data Age," Oxford Internet Institute, December 6, 2013, http://www.oii.ox.ac.uk/news/?id=1013. Craig Mundie, "Privacy Pragmatism," *Foreign Affairs* (March/April 2014), http://www.foreignaffairs.com/articles/140741/craig-mundie/privacy-pragmatism.
6. *Katz v. United States* (389 U.S. 347, 1967).
7. *Terry v. Ohio* (392 U.S. 1, 1968).
8. *United States v. White* (401 U.S. 745, 1971).
9. *United States v. Knotts* (460 U.S. 276, 1983).
10. *United States v. Karo* (468 U.S. 705, 1984).
11. *Kyllo v. United States* (533 U.S. 27, 2001).
12. *United States v. Jones* (565 U.S. ___, 2012).
13. *Florida v. Jardines* (569 U.S. ___, 2013).

14. *United States v. Miller* (425 U.S. 435, 1976).
15. *Smith v. Maryland* (442 U.S. 735, 1979).
16. Stephen E. Henderson, "After *United States v. Jones*, after the Fourth Amendment Third Party Doctrine," *North Carolina Journal of Law & Technology* 14 (2013): 434. "According to Justice Blackmun, writing for the majority, '[t]he switching equipment that processed those numbers [was] merely the modern counterpart of the operator who, in an earlier day, personally completed calls for the subscriber." Orin S. Kerr, "The Case for the Third-Party Doctrine," *Michigan Law Review* 107, 4 (2009): 561–601.
17. Orin S. Kerr, "The Case for the Third-Party Doctrine," 561–601.
18. Richard A. Epstein, "Privacy and the Third Hand: Lessons from the Common Law of Reasonable Expectations," *Berkeley Technology Law Journal* 24, 3 (2009): 2000.
19. "The Taneja Group estimated the total cloud storage hardware market in 2010 was $3.2 billion, growing 31 percent per year to $9.4 billion by 2014." Patrick Scully, "Cloud Storage" *Broadcast Engineering* 54, 11 (2012): 30–33.
20. Craig Mundie, "Data Pragmatism: Focus on Data Use, Not Data Collection," *Foreign Affairs* (March/April 2014), http://www.foreignaffairs.com/articles/140741/craig-mundie/privacy-pragmatism. Thomas H. Davenport, "Who Owns Your Data Exhaust?" *The Wall Street Journal*, November 20, 2013, http://blogs.wsj.com/cio/2013/11/20/who-owns-your-data-exhaust/.
21. Will Thomas DeVries, "Protecting Privacy in the Digital Age," *Berkeley Technology Law Journal* 18, 1 (2003): 291–292, 293.
22. Gerald G. Ashdown, "The Fourth Amendment and the 'Legitimate Expectation of Privacy,'" *Vanderbilt Law Review* 34, 1 (1981): 1289, 1315; Susan W. Brenner & Leo L. Clarke, "Fourth Amendment Protection for Shared Privacy Rights in Stored Transactional Data," *Journal of Law and Policy* 14 (2006): 211; Andrew J. DeFilippis, Note, "Securing Informationships: Recognizing a Right to Privity in Fourth Amendment Jurisprudence," *The Yale Law Journal* 115, 5 (2006): 1086, 1092; Susan Freiwald, "First Principles of Communications Privacy," *Stanford Technology Law Review* 3 (2007); Lewis R. Katz, "In Search of a Fourth Amendment for the Twenty-first Century," *Indiana Law Journal* 65, 3 (1990): 549, 564–66; Matthew D. Lawless, "The Third Party Doctrine Redux: Internet Search Records and the Case for a 'Crazy Quilt' of Fourth Amendment Protection," *UCLA Journal of Law and Technology* (2007): 1, 3; Arnold H. Loewy, "The Fourth Amendment as a Device for Protecting the Innocent," *Michigan Law Review* 81, 5 (1983); Christopher Slobogin, *Privacy at Risk: The New Government Surveillance and the Fourth Amendment* Chicago, University of Chicago Press (2007): 151–164; Scott E. Sundby, "'Everyman's' Fourth Amendment: Privacy or Mutual Trust Between Government and Citizen?" *Columbia Law Review* 94, 6 (1994): 1757–58.
23. "The EU's proposal includes three elements in particular that lend themselves to a property-based conception: consumers are granted clear entitlements to their own data; the data, even after it is transferred, carries a burden that 'runs with it' and binds third parties; and consumers are protected through remedies grounded in 'property rules.'" Jacob M. Victor, "The EU General Data

Protection Regulation: Toward a Property Regime for Protecting Data Privacy," *Yale Law Journal* 123, 2 (2013): 515.
24. "Though the Regulation is framed in the fundamental-human-rights terms typical of European privacy law, this Comment argues that it can also be conceived of in property-rights terms. The Regulation takes the unprecedented step of, in effect, creating a property regime in personal data, under which the property entitlement belongs to the data subject and is partially alienable." Jacob M. Victor, "The EU General Data Protection Regulation: Toward a Property Regime for Protecting Data Privacy," *The Yale Law Journal* 123 (2), November 2013. Available at http://www.yalelawjournal.org/comment/the-eu-general-data-protection-regulation-toward-a-property-regime-for-protecting-data-privacy.
25. Amitai Etzioni, "The Privacy Merchants: What Is To Be Done?" *Journal of Constitutional Law* 14, 4 (2012): 935.
26. For example, restrictions on certain kinds of personal data processing do not apply "where processing of the data is required for the purposes of preventive medicine, medical diagnosis, the provision of care or treatment or the management of health-care services, and where those data are processed by a health professional subject under national law or rules established by national competent bodies to the obligation of professional secrecy or by another person also subject to an equivalent obligation of secrecy." Alternately, "Member States may adopt legislative measures to restrict the scope of the obligations and rights provided for" by the directive "when such a restriction constitutes a necessary measure to safeguard: (a) national security; (b) defence; (c) public security; (d) the prevention, investigation, detection and prosecution of criminal offences, or of breaches of ethics for regulated professions; (e) an important economic or financial interest of a Member State or of the European Union, including monetary, budgetary and taxation matters," or several other dimensions of the common good. See the text of the EU Data Protection Directive at http://www.dataprotection.ie/docs/EU-Directive-95-46-EC-Chapter-2/93.htm.
27. Christopher Millard, "Proposed EC Directives on Data Protection," *The Computer Law and Security Report* 7, 1 (1991): 21.
28. Joris van Hoboken, personal correspondence, April 25, 2014.
29. Craig Mundie, "Privacy Pragmatism," *Foreign Affairs* (March/April 2014): 30.
30. Not everyone agrees that this is the case. In private correspondence, Abraham Newman of Georgetown University wrote, "Many criticize European privacy rules as weak because they do not see large financial sanctions against firms. But this misses the key preventative dimension of such rules for firm compliance. Big players like eBay or IBM work closely with regulators and implement internal data privacy policies in order to head off a data privacy scandal. In other words, few people are ever audited by the IRS but we rarely criticize the IRS as a weak regulator."
31. Eztioni, "A Cyber Age Privacy Doctrine."
32. Many scholars criticize the circular reasoning of the "reasonable expectation of privacy" text outlined in *Katz*. See, e.g., Richard A. Posner, *The Uncertain Protection of Privacy by the Supreme Court*, 1979 Sup. Ct. Rev. 188 (1979) (it is

"circular to say that there is no invasion of privacy unless the individual whose privacy is invaded had a reasonable expectation of privacy; whether he will or will not have such an expectation will depend on what the legal rule is"). See also Richard S. Julie, *High-Tech Surveillance Tools and the Fourth Amendment: Reasonable Expectations of Privacy in the Technological Age*, 37 Am. Crim. L. Rev. 132 (2000); Anthony G. Amsterdam, *Perspectives on the Fourth Amendment*, 58 Minn. L. Rv. 349, 384 (1974); Jed Rubenfeld, *The End of Privacy*, 61 Stan. L. Rev. 106 (2008); Richard H. Seamon, *Kyllo v. United States and the Partial Ascendance of Justice Scalia's Fourth Amendment*, 79 Wash. U. L. Q. 1023–4 (2001). The Court acknowledged this criticism in Kyllo, 121 S. Ct. at 2043.

33. Amitai Etzioni, "A Liberal Communitarian Conception of Privacy," *John Marshall Journal of Information Technology and Privacy Law* 29, no. 419 (2012).
34. Peter P. Swire, "*Katz* Is Dead. Long Live *Katz*," *Michigan Law Review* 102, (2004): 913.
35. *United States v. Windsor* (570 U.S. 12, 2013).
36. For a concept of harm, see Cate, Cullen, and Mayer-Schönberger, "Reinventing Privacy Principles for the Big Data Age," 14.
37. *Berkemer v. McCarty* (468 U.S. 420, 1984). Although the Supreme Court granted certiorari to a case of drunk driving that sought to clarify this distinction, the Court ruled that until the suspect is actually placed under arrest and into a police vehicle the question of whether she is in custody is a function of the extent to which the circumstances of the stop mimic the restraints and stresses of actual arrest.
38. In common law, "impartial" was understood to mean having a lack of familial ties to or financial interest in the outcome of a case; however, today people often interpret "impartial" to mean that jurors know nothing of the case at hand other than the facts presented at trial. Caren Myers Morrison, "Jury 2.0," *Hastings Law Journal* 62, 6 (2011): 1619.
39. *Maynard v. United States*. Orin Kerr, "The Mosaic Theory of the Fourth Amendment," *Michigan Law Review* 111, 3 (2012): 329.
40. Though arguably restrictions or guidelines on the megabytes of information to be collected should vary based on the type of information. This is because the byte is strictly speaking a measure of data, not information. 100 mb of *data*, for example, is enough for thousands of text e-mails but less than five minutes of high-quality video, and the former could provide a much greater amount of private *information* than the latter.
41. "Surveillance Self-Defense: Getting a Court Order Authorizing a Wiretap," Electronic Frontier Foundation, Accessed March 13, 2014, https://ssd.eff.org/wire/govt/wiretapping-authorization.
42. Kevin V. Ryan and Mark L. Krotosi, "Caution Advised: Avoid Undermining the Legitimate Needs of Law Enforcement to Solve Crimes Involving the Internet in Amending the Electronic Communications Privacy Act," *University of San Francisco Law Review* 47, 2 (2012): 321.
43. *United States v. Jones* (2012).
44. To clarify, speed cameras tell only what speed a vehicle is going at a single moment in time—that is, they collect one discrete data point. The same is true

of an airport screening, which detects information about an individual only at one given point in time. A single CCTV camera is limited in its ability to collect information; it cannot collect information about a passing individual except while that person is within range of the camera. By contrast, wiretaps or continuous GPS monitoring collect many data points about the individual over a long range of time, and paint a much more comprehensive picture of the person's movements or associations.
45. Cate, Cullen, and Mayer-Schönberger, "Reinventing Privacy Principles for the Big Data Age."
46. This is a subject about which much has been written; it is therefore not further explored here.
47. Paul M. Schwartz and Daniel J. Solove, "The PII Problem: Privacy and a New Concept of Personally Identifiable Information," *New York University Law Review* 86, 6 (2011): 1816.
48. Joel M. Gora, "The Fourth Amendment at the Airport: Arriving, Departing, or Cancelled," *Villanova Law Review* 18, 6 (1973): 1038.
49. Jay Stanley, "Extreme Traffic Enforcement," ACLU Blog, American Civil Liberties Union, May 24, 2012, https://www.aclu.org/blog/technology-and-liberty-criminal-law-reform/extreme-traffic-enforcement. "ACLU of Iowa Challenges Use of Speed Cameras in Davenport," American Civil Liberties Union, June 14, 2006, https://www.aclu.org/technology-and-liberty/aclu-iowa-challenges-use-speed-cameras-davenport.
50. "Government Proposes Massive Shift In Online Privacy Policy," American Civil Liberties Union, August 10, 2009, https://www.aclu.org/free-speech_technology-and-liberty/government-proposes-massive-shift-online-privacy-policy.
51. "American Civil Liberties Union Privacy Statement," American Civil Liberties Union, January 18, 2013, https://www.aclu.org/american-civil-liberties-union-privacy-statement.
52. Susan Herman, *Taking Liberties: The War on Terror and the Erosion of American Democracy*, New York: Oxford University Press, 2014.
53. David Zeitlyn, "The Talk Goes Outside: Argument, Privacy and Power in Mambila Society, Towards a Sociology of Embedded Praxis," *Africa: The Journal of the International African Institute* 73, 4 (2003): 607.
54. PHI is information, held by health care providers, defined as "1. Name including current, previous, and mother's maiden name, 2. Postal address and all geographical subdivisions smaller than a State . . . except for the initial three digits of a zip code . . . , 3. All elements of dates (except year) for dates directly related to an individual, including birth date, admission date, discharge date, [and so forth], 4. Telephone numbers, 5. Facsimile numbers, 6. Electronic mail addresses, 7. Social security numbers, 8. Medical record numbers, 9. Health plan beneficiary numbers, 10. Account numbers, 11. Certificate/license numbers, 12. Vehicle identifiers and serial numbers, including license plate numbers, 13. Device identifiers and serial numbers, 14. Web Universal Resource Locators (URLs), 15. Internet Protocol (IP) address numbers, 16. Biometric identifiers, including finger and

voice prints, 17. Full face photographic images and any comparable images, [and] 18. Any other unique identifying number, characteristic, or code (other than a unique study ID)." David T. Fetzer and O. Clark West, "The HIPAA Privacy Rule and Protected Health Information: Implications in Research Involving DICOM Image Databases," *Academic Radiology* 15, 3 (2008): 390–395.
55. C.F.R. 164.508 (a) (2) (2003).
56. Italics mine. http://www.hhs.gov/ocr/privacy/hipaa/administrative/privacyrule/privrulepd.pdf.
57. *United States v. Miller* (425 U.S. 435, 1976).
58. U.S. Code § 3401, http://www.law.cornell.edu/uscode/text/12/3401.
59. Harold C. Relyea, "Legislating Personal Privacy Protection: The Federal Response," *The Journal of Academic Leadership* 27, 1 (2001): 43.
60. Pub.L. 110–233, 122 Stat. 881.
61. "The Act prohibits law enforcement officials from searching for or seizing information from people who disseminate information to the public [the media]. Where it applies, the Act requires law enforcement officials to instead rely on compliance with a subpoena." Elizabeth B. Uzelac, "Reviving the Privacy Protection Act of 1980," *Northwestern University Law Review* 107, 3 (2015): 1437–1468.
62. N. J. King and V. T. Raja, "What Do They Really Know About Me in the Cloud? A Comparative Law Perspective on Protecting Privacy and Security of Sensitive Information," *American Business Law Journal* 50, 2 (2013): 424–431.
63. Ibid.
64. Ibid.
65. PHI is further elaborated in the law, with sixteen specific data fields named as patient information that must be deleted from health-care research manuscripts and other publications. Elizabeth Madsen, Daniel R. Masys, and Randolph A. Miller, "HIPAA Possamus," *Journal of the American Medical Informatics Association* 10, 3: 294.
66. Paul M. Schwartz and Daniel J. Solove, "The PII Problem: Privacy and A New Concept of Personally Identifiable Information," *New York University Law Review* 86, 6 (2011): 1821.
67. *United States v. Jones* (565 U.S. ___, 2012).
68. Andrew A. Proia, "A New Approach to Digital Reader Privacy: State Regulations and Their Protection of Digital Book Data," *Indiana Law Journal* 88, 4 (2013): 1608.
69. Amitai Etzioni, "The Privacy Merchants: What Is to Be Done?" *Journal of Constitutional Law* 14 no. 4 (2012): 950. Ted Bridis, "FBI: Data Brokers Probably Act Illegally," *The Washington Post*, June 22, 2006, www.washingtonpost.com/wp-dyn/content/article/2006/06/22/AR2006062200932.html. Martin H. Bosworth, "FBI Uses Data Brokers, 'Risk Scores' to Hunt Terrorists," *Consumer Affairs*, July 11, 2007, http://www.consumeraffairs.com/news04/2007/07/fbi_risk_scores.html.
70. Erik Brynjolfsson and Andrew McAfee, *The Second Machine Age: Work, Progress, and Prosperity in a Time of Brilliant Technologies*, New York: W. W. Norton & Company, 2014.

71. Evan Perez, "Secret Court's Oversight Gets Scrutiny," *The Wall Street Journal*, June 9, 2013, http://online.wsj.com/news/articles/SB10001424127887324904004578535670310514616?mg=reno64-wsj.
72. "Michael Mukasey, who was attorney general under President George W. Bush, said in an interview that the lack of rejections by the FISA court doesn't mean the court is a rubber stamp. He notes the court sometimes modifies orders and that the Justice Department's national-security division is careful about the applications it presents to the court." Evan Perez, "Secret Court's Oversight Gets Scrutiny," *The Wall Street Journal*, June 9, 2013. Available at http://www.wsj.com/articles/SB10001424127887324904004578535670310514616.
73. Sean Sullivan, "NSA Head: Surveillance Helped Thwart More Than 50 Terror Plots," *The Washington Post*, June 18, 2013, http://www.washingtonpost.com/blogs/post-politics/wp/2013/06/18/nsa-head-surveillance-helped-thwart-more-than-50-terror-attempts/.
74. Peter Bergen, David Sterman, Emily Schneider, and Bailey Cahall, "Do NSA's Bulk Surveillance Programs Stop Terrorists?" New America Foundation, January 2014. Available at http://www.lawfareblog.com/wp-content/uploads/2014/01/Bergen_NAF_NSA-Surveillance_1.pdf
75. It should be noted that in a full 28 percent of the cases, the study was *unable to determine* what method initiated the investigation because public records and court records do not reveal this information. The authors *assume* that an undercover informant, a family member, etc. tipped off the police, but the possibility of bulk surveillance playing a role that is not publicly claimed cannot be entirely ruled out. Ellen Nakashima, "NSA phone record collection does little to prevent terrorist attacks, group says," *The Washington Post*, January 12, 2014, http://www.washingtonpost.com/world/national-security/nsa-phone-record-collection-does-little-to-prevent-terrorist-attacks-group-says/2014/01/12/8aa860aa-77dd-11e3-8963-b4b654bcc9b2_story.html; and Peter Bergen, David Sterman, Emily Schneider, and Baily Cahall, "Do NSA's Bulk Surveillance Programs Stop Terrorists?" New America Foundation, January 13, 2014, http://www.newamerica.net/publications/policy/do_nsas_bulk_surveillance_programs_stop_terrorists: "Regular FISA warrants not issued in connection with Section 215 or Section 702, which are the traditional means for investigating foreign persons, were issued in at least 48 (21 percent) of the cases we looked at."
76. Author's personal calculations based on figures from ibid.
77. Dan Eggen, "U.S. Report Divulges Details of Patriot Act's Effectiveness," *The Chicago Tribune* (reprinted from *The Washington Post*), July 14, 2004, http://articles.chicagotribune.com/2004-07-14/news/0407140330_1_library-and-bookstore-records-usa-patriot-act-gen-john-ashcroft.
78. Dan Eggen and Julie Tate, "U.S. Campaign Produces Few Convictions on Terrorism Charges," *The Washington Post*, June 12, 2005, http://www.washingtonpost.com/wp-dyn/content/article/2005/06/11/AR2005061100381.html.
79. Steven C. Bennett et al, *Storm Clouds Gathering for Cross-Border Security and Data Privacy: Cloud Computing Meets the U.S.A. Patriot Act*, 13 Sedona Conf. J. 235, 245, cited in Edward R. Alo, "EU Privacy Protection: A Step Towards

Global Privacy," *Michigan State International Law Review* 22 (3), 2014. Available at http://digitalcommons.law.msu.edu/cgi/viewcontent.cgi?article= 1155 & context=ilr.
80. Emphasis added. Benjamin Wallace-Wells, "Patriot Act," *New York Magazine*, August 27, 2011, http://nymag.com/news/9-11/10th-anniversary/patriot-act/.
81. Jay Stanley, "Christie Use of Tollbooth Data and Why Location Privacy Must Be Protected," ACLU, January 16, 2015. Available at https://www.aclu.org/blog/technology-and-liberty-national-security/christie-use-tollbooth-data-and-why-location-privacy-m.
82. Michael Martinez, "ACLU Raises Privacy Concerns About Police Technology Tracking Drivers," CNN, July 18, 2013. Available at http://www.cnn.com/2013/07/17/us/aclu-license-plates-readers/.
83. Martin Austermuhle, "D.C. Police to Test Body Cameras, But Civil Libertarians Raise Concerns," WAMU, September 24, 2014. Available at http://wamu.org/news/14/09/24/dc_police_officers_to_test_body_cameras.
84. Susan Stellin, "Airport Screening Concerns Civil Liberties Groups," *The New York Times*, March 11, 2013. Available at http://www.nytimes.com/2013/03/12/business/passenger-screening-system-based-on-personal-data-raises-privacy-issues.html?pagewanted=all&_r=0.
85. Lauren C. Williams, "The Next Civil Liberties Fight Could Be Over Breathalyzers," ThinkProgress, November 12, 2014. Available at http://thinkprogress.org/justice/2014/11/12/3590539/breathalyzers/.
86. For example, the ACLU has contended that traffic stops show a pattern of racial bias. See for example "CPD Traffic Stops and Resulting Searches in 2013," ACLU Illinois, December 26, 2014. Available at http://www.aclu-il.org/cpd-traffic-stops-and-resulting-searches-in-2013/.
87. "Workplace Drug Testing," ACLU, March 12, 2002. Available at https://www.aclu.org/racial-justice_womens-rights/workplace-drug-testing.
88. See, for example, Alderman et al. v. United States, 394 U.S. 165 (1969), which addressed electronic surveillance as a collection mechanism but did not comment on the government's right to share that information with others; Berger v. New York, 388 U.S. 41 (1967), which found New York's eavesdropping laws unconstitutional but never called into question the right of the government to share the information among law enforcement officials; Board of Education of Independent School District No. 92 of Pottawatomie County et al v. Earls et al., 536 U.S. 822 (2002), which held that the school district's drug testing policy was unconstitutional, but not on the grounds that banning someone from playing a sport for a positive drug test in effect shares information about that person's drug use with a variety of others; and many more. All of the Fourth Amendment cases read by this author addressed the question of whether an unreasonable search or seizure had occurred, and never asked about the appropriate scope of the government's subsequent use of legally-obtained information.
89. *Schmerber v. California* (384 U.S. 757, 1966). Italics added.
90. Amitai Etzioni, "Eight Nails into *Katz*'s Coffin," *Case Western Reserve Law Review* 65, 2 (2015), forthcoming.

91. *Florida v. Riley* (488 U.S. 445, 1989).
92. *Florida v. Riley* (109 S. Ct. 693, 1989).
93. For additional discussion of this concept, see Amitai Etzioni, "A Cyber Age Privacy Doctrine."
94. Technically, the term "virtual sub-person" would be more appropriate because the virtual parts of personhood are still part of the person. The agent that acts in cyberspace has one or more names of his or her own, a distinct locality and address, manners, and postures that are on the one hand distinct from those of the offline person but also linked. Moreover, if the virtual person commits a crime, the whole person is judged and punished. If the virtual agent is exposed, the offline person is as well.
95. United Sattes v. Place, 462 U.S. 696 (1983).
96. *Florida v. Jardines* (2013). Internal citations omitted.
97. Eve Brensike Primus, "Disentangling Administrative Searches," *Columbia Law Review* 111, 254: 257.
Russell L. Weaver, "Administrative Searches, Technology and Personal Privacy," *The William and Mary Bill of Rights Journal* 22, 2 (2013): 571.
98. "Microsoft and NYPD Announce Partnership Providing Real-Time Counterterrorism Solution Globally," Microsoft, August 8, 2012, http://www.microsoft.com/government/en-us/state/brightside/Pages/details.aspx?Microsoft-and-NYPD-Announce-Partnership-Providing-Real-Time-Counterterrorism-Solution-Globally&blogid=697.
99. Craig Timberg, "New Surveillance Technology Can Track Everyone in an Area for Hours at a Time," *The Washington Post*, February 5, 2014, http://www.washingtonpost.com/business/technology/new-surveillance-technology-can-track-everyone-in-an-area-for-several-hours-at-a-time/2014/02/05/82f1556e-876f-11e3-a5bd-844629433ba3_story.html.
100. Ibid.
101. Ibid.
102. Press Release, N.Y.C. Government, Mayor Bloomberg, Police Commissioner Kelly and Microsoft Unveil New, State-of-the-Art Technology (Aug. 8, 2012), *available at* http://www.nyc.gov/portal/site/nycgov/menuitem.c0935b9a57bb4ef3daf2f1c701c789a0/index.jsp?pageID=mayor_press_release&catID=1194&doc_name=http%3A%2F%2Fwww.nyc.gov%2Fhtml%2Fom%2Fhtml%2F2012b%2Fpr291-12.html&cc=unused1978&rc=1194&ndi=1.
103. "Mayor Bloomberg, Police Commissioner Kelly and Microsoft unveil new, state-of-the-art technology that aggregates and analyzes existing public safety data in real time to provide a comprehensive view of potential threats and criminal activity," New York City Government, August 8, 2012, http://www.nyc.gov/portal/site/nycgov/menuitem.c0935b9a57bb4ef3daf2f-1c701c789a0/index.jsp?pageID=mayor_press_release&catID=1194&doc_name=http%3A%2F%2Fwww.nyc.gov%2Fhtml%2Fom%2Fhtml%2F2012b%2Fpr291-12.html&cc=unused1978&rc=1194&ndi=1.
104. Martin Kaste, "In 'Domain Awareness,' Detractors See Another NSA," National Public Radio, February 21, 2014, http://www.npr.org/blogs/

alltechconsidered/2014/02/21/280749781/in-domain-awareness-detractors-see-another-nsa.
105. "NYPD Domain Awareness System Public Security Privacy Guidelines." Public Intelligence, April 2, 2009, http://publicintelligence.net/nypd-domain-awareness-system-public-security-privacy-guidelines/.
106. "'Future' of NYPD: Keeping Tab(let)s on Crime Data," *Wall Street Journal*, March 4, 2014.
107. Neal Ungerleider, "NYPD, Microsoft Launch All-Seeing 'Domain Awareness System' with Real-Time CCTV, License Plate Monitoring," Fast Company, March 5, 2014, http://www.fastcompany.com/3000272/nypd-microsoft-launch-all-seeing-domain-awareness-system-real-time-cctv-license-plate-monitor.
108. Nadia Kayyali, "EFF Fights Back against Oakland's Disturbing Domain Awareness Center," Electronic Frontier Foundation, March 4, 2014, https://www.eff.org/deeplinks/2014/03/eff-fights-back-against-oaklands-disturbing-domain-awareness-center.
109. Amitai Etzioni, "NSA: National Security vs. Individual Rights," *Intelligence and National Security Journal* (2014). For a copy, please email icps@gwu.edu.
110. Amitai Etzioni, "The Privacy Merchants"; Julia Angwin, *Dragnet Nation: A Quest for Privacy, Security, and Freedom in a World of Relentless Surveillance* (New York: Henry Holt and Company, 2014).
111. Southern Poverty Law Center, "Montana Freemen Trial May Mark End of an Era," *Intelligence Report* Spring 1998 Issue 90, http://www.splcenter.org/get-informed/intelligence-report/browse-all-issues/1998/spring/justice-vs-justus.
112. *United States v. McGuire* (307 F. 3d. 1192, 2002).
113. *United States v. McGuire*, cited at length in *The People v. Leon* (2005), http://www.courts.ca.gov/opinions/revpub/B173851.PDF.
114. Tom Kenworthy, "Freemen Surrender Ends 81-Day Siege, All 16 Give Themselves Up Peacefully to FBI," *Washington Post*, June 14, 1996, archived copy maintained at *The Spokesman-Review*, http://m.spokesman.com/stories/1996/jun/14/freemen-surrender-ends-81-day-siege-all-16-give/.
115. See, for example, the ACLU's writings on and advocacy against the "No Fly List." Their posts on the subject are available at https://www.aclu.org/blog/tag/no-fly-list. More specifically, see "U.S. Government Watchlisting: Unfair Process and Devastating Consequences," ACLU, March 2014, Available at https://www.aclu.org/sites/default/files/assets/watchlist_briefing_paper_v3.pdf.
116. See, for example, Tania Simoncelli and Sheldon Krimsky, "A New Era of DNA Collections: At What Cost to Civil Liberties?" American Constitution Society for Law and Policy, August 2007. Available at http://www.acslaw.org/sites/default/files/Simoncelli__Krimsky_-_DNA_Collection__Civil_Liberties.pdf.
117. Amitai Etzioni, "Give the Spies a Civilian Review Board," *The Huffington Post*, February 1, 2006, http://www.huffingtonpost.com/amitai-etzioni/give-the-spies-a-civilian_b_14793.html.
118. Amitai Etzioni, *How Patriotic is the Patriot Act? Freedom versus Security in the Age of Terrorism* (New York: Routledge, 2005).

Chapter 3

1. Richard A. Posner, "The Uncertain Protection of Privacy by the Supreme Court," *Supreme Court Review* (1979): 188.
2. Richard A. Epstein, *Principles for a Free Society: Reconciling Individual Liberty with the Common Good* (New York: Basic Books, 1998).
3. Anthony G. Amsterdam, "Perspectives on the Fourth Amendment," *Minnesota Law Review* 58 (1974): 349, 384.
4. Jed Rubenfeld, "The End of Privacy," *Stanford Law Review* 61 (2008): 106.
5. Richard H. Seamon, "Kyllo v. United States and the Partial Ascendance of Justice Scalia's Fourth Amendment," *Washington University Law Quarterly* 79 (2001): 1023–4.
6. Ibid.
7. Kyllo, 121 *Supreme Court* at 2043.
8. Shaun B. Spencer, "Reasonable Expectations and the Erosion of Privacy," *Washington Law Review* 79 (2004): 119; see also Marissa A. Lalli, "Spicy Little Conversations: Technology in the Workplace and a Call for a New Cross-doctrinal Jurisprudence," *American Criminal Law Review* 48 (2011): 243. Lalli argues that, given the "growing popularity of employer-provided personal communication devices" of ambiguous shared ownership between employee and employer, the "expectation of privacy" standard undermines the protection of individuals from unreasonable search and seizure by institutions).
9. Ibid. 860.
10. Jed Rubenfeld, "The End of Privacy," *Stanford Law Review* 61 (2008): 101.
11. Erwin Chemerinsky, "Rediscovering Brandeis's Right to Privacy," *Brandeis Law Journal* 45 (2006–2007): 643; see also Raquel Aldana, "Of Katz and 'Aliens': Privacy Expectations and the Immigration Raids," *U.C. Davis Law Review* 41 (2007–2008): 1088. Aldana argues that "immigrants have become so regulated that any Katz expectation of privacy [for immigrants] to occupy spaces in silence without detection becomes unreasonable."
12. Richard S. Julie, "High-tech Surveillance Tools and the Fourth Amendment: Reasonable Expectations of Privacy in the Technological Age," *American Criminal Law Review* 37 (2000): 127.
13. This view relies in part Justice Rehnquist's statement in Rakas v. Illinois (439 U.S. 144 n.12) that "legitimation of expectations of privacy by law must have a source outside of the Fourth Amendment," either by "reference to concepts of real or personal property law or to understandings that are recognized and permitted by society." Empirical data would be used to shed light on the latter.
14. Christopher Slobogin and Joseph E. Schumacher, "Reasonable Expectations of Privacy and Autonomy in Fourth Amendment Cases: An Empirical Look at Understandings Recognized and Permitted by Society," *Duke Law Journal* 42 (1993): 757.
15. Henry F. Fradella et al., "Quantifying Katz: Empirically Measuring 'Reasonable Expectations of Privacy' in the Fourth Amendment Context," *American Journal of Criminal Law* 38 (2010–2011): 293–94.

16. Institute for Statistics Education, "Glossary of Statistical Terms Test-Retest Reliability," available at http://www.statistics.com.
17. See, for example, Oscar H. Gandy Jr., "Public Opinion Surveys and the Formation of Privacy Policy," *Journal of Social Issues* 59 (2003): 283–99 (the difficulty of framing neutral questions is "especially problematic in the realm of privacy policy"); Susan Freiwald, "A First Principles Approach to Communications' Privacy," *Stanford Technology Law Review* (2007): 3 (questions on privacy might be "too complicated and too easily skewed" to give accurate results).
18. Ruut Veenhoven, "Why Social Policy Needs Subjective Indicators," *Econstor*, available at http://www.econstor.eu/handle/10419/50182.
19. Pew Research Center for the People and the Press, "Methodology: Question Wording, " available at http://www.people-press.org/; examples of such bias include "social desirability bias" ("inaccurate answers to questions that deal with sensitive subjects" like drug use or church attendance, especially in face-to-face interviews), "acquiescence bias" (In a poll asking whether military strength was the best way to secure peace, 55 percent were in favor when it was phrased as a "yes or no" question, but only 33 percent were in favor when "diplomacy" was offered as an alternative), and question order effects. (A 2008 poll found that an additional 10 percent of respondents expressed dissatisfaction with current affairs if they were previously, rather than subsequently, asked if they approved of the president's performance). See also Andrew Binder, "Measuring Risk/Benefit Perceptions of Emerging Technologies," *Public Understanding of Science* (2011) accessed at http://pus.sagepub.com/. (Short opinion polls may yield different results than longer academic surveys.)
20. B. J. McNeil et al., "On the Elicitation of Preferences for Alternative Therapies," *New England Journal of Medicine* 306 (1982): 1259.
21. The archetypal example of survey error leading to false results was the famous "Literary Digest Poll" that falsely predicted Roosevelt's loss of the 1936 presidential election results by relying solely on telephone and car owners, a disproportionately Republican group. See also "The War Over Love Heats Up Again," *Los Angeles Times*, October 29, 1987. (A 1987 mail-in survey on love found that 98 percent of women were unhappy in their relationships, while a telephone poll found that 93 percent were happy—possibly because the unhappy had more motivation to mail in their response); Russell D. Renka, "The Good, the Bad, and the Ugly of Public Opinion Polls," *Southeast Missouri State University*. (Internet polls, which tend to attract an unrepresentative sample of the population and to lack safeguards against multiple voting, can be particularly susceptible to this type of errors.)
22. See, for example, Floyd J. Fowler, Jr. *Survey Research Methods*, 4th ed. (Thousand Oaks, CA: SAGE Publications, Inc., 2009). SAGE Research Methods. Web.
23. Jason Zengerle, "The. Polls. Have. Stopped. Making. Any. Sense," *New York Magazine*, (September 30, 2012); Thomas Fitzgerald, "Rethinking Public Opinion," *The New Atlantis*, 21 (Summer 2008): 45–62.

24. Shaun B. Spencer, "Reasonable Expectations and the Erosion of Privacy," *San Diego Law Review* 39 (2002): 843.
25. Amitai Etzioni, *How Patriotic Is the Patriot Act?: Freedom Versus Security in the Age of Terrorism* (New York: Routledge, 2004).
26. Lior Jacob Strahilevitz, "A Social Networks Theory of Privacy," *John M. Olin Law & Economics*. Working Paper no. 230, available at http://www.law.uchicago.edu/.
27. David W. Cunis, "Note, California v. Greenwood: Discarding the Traditional Approach to the Search and Seizure of Garbage," *Catholic University Law Review* 38 (1989): 543, 565.
28. "State Trooper, Fired for Associating with KKK, Argues for Job Back," *Wall Street Journal*, March 6, 2008; "Patriots Cheerleader Fired After Facebook Swastika Photo," *Fox News*, November 6, 2008; "Facebook Chat Gets 13 Virgin Airlines Employees Fired," *Bloomberg News*, November 1, 2008.
29. "Thirty-Seven Percent of Companies Use Social Networks to Research Potential Job Candidates, According to New CareerBuilder Survey," *PRNewswire*, April 18, 2012.
30. Laura Vanderkam, "How Social Media Can Affect Your Job Search," *CNN*, October 9, 2012.
31. Jonathan Dame, "Will Employers Still Ask for Facebook Passwords in 2014?" *USA Today*, January 10, 2014.
32. Jade Pech, "Social Networking Sites and Selection Decisions: The Impact of Privacy Settings of Facebook Profiles on Hiring." Thesis, University of Central Oklahoma, 2013.
33. Kimberly Dozier, "AP Exclusive: CIA following Twitter, Facebook," Associated Press, November 4, 2011.
34. Sean Gallagher, "Staking out Twitter and Facebook, New Service Lets Police Poke Perps," *Ars Technica* (November 13, 2013).
35. California v. Greenwood, 486 U.S. 35 (1988).
36. Thomas K. Clancy, "What Does the Fourth Amendment Protect: Property, Privacy, or Security?" *Wake Forest Law Review* 33 (1998): 307, 316–20.
37. Ibid.
38. Helen Nissenbaum, "Privacy as Contextual Integrity," *Washington Law Review* 79 (2004): 119.
39. Ibid.
40. United States v. Miller, 425 U.S. 435 (1976).
41. Stephen E. Henderson, "Nothing New under the Sun: A Technologically Rational Doctrine of Fourth Amendment Search," *Mercer Law Review* 56 (2004–2005): 510.
42. U.S. Postal Inspection Service, Frequently Asked Questions, accessed at https://postalinspectors.uspis.gov.
43. Orin S. Kerr, "A User's Guide to the Stored Communications Act, and a Legislator's Guide to Amending It," *George Washington Law Review* 72 (2004), http://ssrn.com/abstract=421860.
44. Peter Swire, "Katz Is Dead. Long Live Katz." *Michigan Law Review* 102 (2004): 906.

45. Craig Mundie, "Privacy Pragmatism: Focus on Data Use, Not Data Collection," *Foreign Affairs*, March/April 2014.
46. See, for example, Justice Marshall in 442 U.S. 735 (1979) (arguing that "unless a person is prepared to forgo [...] personal or professional necessity, he cannot help but accept the risk of surveillance [by third parties]," which is of less relevance to privacy than "the risks he should be forced to assume in a free and open society."). See also *United States V. Jones*, 615 F. 3d 544 (Justice Sotomayor argues the third-party doctrine is "ill suited to the digital age").
47. James J. Tomkovicz, "Beyond Secrecy for Secrecy's Sake: Toward an Expanded Vision of the Fourth Amendment Privacy Province," *Hastings Law Journal* 36 (1985) 645, 649; Richard G. Wilkins, "Defining the 'Reasonable Expectation of Privacy': An Emerging Tripartite Analysis," *Vanderbilt Law Review* 40 (1987): 1077, 1087.
48. Anthony G. Amsterdam, "Perspectives on the Fourth Amendment," *Minnesota Law Review* 58 (1974): 349, 382.
49. Orin S. Kerr, "The Fourth Amendment and New Technologies: Constitutional Myths and the Case for Caution," *Michigan Law Review* 102 (2004): 820.
50. 389 U.S. 347, 361.
51. Daniel T. Pesciotta, "I'm Not Dead Yet: Katz, Jones, and the Fourth Amendment in the 21st Century," *Case Western Reserve Law Review* 63 (2012): 188, 243.
52. United States v. Katz, 389 U.S. 352.
53. 468 U.S. 705, 714.
54. Kyllo v. United States, 533 U.S. at 34, 40.
55. United States v. Knotts, 460 U.S. 276 (1983).
56. California v. Ciraolo, 476 U.S. 207 (1986).
57. Dow Chem. Co. v. United States, 476 U.S. 227 (1986).
58. United States v. Jones, 615 F. 3d 544.
59. Pesciotta, "I'm Not Dead Yet," 244.
60. Ibid., 230.
61. Ibid.; Sherry F. Colb, "The Supreme Court Decides the GPS Case, United States v. Jones, and the Fourth Amendment Evolves," *Verdict Justia* (2012).
62. United States v. Jones, 615 F. 3d 544 (2012).
63. Ibid.
64. "New surveillance technology can track everyone in an area for hours at a time," *Washington Post*, February 5, 2014: Persistent Security Systems uses airborne cameras to "track every vehicle and person across an area the size of a small city, for several hours at a time." [...] "Police are supposed to begin looking at the pictures only after a crime has been reported."
65. New York City Government, "Mayor Bloomberg, Police Commissioner Kelly and Microsoft unveil new, state-of-the-art technology that aggregates and analyzes existing public safety data in real time to provide a comprehensive view of potential threats and criminal activity," August 8, 2012: A joint effort of Microsoft and the New York Police Department "aggregates and analyzes existing public safety data streams" from cameras, license plate readers, radiation detectors, and law enforcement databases. The technology helps police

track suspects by providing arrest records, related 911 calls, local crime data, and vehicle locations. Material deemed to have "continuing law enforcement or public safety value or legal necessity" may be retained indefinitely, otherwise it is stored for up to five years. See also Martin Kaste, "In 'Domain Awareness,' Detractors See Another NSA," NPR, February 21, 2014: Expansion of the system to include additional cameras, facial recognition, cell phone and social media tracking is planned.
66. Amitai Etzioni, "A Cyber Age Privacy Doctrine: A Liberal Communitarian Approach," *I/S: A Journal of Law and Policy for the Information Society*, 10, 2 (Summer 2014).

Chapter 4

1. *Katz v. United States*, 389 U.S. 347 (1969).
2. Henry F. Fradella, Weston J. Morrow, Ryan G. Fischer, and Connie Ireland, "Quantifying *Katz*: Empirically Measuring 'Reasonable Expectations of Privacy' in the Fourth Amendment Context," *American Journal of Criminal Law* 38, 3 (2011): 295.
3. Thane Josef Messinger, "A Gentle and Easy Death: From Ancient Greece to Beyond *Cruzan* Toward a Reasoned Legal Response to the Societal Dilemma of Euthanasia," *Denver University of Law Review* 71 (January 1993), cited in Fradella et al., "Quantifying *Katz*," 295.
4. Fradella et al., "Quantifying *Katz*," 296–97.
5. William Cuddihy and B. Carmon Hardy, "A Man's House Was Not His Castle: Origins of the Fourth Amendment to the United States Constitution," *The William and Mary Quarterly* 37, 3 (July 1980): 371.
6. Thomas K. Clancy, "The Framers' Intent: John Adams, His Era, and the Fourth Amendment," *Indiana Law Journal* 86, 3 (2011): 979–80, 1014.
7. Stephanie M. Stern, "The Inviolate Home: Housing Exceptionalism in the Fourth Amendment," *Cornell Law Review* 95, 5 (July 2010): 924–26, 927.
8. Fradellaet al., "Quantifying *Katz*," 301–302.
9. For example, "In *Steagald v. United States*, the Court resolved an important fourth amendment issue by holding that, absent exigent circumstances or consent, a law enforcement officer may not legally search for the subject of an arrest warrant in the home of a third party without a search warrant." G. Andrew Watson, "Fourth Amendment: Balancing the Interests in Third Party Home Arrests," *Journal of Criminal Law and Criminology* 72, 4 (1981): 1263.
10. U.S. Const., amend. IV.
11. "The greatest [Fourth Amendment] protection is given to a citizen's residence." David M. Stout, "Home Sweet Home?! Maybe Not for Parolees and Probationers When It Comes to Fourth Amendment Protection," *Kentucky Law Journal* 95 (January 2006): 812.
12. See, to give but one example, Jordan C. Budd, "A Fourth Amendment for the Poor Alone: Subconstitutional Status and the Myth of the Inviolate Home," *Indiana Law Journal* 85, 2 (2010): 360.

13. Cited in Thomas K. Clancy, "What Does the Fourth Amendment Protect: Property, Privacy, or Security?" *Wake Forest Law Review* 33, 2 (July 1998): 319.
14. Johnson v. United States (333 U.S. 10, 1948).
15. Cited in Charles Hellman, "Secure in Their Houses? Fourth Amendment Rights at Public Housing Projects," *New York Law School Law Review* 40, 1–2 (1995): 200.
16. Silverman v. United States (365 U.S. 505, 1961).
17. Cited in Kristin M. Barone, "Through the Looking Glass of the Fourth Amendment: The Unintended Consequences of Search Reform Leads to a Technological Erosion of Security in the Home," *Loyola Journal of Public Interest Law* 13, 1 (September2011): 159.
18. *Payton v. New York* (445 U.S. 573, 1980).
19. Cited in Hellman, "Secure in Their Houses?, 198, emphasis added.
20. Cited in William E. Mercantel, "Is It Hot in Here? The Eighth Circuit's Reduction of Fourth Amendment Protections in the Home," *Missouri Law Review* 73, 3 (2008): 888.
21. Mercantel, "Is It Hot in Here?," 888.
22. Budd, "A Fourth Amendment for the Poor Alone," 362.
23. *Smith v. Maryland*, 442 U.S. 735 (1979).
24. Matthew L. Zabel, "High-Tech Assault on the Castle: Warrantless Thermal Surveillance of Private Residences and the Fourth Amendment," *Northwestern University Law Review* 90 ,1 (1995): 273.
25. The first draft of the Fourth Amendment was written by James Madison, but it was based heavily on an earlier Massachusetts model created by Adams. Thomas K. Clancy, "The Framers' Intent: John Adams, His Era, and the Fourth Amendment," *Indiana Law Journal* 86, 3 (2011): 979–80, 982.
26. It is agreed that Adams's report of the events may not be accurate. However, it matters not what actually happened, but only how it influenced Adams's intent in influencing the Fourth Amendment. Clancy, "The Framers' Intent," 995. Cuddihy and Hardy, "A Man's House Was Not His Castle," 371.
27. "In order to ascertain the nature of the proceedings intended by the Fourth Amendment to the Constitution under the terms 'unreasonable searches and seizures,' it is only necessary to recall the contemporary or then recent history of the controversies on the subject, both in this country and in England. The practice had obtained in the colonies of issuing writs of assistance to the revenue officers, empowering them, in their discretion, to search suspected places for smuggled goods." *Boyd v. United States* (116 U.S. 616, 1886); "[The Fourth Amendment] arose from the harsh experience of householders having their doors hammered upon by magistrates and writ-bearing agents of the crown. Indeed, the Fourth Amendment is explainable only by the history and memory of such abuse." Cuddihy and Hardy, ," 372.
For a full history of the English practices that led to the colonial rejection of writs of assistance, see William Cuddihy, "Warrantless House-to-House Searches and Fourth Amendment Originalism: A Reply to Professor Davies," *Texas Tech Law Review* 44, 4 (2012): 998.

"Fourth Amendment: Search and Seizure," Government Printing Office, October 1992, available at http://www.gpo.gov/fdsys/pkg/GPO-CONAN-1992/pdf/GPO-CONAN-1992-10-5.pdf.
28. Emily Hickman, "Colonial Writs of Assistance," *The New England Quarterly* 5, 1 (1932): 84.
29. Clancy, "The Framers' Intent," 980.
30. M. Jackson Jones, "The Fourth Amendment and Search Warrant Presentment: Is a Man's House Always His Castle?" *American Journal of Trial Advocacy* 35, 3 (2012): 529–34.
31. The connection in *Wilkes* is more dubious because the warrant in question searched five houses but *also* arrested more than forty individuals, but it still remains. Jones, "The Fourth Amendment and Search Warrant Presentment," 529–34.
32. Antos-Fallon, "The Fourth Amendment and Immigration Enforcement in the Home," 1008; Sean M. Lewis, "The Fourth Amendment in the Hallway: Do Tenants Have a Constitutionally Protected Privacy Interest in the Locked Common Areas of Their Apartment Building?" *Michigan Law Review* 101, 1 (October 2002): 303.
33. Fradella et al., "Quantifying *Katz*," 327.
34. Myra Marx Ferree, "Beyond Separate Spheres: Feminism and Family Research," *Journal of Marriage and the Family* 52, 4 (November 1990): 867.
35. Tracy E. Higgins, "Reviving the Public/Private Distinction in Feminist Theorizing," *Chicago-Kent Law Review* 75, 3 (2000): 847.
36. Leila J. Rupp, cited in Colin Koopman, "Public and Private in Feminism and Pragmatism," *International Studies in Philosophy* 40, 2 (2008), 49.
37. Raia Prokhovnik, cited in Ronnie Cohen and Shannon O'Byrne, "'Can You Hear Me Now . . . Good!' Feminism(s), the Public/Private Divide, and *Citizens United v. FEC*," *UCLA Women's Law Journal* 20, 1, (2013): 39.
38. Cited in Colin Koopman, "Public and Private in Feminism and Pragmatism," *International Studies in Philosophy* 40, 2008): 49.
39. Ruth Gavison, "Feminism and the Public/Private Distinction," *Stanford Law Review* 45, 1 (November 1992): 5–7.
40. Cohen and O'Byrne, "'Can You Hear Me Now . . . Good!,'" 41.
41. Tracy E. Higgins, "Reviving the Public/Private Distinction in Feminist Theorizing," *Chicago-Kent Law Review* 75, 3 (January 2000): 848.
42. Gavison, "Feminism and the Public/Private Distinction," 21.
43. Mary Dietz, cited in Koopman, "Public and Private in Feminism and Pragmatism," 53.
44. Gavison, "Feminism and the Public/Private Distinction," 3.
45. Higgins, "Reviving the Public/Private Distinction in Feminist Theorizing," 851.
46. Cited in Gavison, "Feminism and the Public/Private Distinction," 1–2.
47. Higgins, "Reviving the Public/Private Distinction in Feminist Theorizing," 851.
48. Gavison, "Feminism and the Public/Private Distinction," 22.

49. Cohen and O'Byrne, "'Can You Hear Me Now . . . Good!'" 40.
50. Koopman, "Public and Private in Feminism and Pragmatism," 52.
51. Chris Armstrong and Judith Squires, "Beyond the Public/Private Dichotomy: Relational Space and Sexual Inequalities," *Contemporary Political Theory* 1 (2002): 267.
52. "*Wyman v. James*: Welfare Home Visits and a Strict Construction of the Fourth Amendment," *Northwestern University Law Journal* 66 (1971): 719.
53. Budd, "A Fourth Amendment for the Poor Alone, 365–66.
54. Stout, "Home Sweet Home?!"
55. Antos-Fallon, "The Fourth Amendment and Immigration Enforcement in the Home,"1000.
56. Terrence P. Jeffrey, "HHS Report: Percentage of Americans on Welfare Hits Record High," *CSNews.com*, July 8, 2014, available at http://cnsnews.com/news/article/terence-p-jeffrey/hhs-report-percentage-americans-welfare-hits-recorded-high.
57. Budd, "A Fourth Amendment for the Poor Alone," 355–408. David Reichbach, "The Home Not the Homeless: What the Fourth Amendment has Historically Protected and Where the Law is Going After *Jones*," *University of San Francisco Law Review* 47, 2 (2012–2013). Andrew Guthrie Ferguson, "Personal Curtilage: Fourth Amendment Security in Public," *William & Mary Law Review* 55, 4, 2014.
58. Bryce Covert, "More Than 600,000 Americans Are Homeless on Any Given Night," Think Progress, November 22, 2013, available at http://thinkprogress.org/economy/2013/11/22/2982691/hud-homeless-count/.
59. Mark A. Godsey, "Privacy and the Growing Plight of the Homeless: Reconsidering the Values Underlying the Fourth Amendment," *Ohio State Law Journal* 53, 3 (1992): 869–70.
60. Michael D. Granston, "From Private Places to Private Activities: Toward a New Fourth Amendment House for the Shelterless," *The Yale Law Journal* 101, 6 (April 1992): 1316.
61. Granston, "From Private Places to Private Activities," 1317.
62. Amitai Etzioni, "The Bankruptcy of Liberalism and Conservatism," *Political Science Quarterly* 128, 1 (April 2013): 39–65.
63. Kim Zetter, "Yahoo, Verizon: Our Spy Capabilities Would 'Shock,' 'Confuse' Consumers," *Wired*, December 1, 2009, available at http://www.wired.com/2009/12/wiretap-prices/. Jay Stanley, *The Surveillance-Industrial Complex: How the American Government is Conscripting Businesses and Individuals in the Construction of a Surveillance Society*, American Civil Liberties Union, 2004, available at http://www.aclu.org/FilesPDFs/surveillance_report.pdf.
64. "911 Wireless Services," FCC, accessed October 7, 2014, at http://www.fcc.gov/guides/wireless-911-services.
65. Kevin Emas and Tamara Pallas, "*United States v. Jones*: Does *Katz* Still Have Nine Lives?" *St. Thomas Law Review* 24, 2 (2012): 172.
66. Edmund W. Kitch, "*Katz v. United States*: The Limits of the Fourth Amendment," *The Supreme Court Review* (1968): 133.

67. D. C. Roth, "*Florida v. Jardines*: Trespassing on the Reasonable Expectation of Privacy," *Denver University Law Review* 91, 2 (2014): 554.
68. Cynthia Lee, "Package Bombs, Footlockers, and Laptops: What the Disappearing Container Doctrine Can Tell Us About the Fourth Amendment," *The Journal of Criminal Law and Criminology* 100, 4 (2010): 1415.
69. Ibid., 1405.
70. Ibid., 1414.
71. *Ex Parte Jackson*, 96 U.S. 727 (1828).
72. Amitai Etzioni, "A Cyber Age Privacy Doctrine: A Liberal Communitarian Approach," *I/S: A Journal of Law and Policy for the Information Society* 10, 2 (2014).
73. Arguably, restrictions or guidelines on the megabytes of information to be collected should vary based on the type of information because the byte is, strictly speaking, a measure of data, not information. For example, 100 mb of *data* is enough for thousands of text e-mails but less than five minutes of high-quality video, and the former could provide a much greater amount of private *information* than the latter.
74. *Riley v. California*, 134 S. Ct. 2473 (2014).
75. Ibid.
76. Ibid.
77. National Conference of State Legislatures, "Genetic Privacy Laws" (2008), http://www.ncsl.org/research/health/genetic-privacy-laws.aspx.
78. "The Act prohibits law enforcement officials from searching for or seizing information from people who disseminate information to the public [the media]. Where it applies, the Act requires law enforcement officials to instead rely on compliance with a subpoena." Elizabeth B. Uzelac, "Reviving the Privacy Protection Act of 1980," *Northwestern University Law Review* 107, 3 (2013): 1437–68.
79. N. J. King and V. T. Raja, "What Do They Really Know About Me in the Cloud? A Comparative Law Perspective on Protecting Privacy and Security of Sensitive Information," *American Business Law Journal* 50,2 (2013): 424–31.
80. Assume holding constant the level of public interest. The said markers would be recollected, for instance, when a terrorist attack is imminent or for other significant changes in public concerns. For more on this see Amitai Etzioni, *Limits of Privacy* (Basic Books: New York, 1999).

Chapter 5

1. Julia Angwin, "The Web's New Gold Mine: Your Secrets," *Wall Street Journal*, July 30, 2010, http://online.wsj.com/article/SB10001424052748703940904575395073512989404.html.
2. Ibid.
3. Justin Scheck, "Stalkers Exploit Cell Phone GPS," *Wall Street Journal*, August 3, 2010, http://online.wsj.com/article/SB1000142405274870346730457538352231 8244234.html.

4. Noam Cohen, "It's Tracking Your Every Move, and You May Not Even Know," *New York Times*, March 26, 2011, A1.
5. "They're Watching You," *Business Week*, January 23, 2005, http://www.businessweek.com/magazine/content/05_04/b3917056_mz005.htm.
6. Christopher Slobogin, "Government Data Mining and the Fourth Amendment," *University of Chicago Law Review* 75 (2008): 317, 320.
7. Noam Cohen, "Law Students Teach Scalia about Privacy and the Web," *New York Times*, May 18, 2009, B3.
8. Emily Steel, "A Web Pioneer Profiles Users by Name," *Wall Street Journal*, October 25, 2010, http://online.wsj.com/article/SB10001424052702304410504575560243259416072.html.
9. Frank Pasquale, "The Dark Market for Personal Data," *The New York Times*, October 17, 2014.
10. Riva Richmond, "How to Fix (or Kill) Web Data About You," *New York Times*, April 14, 2011, B6.
11. Jack Lindamood, et al., *Inferring Private Information Using Social Network Data*, Paper presented at the 18th International World Wide Web Conference, Madrid, April 20-24 2009, http://www.utdallas.edu/~muratk/publications/www09pp242-lindamood.pdf.
12. Julia Angwin and Steve Stecklow, "Scrapers' Dig Deep for Data on Web," *Wall Street Journal*, October 12, 2010, http://online.wsj.com/article/SB10001424052748703358504575544381288117888.html.
13. Ibid.
14. Eli Pariser, "What the Internet Knows about You," *CNN*, May 22, 2011, http://articles.cnn.com/2011-05-22/opinion/pariser.filter.bubble.
15. Steel, "A Web Pioneer Profiles Users by Name," note 10.
16. Ibid.
17. Steve Stecklow and Paul Sonn, "Shunned Profiling Technology on the Verge of Comeback," *Wall Street Journal*, November 24, 2010, http://online.wsj.com/article/SB10001424052748704243904575630751094784516.html.
18. Jessica Guynn, "T. Rowe Price Invests in Facebook," *Los Angeles Times*, April 15, 2011, http://latimesblogs.latimes.com/technology/2011/04/t-rowe-price-invests-in-facebook.html.
19. Pascal Emmanuel Gobry, "Facebook: Now 700 Million Strong?" *Business Insider*, May 31, 2011, http://www.businessinsider.com/facebook-700-million-2011-5.
20. "Facebook Faces Criticism over Privacy Change," BBC News, December 10, 2009, http://news.bbc.co.uk/go/pr/fr/-/2/hi/technology/8405334.stm.
21. Juliana Gruenwald, "Facebook Defends Privacy Policies," *National Journal*, July 27, 2010, http://techdailydose.nationaljournal.com/2010/07/facebook-defends-privacy-polic.php.
22. Emily Steel and Geoffrey A. Fowler, "Facebook in Privacy Breach," *Wall Street Journal*, October 18, 2010.
23. Ibid.
24. Ibid.
25. Miguel Helft, "Marketers Can Glean Private Data on Facebook," *New York Times*, October 23, 2010, B1.

26. Amir Efrati, "'Like' Button Follows Web Users," *Wall Street Journal*, May 19, 2011, B1.
27. Ibid.
28. Ibid.
29. Christopher Hoofnagle, "Big Brother's Little Helpers: How ChoicePoint and Other Commercial Data Brokers Collect, Process, and Package Your Data for Law Enforcement," *North Carolina Journal of International Law and Commercial Regulation* 29 (2004): 595, 611.
30. Daniel Solove, "The Digital Person: Technology and Privacy in the Information Age" (New York: New York University Press, 2004), 169.
31. Ibid., 167.
32. Christopher Hoofnagle, "Big Brother's Little Helpers," 611.
33. The American Civil Liberties Union, "The Surveillance-Industrial Complex: How the American Government is Conscripting Businesses and Individuals in the Construction of a Surveillance Society" 26 (August 2004), available at http://www.aclu.org/FilesPDFs/surveillance_report.pdf.
34. Christopher Slobogin, "Government Data Mining and the Fourth Amendment," *University of Chicago Law Review* 75 (2008): 320.
35. Arshad Mohammed and Sara Kehaulani Goo, "Government Increasingly Turning to Data Mining," *Washington Post*, June 15, 2006, http://www.washingtonpost.com/wp-dyn/content/article/2006/06/14/AR2006061402063.html.
36. Ibid.
37. Frank Pasquale, "The Dark Market for Personal Data," *New York Times*, October 17, 2014.
38. Julia Angwin, *Dragnet Nation: A Quest for Privacy, Security, and Freedom in a World of Relentless Surveillance* (New York: Times Books, 2014), 93.
39. Ibid., 95.
40. Ibid.
41. "Data Mining: Federal Efforts Cover a Wide Range of Uses," *Government Accountability Office*, GAO-04-548 (May 2004), http://www.gpo.gov/fdsys/pkg/GAOREPORTS-GAO-04-548/html/GAOREPORTS-GAO-04-548.htm.
42. Charlie Savage, "FBI Agents Get Leeway to Push Privacy Bounds," *New York Times*, June 13, 2011, http://www.nytimes.com/2011/06/13/us/13fbi.html.
43. Google Transparency Report (June 2011), http://www.google.com/transparencyreport/governmentrequests.
44. Polly Sprenger, "Sun On Privacy: 'Get Over It,'" *Wired*, January 26, 1999, http://www.wired.com/politics/law/news/1999/01/17538.
45. Bobbie Johnson, "Privacy No Longer a Social Norm, says Facebook Founder," *The Guardian*, January 11, 2010, http://www.guardian.co.uk/technology/2010/jan/11/facebook-privacy.
46. Ian Paul, "Facebook CEO Challenges the Social Norm of Privacy," *PC World*, January 11, 2010, http://www.pcworld.com/article/186584/facebook_ceo_challenges_the_social_norm_of_privacy.html.
47. L. Gordon Crovitz, "The 0.00002% Privacy Solution," *Wall Street Journal*, March 28, 2011, A15.

NOTES 205

48. Ibid.
49. Ibid.
50. Joseph Turow, Jennifer King, Chris Jay Hoofnagle, Amy Bleakley, and Michael Hennessy. *Americans Reject Tailored Advertising and Three Activities that Enable It*, September 29, 2009, http://repository.upenn.edu/asc_papers/137.
51. Alan Westin, "'Whatever Works': The American Public's Attitudes toward Regulation and Self-Regulation on Consumer Privacy Issues, in National Telecommunication & Information Administration," U.S. Department of Commerce, Privacy and Self-Regulation in the Information Age ch. 1, § F (1997), http://www.ntia.doc.gov/reports/privacy/selfreg1.htm#1F.
52. Bob Tedeschi, "Everybody Talks About Online Privacy, But Few Do Anything About It," *New York Times*, June 3, 2003, C6.
53. Matt Carmichael, "What Consumers Want from Brands Online," *Advertising Age*, February 27, 2011, http://adage.com/article/digital/consumers-seek-brand-discounts-facebook-preferred-platform/149095.
54. For further discussion, see A. Michael Froomkin, Symposium, "The Death of Privacy?" *Stanford Law Review* 52 (2000); and Eugene Volokh, "Freedom of Speech and Information Privacy: The Troubling Implications of a Right to Stop People from Speaking About You," *Stanford Law Review* 52 (2000): 1051.
55. Susanna Kim Ripken, "The Dangers and Drawbacks of the Disclosure Antidote: Toward a More Substantive Approach to Securities Regulation," *Baylor Law Review* 58 (2006): 186, 195.
56. For further discussion on this subject, see Dan Ariely, *Predictably Irrational: The Hidden Forces That Shape Our Decisions* (New York: Harper Collins, 2008), 243.
57. Chris Hoofnagle, "Can Privacy Self-Regulation Work for Consumers?" *TAP*, January 26, 2011, http://www.techpolicy.com/CanPrivacySelf-Regulation-Work-Hoofnagle.aspx.
58. Adam Satariano and Katie Hoffmann, "Apple Denies Tracking iPhone Locations, Will Update Software," *Bloomberg* (April 27, 2011), http://www.bloomberg.com/news/2011-04-27/apple-denies-tracking-iphone-locations-will-reduce-data-storage-capacity.html.
59. L. Gordon Crovitz, "The 0.00002% Privacy Solution," A15.
60. Ibid.
61. Federal Trade Commission, *FTC Staff Issues Privacy Report, Offers Framework for Consumers, Businesses, and Policymakers* (December 1, 2010),http://www.ftc.gov/opa/2010/12/privacyreport.shtm.
62. Joseph Turow, "Americans and Online Privacy: The System Is Broken," *Annenberg Public Policy Center Report* (June 2003), http://www.asc.upenn.edu/usr/jturow/internet-privacy-report/36-page-turow-version-9.pdf.
63. Paul M. Schwartz, "Preemption and Privacy," *Yale Law Journal* 118 (2009): 902, 921.
64. Ibid., 929.
65. *The Need for a Comprehensive Approach to Protecting Consumer Privacy: Hearing on the State of Online Consumer Privacy Before the Senate Comm. On*

Commerce, Science & Transportation, 112th Cong. 6 (2011) (statement of Erich Anderson, Deputy General Counsel, Microsoft Corporation).
66. Ibid., 8 [emphasis in the original].
67. H.B. 5765, General Assembly, February Session (Conn. 2008).
68. Paul M. Schwartz, "Preemption and Privacy," *Yale Law Journal* 118 (2009): 902, 921.
69. Hoofnagle, "Can Privacy Self-Regulation Work for Consumers?".
70. For further discussion of consent-based approaches to privacy and information "ownership," see Julie E. Cohen, "Information Rights and Intellectual Freedom" in *Ethics and the Internet,* ed. Anton Vedder (Antwerp: Intersentia, 2001), 11–32.
71. Julia M. Fromholz, "The European Union Data Privacy Directive," *Berkeley Technology Law Journal* 15 (2000): 461, 462.
72. Fred H. Cate, *Privacy in the Information Age* (Washington, DC: Brookings Institution Press, 1997), 36.
73. "EU Data Protection Directive," *Electronic Privacy Information Center,* http://epic.org/privacy/intl/eu_data_protection_directive.html.
74. Erica Newland, "CDT Comments on EU Data Protection Directive," *The Center for Democracy and Technology* (January 20, 2011), http://www.cdt.org/blogs/erica-newland/cdt-comments-eu-data-protection-directive; see also The Center for Democracy and Technology, "Comments of the Center For Democracy and Technology to the European Commission in the Matter of Consultation on the Commission's Comprehensive Approach on Personal Data Protection in the European Union" (January 15, 2011), http://cdt.org/files/pdfs/CDT_DPD_Comments.pdf.
75. Julia M. Fromholz, "The European Union Data Privacy Directive," *Berkeley Technology Law Journal* 15 (2000): 467–68.
76. Fred H. Cate, *Privacy in the Information Age* (1997), 36, 37.
77. Ibid.
78. Ibid, 36.
79. Fred H. Cate, "The EU Data Protection Directive, Information Privacy, and the Public Interest," *Iowa Law Review* 80 (1995): 431, 437.
80. Erica Newland, "CDT Comments on EU Data Protection Directive," *The Center for Democracy and Technology* (January 20, 2011), 75, http://www.cdt.org/blogs/erica-newland/cdt-comments-eu-data-protection-directive.
81. Article 13 of Council Directive 95/46/EC of the European Parliament and of the Council of 24 on the protection of individuals with regard to the processing of personal data and on the free movement of such data, 1995 O.J. L 281/31.
82. Ibid.
83. For a discussion of this topic, see Ellen Mastenbroek, "EU Compliance: Still a 'Black Hole'?" *Journal of European Public Policy* 12 (2005): 1103–20; see also, Maria Mendrinou, "Non-compliance and the European Commission's Role in Integration," *Journal of European Public Policy* 3 (1996): 1–22.
84. 5 U.S.C. § 552a(e)(7).
85. Amitai Etzioni, "DNA Tests and Databases in Criminal Justice Individual Rights and the Common Good," in *DNA and the Criminal Justice System: The Technology of Justice* (MIT Press, 2004), 197–223.
86. Gina Stevens, "Privacy Protections for Personal Information Online," *Congressional Research Service Report for Congress* (April 6, 2011).

87. "Katie Kindelan, John McCain, and John Kerry Propose 'Online Privacy Bill of Rights,'" *Social Times* (March 10, 2011), http://socialtimes.com/john-mccain-and-john-kerry-propose-online-privacy-bill-of-rights_b41604.
88. Tony Romm, "Will FTC Get the Funds It Needs to Police Internet?" *Politico* (June 3, 2011), http://www.politico.com/news/stories/0611/56134.html.
89. Marcy Peek, "Passing Beyond Identity on the Internet: Espionage and Counterespionage in the Internet Age," *Vermont Law Review* 28 (2003): 91, 94.
90. Marcia Stepanek, "Weblining," *Business Week*, April 3, 2000, http://www.businessweek.com/2000/00_14/b3675027.htm.
91. Nicholas Carr, "The Dangers of Web Tracking," *Wall Street Journal*, August 7, 2010, W1.
92. Jennifer Golbeck, Christina Robles, and Karen Turner, "Predicting Personality with Social Media," CHI Extended Abstracts (2011): 253–62.

Chapter 6

1. James Lewis and Stephen Baker, "The Economic Impact of Cybercrime and Cyber Espionage," *Center for Strategic and International Studies* (July 2013), http://www.mcafee.com/us/resources/reports/rp-economic-impact-cybercrime.pdf.
2. Michael A. Riley and Ashlee Vance, "China Corporate Espionage Boom Knocks Wind Out of U.S. Companies," *Bloomberg*, http://www.bloomberg.com/news/2012-03-15/china-corporate-espionage-boom-knocks-wind-out-of-u-s-companies.html (accessed June 29, 2014).
3. James A. Lewis, "China's Economic Espionage," *Foreign Affairs*, http://www.foreignaffairs.com/articles/138427/james-a-lewis/chinas-economic-espionage (accessed June 29, 2014).
4. Sid Kircheimer, "Cybercrime Costs 508,000 U.S. Jobs," *AARP*, http://blog.aarp.org/2013/07/25/cybercrime-costs-508000-u-s-jobs/ (accessed June 29, 2014).
5. Joshua Phillip, "The Staggering Cost of Economic Espionage Against the US," *The Epoch Times*, http://www.theepochtimes.com/n3/326002-the-staggering-cost-of-economic-espionage-against-the-us/ (accessed June 29, 2014).
6. Carrie Lukas, "It's Time for the U.S. to Deal with Cyber-Espionage," *US News*, http://www.usnews.com/opinion/articles/2013/06/04/chinas-industrial-cyberespionage-harms-the-us-economy (accessed June 29, 2014).
7. Jamil Anderlini, Peter Marsh, John Reed, Joseph Menn, Peggy Hollinger, and Daniel Schäfer, "Industrial Espionage: Data Out of the Door," *Financial Times*, http://www.ft.com/intl/cms/s/0/ba6c82c0-2e44-11e0-8733-00144feabdc0.html#axzz35DQLxMz4 (accessed June 29, 2014).
8. Danny Yadron, "Companies Wrestle with the Cost of Cybersecurity," *Wall Street Journal* http://online.wsj.com/news/articles/SB10001424052702304834704579403421539734550 (accessed June 29, 2014).
9. *The Economist*, "White Hats to the Rescue," http://www.economist.com/news/business/21596984-law-abiding-hackers-are-helping-businesses-fight-bad-guys-white-hats-rescue (accessed June 29, 2014).
10. *Business Software Alliance*, "Security," http://www.bsa.org/advocacy/security (accessed June 29, 2014).

11. However, the U.S. Chamber of Commerce endorsed the Cybersecurity Act of 2013, which "would codify NIST's role in developing the Cybersecurity Framework." Hogan Lovells Privacy Team, "U.S. Cybersecurity Policy Developments: A Year-to-Date Roundup," *The International Association of Privacy Professionals* https://www.privacyassociation.org/privacy_tracker/post/u.s._cybersecurity_policy_developments_a_year_to_date_roundup (accessed June 29, 2014).
12. James A. Lewis, "Innovation and Cybersecurity Regulation," *Center for Strategic and International Studies*, http://csis.org/files/media/csis/pubs/090327_lewis_innovation_cybersecurity.pdf (accessed June 29, 2014). Here, faith-based refers to the assumption that the private sector will act in good faith to secure its networks and computers against cyber attacks.
13. James A. Lewis, "Innovation and Cybersecurity Regulation".
14. Daniel Kahneman, *Thinking, Fast and Slow* (New York: Farrar, Straus and Giroux, 2011).
15. Danny Yadron, "Boards Race to Fortify Cybersecurity," *The Wall Street Journal*, http://www.wsj.com/articles/boards-race-to-bolster-cybersecurity-1404086146 (accessed June 30, 2014).
16. Nathan Alexander Sales, "Regulating Cyber-Security," *Northwestern University Law Review* 107, 4 (Summer 2013): 1508.
17. Danny Yadron, "Boards Race to Fortify Cybersecurity."
18. Ken Dilanian, "U.S. Chamber of Commerce Leads Defeat of Cyber-security Bill," *Los Angeles Times*, http://articles.latimes.com/2012/aug/03/nation/la-na-cyber-security-20120803 (accessed June 29, 2014).
19. Danny Yadron, "Companies Wrestle with the Cost of Cybersecurity."
20. Kevin Coleman, "Meeting the Cost of Cybersecurity," *Defense News*. http://www.defensenews.com/article/M5/20140325/C4ISRNET18/303250028/Meeting-cost-cybersecurity (accessed June 29, 2014).
21. Amitai Etzioni, "Cybersecurity in the Private Sector," *Issues in Science and Technology* 28,1 (Fall 2011): 58–62.
22. Alexander Botting, "Cybersecurity in the Private Sector—Playing Catch-up," *The Hill*, http://thehill.com/blogs/congress-blog/technology/205883-cybersecurity-in-the-private-sector-playing-catch-up (accessed June 29, 2014).
23. Emily R. Caron, "Target Data Breach and NIST Cybersecurity Framework Raise Tough Insurance Questions," *Lathrop & Gage, LLP*, https://law.ku.edu/sites/law.ku.edu/files/docs/media_law/2014/Media_Privacy_Beyond.pdf (accessed June 29, 2014).
24. Ariel Yehezkel and Thomas Michael, "Cybersecurity: Breaching the Boardroom," *Sheppard Mullin Richter & Hampton LLP*, http://www.sheppardmullin.com/media/article/1280_MCC-Cybersecurity-Breaching%20The%20Boardroom.pdf (accessed June 29, 2014).
25. Alina Selyukh, Ros Krasny, and Chris Reese, "Senate Cybersecurity Bill Gives Firms Liability Protection for Sharing Data," *Insurance Journal*, http://www.insurancejournal.com/news/national/2014/04/30/327968.htm (accessed June 29, 2014).
26. Alina Selyukh, Ros Krasny, and Chris Reese, "Senators Ready to Try Again on U.S. Cybersecurity Legislation," *Reuters*, http://www.reuters.com/article/2014/04/30/

us-usa-cybersecurity-congress-idUSBREA3T0QF20140430 (accessed June 29, 2014).
27. Alex Wilhelm, "Sen. Rockefeller Blasts Granting Firms Liability Protection for Following Voluntary Cybersecurity Standards," *The Next Web*, http://thenextweb.com/us/2013/06/05/sen-rockefeller-blasts-granting-firms-liability-protection-for-following-voluntary-cybersecurity-standards/ (accessed June 29, 2014).
28. Amitai Etzioni, "The Bankruptcy of Liberalism and Conservatism," *Political Science Quarterly* 128, 1 (Spring 2013): 39–65. Internal quotation marks omitted.
29. Ken Dilanian, "U.S. Chamber of Commerce Leads Defeat of Cyber-security Bill," *Los Angeles Times*, http://articles.latimes.com/2012/aug/03/nation/la-na-cyber-security-20120803 (accessed June 29, 2014).
30. Grant Gross, "Feds Explore Cybersecurity Incentives for Private Sector," *Computer World*, http://www.computerworld.com/s/article/9241407/Feds_explore_cybersecurity_incentives_for_the_private_sector (accessed June 29, 2014).
31. Alexander Botting, "Cybersecurity in the Private Sector."
32. Trisha Leon, "U.S. Launches Initiative for Procurement Cybersecurity," *Business Solutions*. http://www.bsminfo.com/doc/u-s-launches-initiative-for-procurement-cybersecurity-0001 (accessed June 29, 2014).
33. Alexander Botting, "Cybersecurity in the Private Sector."
34. Danielle Ivory, "Federal Contracts Plunge, Squeezing Private Companies," *New York Times*, http://www.nytimes.com/2014/01/16/business/federal-contracts-plunge-squeezing-private-companies.html (accessed June 29, 2014).
35. Robert O'Harrow, Jr., Dana Priest, and Marjorie Censer, "NSA Leaks Put Focus on Intelligence Apparatus's Reliance on Outside Contractors," *Washington Post*, http://www.washingtonpost.com/business/nsa-leaks-put-focus-on-intelligence-apparatuss-reliance-on-outside-contractors/2013/06/10/e940c4ba-d20e-11e2-9f1a-1a7cdee20287_story.html (accessed June 29, 2014).
36. The Associated Press, "Case Against Contractors Resurfaces," http://www.nytimes.com/2013/10/18/us/case-against-contractors-resurfaces.html?_r=0 (accessed June 29, 2014).
37. Jeremy Scahill, "Blackwater's Secret Ops," *The Nation*, http://www.thenation.com/article/154739/blackwaters-black-ops# (accessed June 29, 2014).
38. Michael S. Schmidt and David E. Sanger, "5 in China Army Face U.S. Charges of Cyberattacks," *New York Times*, http://www.nytimes.com/2014/05/20/us/us-to-charge-chinese-workers-with-cyberspying.html (accessed June 29, 2014).
39. Bill Gertz, "Indictment of China Military Hackers Reveals New Details of Cyber Attack Methods," *The Washington Free Beacon*, http://freebeacon.com/national-security/obama-administration-indictment-of-army-hackers-seeks-to-deter-cyber-attacks/ (accessed June 29, 2014).
40. Eloise Lee and Robert Johnson, "The 25 Biggest Defense Companies in America," *Business Insider*, http://www.businessinsider.com/top-25-us-defense-companies-2012-2?op=1 (accessed June 29, 2014).

41. Bill Gertz, "Top Gun Takeover: Stolen F-35 Secrets Showing up in China's Stealth Fighter," *The Washington Times*, http://www.washingtontimes.com/news/2014/mar/13/f-35-secrets-now-showing-chinas-stealth-fighter/?page=all (accessed June 29, 2014).
42. Richard A. Clarke, *Cyber War: The Next Threat to National Security and What to Do About It* (New York: Harper Collins, 2010).
43. Financial Stability Oversight Council, "2014 Annual Report," http://www.treasury.gov/initiatives/fsoc/Documents/FSOC%202014%20Annual%20Report.pdf (accessed June 29, 2014).
44. United States Government Accountability Office, "Maritime Critical Infrastructure Protection: DHS Needs to Better Address Port Security," http://www.gao.gov/assets/670/663828.pdf (accessed June 29, 2014).
45. Amitai Etzioni, "The Bankruptcy of Liberalism and Conservatism," 39–65.
46. "Cybersecurity: Coming Soon to a Government Contract Near You," *Venable LLP*, http://www.venable.com/cybersecurity-coming-soon-to-a-government-contract-near-you-02-04-2014/ (accessed 30 June 2014).

Chapter 7

1. I am indebted to Jesse Spafford for his extensive research assistance on this chapter and to Ashley McKinless and Erin Syring for comments on a previous draft.
2. See Amitai Etzioni, *The New Golden Rule: Community and Morality in a Democratic Society* (New York: Basic Books, 1996).
3. I have previously discussed this balance in the context of privacy and public health, public safety, sex offenders, and freedom of the press, among other rights. See Amitai Etzioni, *The Limits of Privacy* (New York: Basic Books, 1999); Amitai Etzioni, "The Privacy Merchants: What Is To Be Done?" *Journal of Constitutional Law* 14, 4 (March 2012): 929–51; and Amitai Etzioni, *How Patriotic Is the Patriot Act?: Freedom versus Security in the Age of Terrorism* (New York: Routledge, 2004).
4. Gerald Gaus and Shane D. Courtland, "Liberalism," in Edward N. Zalta, ed., *The Stanford Encyclopedia of Philosophy* (Spring 2011), http://plato.stanford.edu/entries/liberalism/. Also: John Rawls, *A Theory of Justice*, rev. ed. (Cambridge, MA: Belknap Press, 1999).
5. Amitai Etzioni, "Communitarianism,"*Encyclopædia Britannica*, Online Academic Edition, http://www.britannica.com/EBchecked/topic/1366457/communitarianism (accessed June 21, 2013).
6. David R. Jones, "Party Polarization and Legislative Gridlock," *Political Research Quarterly* 54, 1 (March 2001): 125–41.
7. Private communication with Strossen.
8. Stewart Baker, *Skating on Stilts: Why We Aren't Stopping Tomorrow's Terrorism* (Stanford, CA: Hoover Institution Press, 2010): 27.
9. Marc Rotenberg, "Restoring a Public Interest Vision of Law in the Age of the Internet," *Duke Law & Technology Review* 7 (2004): 7–15.

10. Larry Abramson, "Privacy Board to Scrutinize Surveillance Programs," *NPR*, July 9, 2013, http://www.npr.org/2013/07/09/200285740/privacy-board-to-hold-first-meeting.
11. See Amitai Etzioni, *The Limits of Privacy*.
12. Sara Carter, "Al Qaeda Gaining Strength in Mali, North Africa," *The Washington Times*, March 26, 2013, http://www.washingtontimes.com/news/2013/mar/26/key-mali-lawmaker-challenges-obama-on-al-qaida-thr/?page=all. See also, Sudarsan Raghavan, "Nigerian Islamist Militants Return from Mali with Weapons, Skills," *The Washington Post*, May 31, 2013, http://articles.washingtonpost.com/2013-05-31/world/39642133_1_northern-mali-boko-haram-nigerian-islamist; and Adam Entous, Drew Hinshaw, and David Gauthier-Villars, "Militants, Chased From Mali, Pose New Threats," *The Wall Street Journal*, May 24, 2013, http://online.wsj.com/article/SB10001424127887323336104578503464066163002.html.
13. Cory Bennett, "How Al-Qaida in Yemen Became the Biggest Terrorist Threat to the U.S.," *National Journal*, May 30, 2013, http://www.nationaljournal.com/political-landscape-podcast/how-al-qaida-in-yemen-became-the-biggest-terrorist-threat-to-the-u-s-20121214. See also, Douglas A. Pryer, "The Rise of the Machines," *Military Review* (March-April 2013): 17, http://usacac.army.mil/CAC2/MilitaryReview/Archives/English/MilitaryReview_20130430_art005.pdf.
14. Bruce Riedel, "Al Qaeda Comeback," *The Daily Beast*, April 12, 2013, http://www.thedailybeast.com/articles/2013/04/12/al-qaeda-comeback.html.
15. For a detailed discussion of this point, see Paul K. Kerr and Mary Beth Nikitin, "Pakistan's Nuclear Weapons: Proliferation and Security Issues," Congressional Research Service, RL34248 (March 19, 2013), http://www.fas.org/sgp/crs/nuke/RL34248.pdf; and Amy F. Woolf, "Nonstrategic Nuclear Weapons," Congressional Research Service, RL32572 (December 19, 2012), http://www.fas.org/sgp/crs/nuke/RL32572.pdf.
16. Shaun Gregory, "The Terrorist Threat to Pakistan's Nuclear Weapons" *CTC Sentinel*, July 15, 2009: 2, 7.
17. Sean M. Joyce, as quoted in "House Select Intelligence Committee Holds Hearing on Disclosure of National Security Agency Surveillance Programs," Federation of American Scientists, June 18, 2013, 10–1, https://www.fas.org/irp/congress/2013_hr/disclosure.pdf.
18. Ibid.
19. Ibid.
20. Ibid.; see also, Erin McClam, "Surveillance Helped Stop Plots against NYSE and New York Subway, Official Says," *NBC News*, June 18, 2013, http://usnews.nbcnews.com/_news/2013/06/18/19022364-surveillance-helped-stop-plots-against-nyse-and-new-york-subway-official-says?lite.
21. Keith Alexander, as quoted in "House Select Intelligence Committee Holds Hearing on Disclosure of National Security Agency Surveillance Programs," Federation of American Scientists, June 18, 2013, 11–13, https://www.fas.org/irp/congress/2013_hr/disclosure.pdf.

22. This is a bit of a simplification, but largely captures the NSA's operating procedures. For a more nuanced discussion, see Marc Ambinder, "How the NSA Uses Your Telephone Records," *The Week*, June 6, 2013, http://theweek.com/article/index/245285/how-the-nsa-uses-your-telephone-records.
23. Jack Nicas, "TSA to Halt Revealing Body Scans at Airports," *Wall Street Journal*, January 18, 2013.
24. Legal Information Institute, "Fourth Amendment," Cornell University Law School. http://www.law.cornell.edu/wex/fourth_amendment (accessed 12 July 2013).
25. See *Electronic Privacy Information Center v. United States Department of Homeland Security*, 653 F.3d 1, 10–11 (D.C. Cir. 2011); and *National Treasury Employees Union v. Von Raab*, 489 U.S. 656, 674–675 & n.3 (1989).
26. See *Michigan Department of State Police v. Sitz*, 110 S. Ct. 2481 (1990).
27. See *Skinner v. Railway Labor Executives' Association*, 489 U.S. 602 (1989); and *National Treasury Employees Union v. Von Raab*, 489 U.S. 656 (1989).
28. USA Patriot Act. Pub. L. 107-56. 115 Stat. 272. October 26, 2011. Accessed at http://www.gpo.gov/fdsys/pkg/PLAW-107publ56/html/PLAW-107publ56.htm
29. Scott Shane and David E. Sanger, "Job Title Key to Inner Access Held by Snowden," *The New York Times*, June 30, 2013, http://www.nytimes.com/2013/07/01/us/job-title-key-to-inner-access-held-by-snowden.html?pagewanted=all.
30. Jeffrey Rosen, "The Naked Crowd: Balancing Privacy and Security in an Age of Terror," *Arizona Law Review* 46 (2004): 611.
31. Beth Givens, "Public Records on the Internet: The Privacy Dilemma," Privacy Rights Clearinghouse, http://www.cfp2002.org/proceedings/proceedings/givens.pdf.
32. See Amitai Etzioni and Radhika Bhat, "Second Chances, Social Forgiveness, and the Internet," *The American Scholar* (Spring 2009), http://theamericanscholar.org/second-chances-social-forgiveness-and-the-internet/#.UdX70DtilJk.
33. Most recent numbers from 2011. Federal Bureau of Investigation, "Clearances," *Crime in the United States*, 2011, http://www.fbi.gov/about-us/cjis/ucr/crime-in-the-u.s/2011/crime-in-the-u.s.-2011/clearances.
34. Matthew C. Waxman, in an interview with Jonathan Masters, "Has the FISA Court Gone Too Far?" Council on Foreign Relations, July 12, 2013, http://www.cfr.org/intelligence/has-fisa-court-gone-too-far/p31095. See also, Shaun Waterman, "Officials Say Americans Protected by Prism Surveillance Program," *The Washington Times*, June 10, 2013, http://www.washingtontimes.com/news/2013/jun/10/officials-say-americans-protected-by-prism-surveil/?page=all.
35. See, for example, GAO-05-866 "Agencies have Taken Key Steps to Protect Privacy in Selected Efforts, but Significant Compliance Issues Remain" (August 2005); GAO-08-536 "Alternatives Exist for Enhancing Protection of Personally Identifiable Information" (May 2008); GAO-12-961T "Federal Law Should Be Updated to Address Changing Technology Landscape" (July 2012); or GAO-12-981 "Measuring Progress and Addressing Potential Privacy Concerns Would Facilitate Integration into the National Airspace System" (September 2012).

36. David Jackson, "Obama: NSA Surveillance Programs Are 'Transparent,'" *USA TODAY*, June 18, 2013, http://www.usatoday.com/story/theoval/2013/06/18/obama-charlie-rose-program-nsa-surveillance/2433549/.
37. Peter Baker, "After Leaks, Obama Leads Damage Control Effort," *The New York Times*, June 28, 2013, http://www.nytimes.com/2013/06/29/us/politics/after-leaks-obama-leads-damage-control-effort.html?pagewanted=all.
38. Trevor Timm, "The NSA Leaks are Forcing More Transparency on Both Companies and the Government," Freedom of the Press Foundation, June 15, 2013, https://pressfreedomfoundation.org/blog/2013/06/nsa-leaks-are-forcing-more-transparency-both-companies-and-government.
39. Ellen Nakashima, "Bipartisan Group of Senators Urges Transparency on Phone Record Surveillance," *The Washington Post*, June 28, 2013, http://articles.washingtonpost.com/2013-06-28/world/40251889_1_phone-records-bulk-collection-senators.
40. Scott Shane and David E. Sanger, "Job Title Key to Inner Access Held by Snowden," *The New York Times*, June 30, 2013, http://www.nytimes.com/2013/07/01/us/job-title-key-to-inner-access-held-by-snowden.html?pagewanted=all.
41. Vindu Goel & Claire Cain Miller, "More Data on Privacy, but Picture Is No Clearer," *The New York Times,* June 17, 2013, http://www.nytimes.com/2013/06/18/technology/more-data-on-privacy-but-picture-is-no-clearer.html.
42. Spencer Ackerman, "Senators Press NSA Director for Answers on Secret Surveillance Program," *The Guardian,* June 12, 2013, http://www.guardian.co.uk/world/2013/jun/12/senate-nsa-director-keith-alexander.
43. Leonard H. Schrank and Juan C. Zarate, "Data Mining, without Big Brother," *The New York Times*, July 2, 2013, http://www.nytimes.com/2013/07/03/opinion/data-mining-without-big-brother.html?_r=0.
44. Ibid.
45. Ibid.
46. In 2001, six men from Buffalo, New York, took a trip to Pakistan for a spiritual retreat sponsored by Tablighi Jamaat—a group that, while associated with radicalism, was not designated as a terrorist organization. While there, however, the six men were accused of attending a terrorist training camp called Al Farooq and supposedly listened to a speech delivered by Osama bin Laden. No evidence was presented of a forthcoming plot on their part. There were no weapons found, no history of violence uncovered, nor was there any "clear and convincing evidence" that the six men were planning any sort of terrorist act. Yet they were still charged under the Antiterrorism and Effective Death Penalty act with a possible fifteen years in prison and $250,000 fine for their activities. JoAnn Wypijewski, "Living in an Age of Fire," *Mother Jones* (March/April 2003), http://www.motherjones.com/politics/2003/03/living-age-fire.
47. Kim Dotcom, "Prism: Concerns over Government Tyranny Are Legitimate," *The Guardian*, June 13, 2013, http://www.guardian.co.uk/commentisfree/2013/jun/13/prism-utah-data-center-surveillance.

Chapter 8

1. Alex Seitz-Wald and Elahe Izadi, "Criminal-Justice Reform, Brought to You by CPAC," *The National Journal* (March 7, 2014), http://www.nationaljournal.com/domesticpolicy/criminal-justice-reform-brought-to-you-by-cpac-20140307.
2. Charles Rangel, "Advancing the Dream Through Education," *Huffington Post*, April 4, 2013, http://www.huffingtonpost.com/rep-charles-rangel/mlk-assassination-anniversary_b_3014441.html.
3. EurWeb, "El DeBarge Debuts Music From New Album 'Second Chance' on 'BET Awards' Show" June 27, 2010, http://www.eurweb.com/2010/06/el-debarge-debuts-music-from-new-album-second-chance-on-bet-awards-show/.
4. Bernard Barsky "A Second Chance" *The Dayton Jewish Observer*, http://www.jewishdayton.org/observer/a-second-chance/.
5. Emily Gibb, "Program Supports Convicts and Helps Them after Prison" *Pittsburg Post-Gazette*, October 30, 2010, http://www.post-gazette.com/local/city/2010/10/30/Program-supports-convicts-and-helps-them-after-prison/stories/201010300239.
6. Ann Zimmerman And Kortney Stringer, "As Background Checks Proliferate, Ex-Cons Face a Lock on Jobs," *Wall Street Journal*, August 26, 2004.
7. Beth Givens, "Public Records on the Internet: The Privacy Dilemma," *Privacy Rights Clearinghouse* (2002), http://www.cfp2002.org/proceedings/proceedings/givens.pdf.
8. Julia Powles, "What Did the Media Miss with the 'Right to Be Forgotten' Coverage?" *The Guardian*, May 21, 2014.
9. Gary Fields and John R. Emshwiller, "As Arrest Records Rise, Americans Find Consequences Can Last a Lifetime," *Wall Street Journal*, August 18, 2014, http://online.wsj.com/articles/as-arrest-records-rise-americans-find-consequences-can-last-a-lifetime-1408415402.
10. "3 in 4 Former Prisoners in 30 States Arrested within 5 Years of Release," *Bureau of Justice Statistics*, April 22, 2014, http://www.bjs.gov/content/pub/press/rprts05p0510pr.cfm.
11. "Recidivism of Prisoners Released in 1994," *Bureau of Justice Statistics*, June 2002, http://www.bjs.gov/content/pub/pdf/rpr94.pdf.
12. Marshall Allen, "Colorado Transparency Unique," *Las Vegas Sun*, September 19, 2010, http://www.lasvegassun.com/news/2010/sep/19/colorado-transparency-unique/.
13. "How to Get Started," *U.S. Department of Health and Human Services, National Practitioner Data Bank*, http://www.npdb.hrsa.gov/hcorg/howToGetStarted.jsp.
14. Marian Wang, "How Complaints from a Single Doctor Caused the Gov't to Take Down a Public Database," *ProPublica*, November 10, 2011, http://www.propublica.org/article/how-complaints-from-a-doctor-caused-the-govt-to-take-down-a-public-database.
15. See Chapter 7, this volume.

16. See, for example, Amitai Etzioni, ed., *Civic Repentance* (Lanham: Rowman & Littlefield, 1999); Amitai Etzioni and David Carney, eds., *Repentance: A Comparative Perspective* (Lanham: Rowman & Littlefield, 1997).
17. Jeffrey Rosen, "The Right to Be Forgotten," *Stanford Law Review Online* 64 (2012): 88.
18. Viviane Reding, "The EU Data Protection Reform 2012: Making Europe the Standard Setter for Modern Data Protection Rules in the Digital Age" (speech, Munich, Germany, January 22, 2012), *European Commission*, http://europa.eu/rapid/press-release_SPEECH-12-26_en.htm.
19. Jeffrey Rosen, "The Right to Be Forgotten," 88.
20. John Hendel, "Why Journalists Shouldn't Fear Europe's 'Right to be Forgotten,'" *The Atlantic*, January 25, 2012, http://www.theatlantic.com/technology/archive/2012/01/why-journalists-shouldnt-fear-europes-right-to-be-forgotten/251955/?single_page=true.
21. Jeffrey Toobin, "The Solace of Oblivion," *New Yorker*, September 29, 2014, http://www.newyorker.com/magazine/2014/09/29/solace-oblivion.
22. Caitlin Dewey, "Pianist Asks *The Washington Post* to Remove a Concert Review under the E.U.'s 'Right to Be Forgotten' Ruling," *Washington Post*, October 31, 2014, http://www.washingtonpost.com/news/the-intersect/wp/2014/10/31/pianist-asks-the-washington-post-to-remove-a-concert-review-under-the-e-u-s-right-to-be-forgotten-ruling/.
23. "European privacy requests for search removals," *Google*, updated November 14, 2014, https://www.google.com/transparencyreport/removals/europeprivacy/.
24. David Kravets, "Google Has Removed 170,000-plus URLs under "Right to Be Forgotten" edict," *Ars Technica*, October 10, 2014, http://arstechnica.com/tech-policy/2014/10/google-has-removed-170000-plus-urls-under-right-to-be-forgotten-edict/.
25. Giancarlo Frosio, "EU Data Protection Authority Adopts Guidelines on the Implementation of the Right to Be Forgotten," The Center for Internet and Society at Stanford Law School, November 28, 2014, available at http://cyberlaw.stanford.edu/blog/2014/11/eu-data-protection-authority-adopts-guidelines-implementation-right-be-forgotten.

Chapter 9

1. To qualify as legal, the program is required to not target Americans. Thus, PRISM searches are carried out only when there is at least "51 percent confidence in a target's 'foreignness.'"
Timothy B. Lee, "How Congress Unknowingly Legalized PRISM in 2007," *The Washington Post*, June 6, 2013, http://www.washingtonpost.com/blogs/wonkblog/wp/2013/06/06/how-congress-unknowingly-legalized-prism-in-2007/.
2. See Amitai Etzioni, *The New Golden Rule: Community and Morality in a Democratic Society* (New York: Basic Books, 1996).

3. I have previously discussed this balance in the context of privacy and public health, public safety, sex offenders, and freedom of the press, among other rights. See Amitai Etzioni, *The Limits of Privacy* (New York: Basic Books, 1999); "The Privacy Merchants: What Is To Be Done?" *Journal of Constitutional Law* 14, 4 (2012): 929–51; and *How Patriotic Is the Patriot Act?: Freedom Versus Security in the Age of Terrorism* (NY: Routledge, 2004).
4. Gerald Gaus and Shane D. Courtland, "Liberalism," in Edward N. Zalta (ed.), *The Stanford Encyclopedia of Philosophy* (Spring 2011 Edition), http://plato.stanford.edu/entries/liberalism/. See also, John Rawls, *A Theory of Justice* (Cambridge, MA: Belknap Press, 1999).
5. Amitai Etzioni, "Communitarianism," *Encyclopædia Britannica*, Online Academic Edition, http://www.britannica.com/EBchecked/topic/1366457/communitarianism.
6. For a broader discussion of this strand of communitarianism, see Russell A. Fox, "Confucian and Communitarian Responses to Liberal Democracy," *The Review of Politics* 59, 3 (1997): 561–92. See also, Daniel Bell, "Daniel Bell on Confucianism and Free SpeechSpeech," audio interview with Free Speech Debate, (February 16, 2012), http://freespeechdebate.com/en/media/daniel-bell-on-confucianism-free-speech/; and Francis Fukuyama, "Confucianism and Democracy," *Journal of Democracy* 6, 2 (1995): 20–33.
7. Jed Rubenfeld, "The Right of Privacy," *Harvard Law Review* 102, 4 (1989): 740. The development of a right to privacy with respect to torts dates back a bit further to 1890 with the publication of Warren and Brandeis's "The Right to Privacy." See Richard A. Posner, "The Right of Privacy," *Georgia Law Review* 12, 3 (1978): 409.
See also Samuel D. Warren and Louis D. Brandeis, "The Right to Privacy," *Harvard Law Review* 4, 5 (1890): 193–220.
The exact emergence of the notion of a *Constitutional* right to privacy is a bit more difficult to exactly pinpoint. For more genealogy of constitutional right, see William M. Beaney, "The Constitutional Right to Privacy in the Supreme Court," *The Supreme Court Review* (1962): 212–51.
8. Anthony Lewis, *Freedom for the Thought We Hate: A Biography of the First Amendment* (New York: Basic Books, 2007), 23.
9. *Black's Law Dictionary*, "What Is the Public Interest?" *Black's Free Online Legal Dictionary*, 2nd ed., available at http://thelawdictionary.org/public-interest/.
10. See, for example, *United States v. Hartwell*, 436 F.3d 174, 180 (3d Cir. Pa. 2006); *Skinner v. Railway Labor Executives' Association*, 489 U.S. 602 (1989); and *National Treasury Employees Union v. Von Raab*, 489 U.S. 656 (1989).
11. *New York Times Co. v. United States*, 403 U.S. 713 (1971).
12. *United States v. Hartwell*, 436 F.3d 174, 180 (3d Cir. Pa. 2006).
13. See, for example, Bruce Schneier, "It's Smart Politics to Exaggerate Terrorist Threats," *CNN*, May 20, 2013, http://www.cnn.com/2013/05/20/opinion/schneier-security-politics/index.html.
14. See, for example, Randy E. Barnett, "The NSA's Surveillance Is Unconstitutional," *The Wall Street Journal*, July 11, 2013, http://online.wsj.com/article/SB10001

24127887323823004578593591276402574.html. See also, Conor Friedersdorf, "Lawbreaking at the NSA: Bring On a New Church Committee," *The Atlantic*, August 16, 2013, http://www.theatlantic.com/politics/archive/2013/08/lawbreaking-at-the-nsa-bring-on-a-new-church-committee/278750/.
15. Frank Thorp and Carrie Dann, "House Narrowly Votes Down Move to Gut NSA Data-Collection Program," *NBC News*, July 24, 2013, http://nbcpolitics.nbcnews.com/_news/2013/07/24/19658896-house-narrowly-votes-down-move-to-gut-nsa-data-collection-program?lite.
16. For example, *The New York Times*, "President Obama's Dragnet," June 6, 2013, http://www.nytimes.com/2013/06/07/opinion/president-obamas-dragnet.html?pagewanted=all.
17. Karen J. Greenberg, Susan Quatrone, et al., "Terrorist Trial Report Card: September 11, 2001–September 11, 2011," *Center on Law and Security, NYU School of Law* (2011), http://www.lawandsecurity.org/Portals/0/Documents/TTRC%20Ten%20Year%20Issue.pdf.
18. Anthony D. Romero, "Terrorists Are Criminals and Should be Tried in Civilian Court," *U.S. News & World Report*, February 16, 2010, http://www.usnews.com/opinion/articles/2010/02/16/terrorists-are-criminals-and-should-be-tried-in-civilian-court.
19. Paige Lavender, "Eric Holder Defends Civilian Trials for Terrorists," *The Huffington Post*, June 16, 2011, http://www.huffingtonpost.com/2011/06/16/eric-holder-civilian-trials-terrorism_n_878750.html.
20. Melanie Getreuer, "Why Civilian Courts Are Best for Terror Trials, Especially Boston Bombing Suspect," *The Christian Science Monitor*, April 30, 2013, http://www.csmonitor.com/Commentary/Opinion/2013/0430/Why-civilian-courts-are-best-for-terror-trials-especially-Boston-bombing-suspect.
21. Barack Obama, "Remarks by the President at the National Defense University," May 23, 2013, *The White House Office of the Press Secretary*, http://www.whitehouse.gov/the-press-office/2013/05/23/remarks- president-national-defense-university.
22. Barack Obama, as quoted in "Obama's Remarks at a News Conference," *The New York Times*, August 9, 2013, http://www.nytimes.com/2013/08/10/us/politics/obamas-remarks-at-a-news-conference.html?pagewanted=all&_r=0.
23. Mark Mazzetti, "Interpol Asks Nations to Help Track Terror Suspects Freed in Prison Breaks," *The New York Times*, August 3, 2013, http://www.nytimes.com/2013/08/04/world/interpol-issues-alert-on-prison-breaks-in-9-nations.html?_r=0.
24. Hillary Clinton, "America's Pacific Century," *Foreign Policy* (2011) http://www.foreignpolicy.com/articles/2011/10/11/americas_pacific_century?print=yes&hidecomments=yes&page=full.
25. Douglas A. Pryer, "The Rise of the Machines," *Military Review* (2013): 17, http://usacac.army.mil/CAC2/MilitaryReview/Archives/English/MilitaryReview_20130430_art005.pdf.
26. Lindsey Boerma, "Al Qaeda Embassy Plot Among 'Most Specific and Credible Threats' Since 9/11, McCaul says," *CBS News*, August 4, 2013, http://www.

cbsnews.com/8301-3460_162-57596909/al-qaeda-embassy-plot-among-most-specific-and-credible-threats-since-9-11-mccaul-says/.
27. Katherine Zimmerman, "Al Qaeda and Its Affiliates in 2013," *American Enterprise Institute* (2013): 2, http://www.criticalthreats.org/al-qaeda/al-qaeda-affiliates.
28. There is a debate regarding the nature of the relationship between al Qaeda and what are often designated its subsidiaries. For more on this point, see Leah Farrall, "Forward Focus: Assessing Al-Qaeda's In-Theater Capabilities," *IHS Defense, Security and Risk Consulting* (2012): 14–19, http://allthingsct.files.wordpress.com/2012/03/janes-article-2012.pdf.
29. Oren Dorell, "Al-Qaeda On the Run? No Way, Say Experts," *USA Today*, August 6, 2013, http://www.usatoday.com/story/news/world/2013/08/06/al-qaeda-middle-east/2623475/.
30. Sara Carter, "Al Qaeda Gaining Strength in Mali, North Africa," *The Washington Times*, March 26, 2013, http://www.washingtontimes.com/news/2013/mar/26/key-mali-lawmaker-challenges-obama-on-al-qaida-thr/?page=all. See also, Sudarsan Raghavan, "Nigerian Islamist Militants Return from Mali with Weapons, Skills," *The Washington Post*, May 31, 2013, http://articles.washingtonpost.com/2013-05-31/world/39642133_1_northern-mali-boko-haram-nigerian-islamist. See also, Adam Entous, Drew Hinshaw, and David Gauthier-Villars, "Militants, Chased from Mali, Pose New Threats," *The Wall Street Journal*, May 24, 2013, http://online.wsj.com/article/SB10001424127887323336104578503464066163002.html.
31. Zimmerman, "Al Qaeda and its Affiliates in 2013," 3.
32. *The Economist*, "The Unquenchable Fire," September 28, 2013, 21–23.
33. Zimmerman, "Al Qaeda and its Affiliates in 2013," 3.
34. Ibid.
35. Ibid.
36. "Islamic State Crisis: '3,000 European Jihadists Join Fight,'" BBC News, September 26 2014, http://www.bbc.com/news/world-middle-east-29372494.
37. Mark Mazzetti and Helene Cooper, "U.S. Officials and Experts at Odds on Threat Posed by ISIS," *New York Times*, August 22, 2014.
38. Liz Sly, "Al-Qaeda Expands in Syria via Islamic State," *The Washington Post*, August 12, 2013, http://www.washingtonpost.com/world/al-qaeda-expands-in-syria-via-islamic-state/2013/08/12/3ef71a26-036a-11e3-9259-e2aaf-e5a5f84_story.html.
39. Ibid.
40. Mark Mazzetti, "Interpol Asks Nations to Help Track Terror Suspects Freed in Prison Breaks," *The New York Times*, August 3, 2013, http://www.nytimes.com/2013/08/04/world/interpol-issues-alert-on-prison-breaks-in-9-nations.html?_r=0.
41. Ibid.
42. Ibid.
43. Carol J. Williams, "Spree of Jailbreaks Stirs Fear of New Al Qaeda Threat," *The Los Angeles Times*, July 31, 2013, http://www.latimes.com/news/world/worldnow/la-fg-wn-prison-breakouts-al-qaeda-20130730,0,3702148.story.

See also, Kareem Raheem and Ziad al-Sinjary, "Al Qaeda Prison Break: Hundreds of Militants Flee Iraq's Notorious Abu Ghraib jail," *NBC News*, July 22, 2013, http://worldnews.nbcnews.com/_news/2013/07/22/19615653-al-qaeda-prison-break-hundreds-of-militants-flee-iraqs-notorious-abu-ghraib-jail?lite.
44. *The Economist*, "The Unquenchable Fire," 21–23.
45. Tom Whitehead and Peter Foster, "Al-Shabaab Calls for Attacks on Oxford Street and Westfield Centres in New Terror Threat," *The Telegraph*, February 22, 2015.
46. For a detailed discussion of this point, see Paul K. Kerr and Mary Beth Nikitin, "Pakistan's Nuclear Weapons: Proliferation and Security Issues," *Congressional Research Service*, RL34248, March 19, 2013, http://www.fas.org/sgp/crs/nuke/RL34248.pdf; and Amy F. Woolf, "Nonstrategic Nuclear Weapons," *Congressional Research Service*, RL32572 (2012), http://www.fas.org/sgp/crs/nuke/RL32572.pdf.
47. Shaun Gregory, "The Terrorist Threat to Pakistan's Nuclear Weapons," *CTC Sentinel* 2, 7 (2009). See also, Dean Nelson and Tom Hussain, "Militants Attack Pakistan Nuclear Air Base," *The Telegraph*, August 16, 2012, http://www.telegraph.co.uk/news/worldnews/asia/pakistan/9479041/Militants-attack-Pakistan-nuclear-air-base.html; and Kapil Komireddi, "Take Pakistan's Nukes, Please," *Foreign Policy*, May 24, 2011, http://www.foreignpolicy.com/articles/2011/05/24/take_ pakistans_nukes_please.
48. Joseph Goldstein, "Judge Rejects New York's Stop-and-Frisk Policy," *The New York Times*, August 12, 2013, http://www.nytimes.com/2013/08/13/nyregion/stop-and-frisk-practice-violated-rights-judge-rules.html?pagewanted=all&_r=0.
49. *The New York Times*, "Stop-and-Frisk on Trial," May 21, 2013, http://www.nytimes.com/2013/05/22/opinion/stop-and-frisk-on-trial.html?ref=stopandfrisk.
50. Adam Serwer, "Holder Defends Civilian Courts," *The American Prospect*, March 16, 2010; Lavender, "Eric Holder Defends Civilian Trials for Terrorists"; and *The Associated Press*, "Eric Holder: Critics of Civilian Courts Handling Terrorism Cases 'Are Simply Wrong,'" *The Huffington Post*, May 11, 2013, http://www.huffingtonpost.com/2013/05/11/eric-holder-terrorism-cases_n_3260432.html.
51. See Matthew Kroenig and Barry Pavel, "How to Deter Terrorism," *The Washington Quarterly* 35, 2 (2012): 21–36, http://dx.doi.org/10.1080/0163660X.2012.665339: "In contrast [to the Cold War], deterrence against terrorism can only be partial at best. The United States cannot deter all terrorist activity, but as long as Washington can deter certain types of terrorists from engaging in certain types of terrorist activity, deterrence can contribute to national security goals."
52. Robert Pape, *Dying to Win: The Strategic Logic of Suicide Terrorism* (New York: Random House, 2006) ch. 2 and 5.
53. Clearly jihadists do not have a monopoly on this type of fanaticism, and the American criminal court system handles domestic terrorists, like Wade Michael Page who killed six worshippers in a Sikh temple in 2012. But zealots

such as these are also best dealt with in a preventative measure, and while they make up a tiny percentage of American criminals, they are a large part of the terrorist population, large enough to justify a different level of legal protection.
54. Matthew Waxman writes "criminal justice also has a preventive component . . . criminal law is generally retrospective in focus, in that it addresses past acts" in "Administrative Detention of Terrorists: Why Detain, and Detain Whom?" *Journal of National Security Law and Policy* 3 (2009): 12–13.
55. Coleen Rowley, "Memo to FBI Director Robert Mueller," May 21, 2002, http://globalresearch.ca/articles/ROW205A.html.
56. The FBI "provides guidance for law enforcement officers confronted with an emergency that may require interrogating a suspect held in custody about an imminent threat to public safety without providing Miranda warnings." Carl A. Benoit, "The 'Public Safety' Exception to Miranda," *FBI Law Enforcement Bulletin* (2011), http://www.fbi.gov/stats-services/publications/law-enforcement-bulletin/february2011/legal_digest.
57. John Yoo, "The Legality of the National Security Agency's Bulk Data Surveillance Programs," 9 *I/S: A Journal of Law and Policy for the Information Society* (2014): 301.
58. El-Motassadeq was later re-tried and convicted but the case demonstrates that "even in the most obvious and dramatic instances of terrorist involvement, substantial conviction cannot always be achieved." Brian Whitaker, "Member of 9/11 Terror Cell Jailed," *The Guardian*, August 19, 2005, http://www.guardian.co.uk/world/2005/aug/20/september11.usa.
59. Lucian E. Dervan, "The Surprising Lessons from Plea Bargaining in the Shadow of Terror," *Georgia State University Law Review* 27, 2 (2011): 239–98.
60. *The New York Times*, "Ali Saleh Kahlah al-Marri," May 1, 2009, http://topics.nytimes.com/top/reference/timestopics/people/m/ali_saleh_kahlah_al_marri/index.html.
61. See, for example: Mark A. Rothstein, "Privacy and Technology in the Twenty-First Century," *University of Louisville Law Review* 52 (2014): 333, 339.
62. See, for example: Jameel Jaffer, "Needles are Harder to Find in Bigger Haystacks," *The New York Times*, June 10, 2013, http://www.nytimes.com/roomfordebate/2013/06/09/is-the-nsa-surveillance-threat-real-or-imagined; Ron Wyden and Mark Udall, "Wyden, Udall Issue Statement on Effectiveness of Declassified NSA Programs," June 19, 2013, http://www.wyden.senate.gov/news/press-releases/wyden-udall-issue-statement-on-effectiveness-of-declassified-nsa-programs; Kevin Drum, "The NSA's Massive Call Record Surveillance Program Barely Accomplishes Anything," *Mother Jones*, July 31, 2013, http://www.motherjones.com/kevin-drum/2013/07/nsa-surveillance-call-record-program; and Robert Zubrin, "PRISM Costs Lives," *National Review Online*, June 21, 2013, http://www.nationalreview.com/article/351622/prism-costs-lives-robert-zubrin.
63. Keith Alexander, as quoted in "House Select Intelligence Committee Holds Hearing on Disclosure of National Security Agency Surveillance Programs," Federation of American Scientists, June 18, 2013, pp. 5, 11–13, https://www.fas.org/irp/congress/2013_hr/disclosure.pdf.

64. Jaffer, "Needles are Harder to Find in Bigger Haystacks."
65. Matthew Waxman, "How to Measure the Value of NSA Programs?" *Lawfare*, August 12, 2013, http://www.lawfareblog.com/2013/08/how-to-measure-the-value-of-nsa-programs/.
66. Wyden and Udall, "Wyden, Udall Issue Statement on Effectiveness of Declassified NSA Programs"; Drum, "The NSA's Massive Call Record Surveillance Program Barely Accomplishes Anything"; andJosh Gerstein, "The Metadata Muddle: How Effective Is Call-tracking?" *Politico*, June 19, 2013, http://www.politico.com/story/2013/06/nsa-surveillance-93075.html.
67. Ibid; and Waxman, "How to Measure the Value of NSA Programs?"
68. John Mueller and Mark G. Stewart, "Secret without Reason and Costly without Accomplishment: Questioning the National Security Agency's Metadata Program," *I/S: A Journal of Law and Policy for the Information Society* 10, 1 (2014): 407.
69. See Mark D. Young, "National Insecurity: The Impacts of Illegal Disclosures of Classified Information," *I/S: A Journal of Law and Policy for the Information Society*, 10, 1 (2014): 367: "The complexities, technology, and ambiguity of the modern security environment make it unlikely that any single intelligence source or program will provide a "smoking gun" on a national security threat [. . .] To overcome these realities, the Intelligence Community must apply a dizzying set of analytic techniques [. . .] This is no small task and it requires a mosaic of information, to include bulk metadata."
70. Peter L. Bergen, *The Osama bin Laden I Know* (New York: Free Press, 2006), 397; Jason Burke and Ian Black, "Al-Qaida: Tales from Bin Laden's Volunteers," *The Guardian*, September 10, 2009, http://www.theguardian.com/world/2009/sep/10/al-qaida-terrorism-bin-laden; Matthew Schofield, "Osama bin Laden Was Angry, Increasingly Irrelevant in Final Years, Letters Show," *McClatchy*, May 3, 2012, http://www.mcclatchydc.com/2012/05/03/v-print/147573/letters-show-bin-laden-was-angry.html.
71. Peter Finn and Anne E. Kornblut, "Al-Qaeda Couriers Provided Trail That Led to bin Laden," *The Washington Post*, May 2, 2011, http://articles.washingtonpost.com/2011-05-02/national/35264458_1_al-qaeda-couriers-osama-bin-laden-abu-faraj.
72. Sibohan Gorman, Evan Perez, and Janet Hook, "U.S. Collects Vast Data Trove," *The Wall Street Journal*, June 7, 2013, http://online.wsj.com/article/SB10001424127887324299104578529112289298922.html.
73. Dianne Feinstein, "Make NSA Programs More Transparent," *The Washington Post*, July 30, 2013, http://articles.washingtonpost.com/2013-07-30/opinions/40893423_1_nsa-analyst-national-security-agency-fisa-court; Bob Cesca, "CNET Reporter Posts Wildly Inaccurate Yet Totally Viral "Bombshell" About NSA Eavesdropping," *The Daily Banter*, June 16, 2013, http://thedailybanter.com/2013/06/cnet-reporter-posts-wildly-inaccurate-yet-totally-viral-bombshell-about-nsa-eavesdropping/. Examples of critics include: Glenn Greenwald, "Fisa Court Oversight: A Look Inside a Secret and Empty Process," *The Guardian*, June 18, 2013,

http://www.theguardian.com/commentisfree/2013/jun/19/fisa-court-oversight-process-secrecy; Conor Friedersdorf, "The NSA Scandal Is *All That*: A Polite Rebuttal to Marc Ambinder," *The Atlantic*, August 22, 2013, http://www.theatlantic.com/politics/archive/2013/08/the-nsa-scandal-is-em-all-that-em-a-polite-rebuttal-to-marc-ambinder/278886/.
74. Barton Gellman and Ashkan Soltani, "NSA Tracking Cellphone Locations Worldwide, Snowden Documents Show," *Washington Post*, December 4, 2013.
75. Information voluntarily handed over to another party does not receive Fourth Amendment protection "even if the information is revealed on the assumption that it will be used only for a limited purpose and the confidence placed in the third party will not be betrayed." *United States v. Miller*, 425 U.S. 435, 443 (1976); see also, Orin Kerr, "The Case for the Third Party Doctrine," *Michigan Law Review* 107 (2009): 561, 569–70. Earlier cases that built up this doctrine include *Lee v. United States* 343 U.S. 747 (1952) and *Couch v. United States* 409 U.S. 322 (1973).
76. *United States v. Miller*, 425 U.S. 435 (1976).
77. *Smith v. Maryland*, 442 U. S. 735 (1979).
78. Robert Litt, "General Counsel Litt's Remarks on Intelligence Collection," *Council on Foreign Relations,* July 18, 2013, http://www.cfr.org/intelligence/general-counsel-litts-remarks-intelligence-collection/p31130?cid=rss-primarysources-general_counsel_litt_s_remarks-071813.
79. As Orin Kerr notes: "The third-party doctrine is the Fourth Amendment rule scholars love to hate. It is the *Lochner* of search and seizure law, widely criticized as profoundly misguided . . . The verdict among commentators is has been frequent and apparently unanimous: The third-party doctrine is not only wrong, but horribly wrong. Even many state court judges have agreed. Over a dozen state Supreme Courts have rejected the doctrine under parallel provisions of their state constitutions. . . . Remarkably, even the U.S. Supreme Court has never offered a clear argument in its favor. Many Supreme Court opinions have applied the doctrine; few have defended it" ("The Case for the Third-Party Doctrine," 563–64). Though Kerr highlights the many criticisms of the doctrine, the cited paper attempts to defend the doctrine by defusing prominent criticism and presenting positive reasons for accepting the doctrine, e.g., it preserves the Fourth Amendment's technological neutrality and ensures its ex ante clarity.
80. Matthew Tokson, "Automation and the Fourth Amendment," *Iowa Law Review* 96 (2011): 581, 586.
81. Greenwald, "Fisa Court Oversight."
82. Friedersdorf, "The NSA Scandal Is *All That*: A Polite Rebuttal to Marc Ambinder."
83. *Pew Research,* "Few See Adequate Limits on NSA surveillance programs," July 26, 2013, http://www.people-press.org/2013/07/26/few-see-adequate-limits-on-nsa-surveillance-program/.
84. David Ignatius, "NSA Weighs Its Options," *The Washington Post*, July 26, 2013, http://articles.washingtonpost.com/2013-07-26/opinions/40859128_1_national-security-agency-surveillance-programs-calling-records.

85. Keith Alexander, as quoted in "Clear and Present Danger: Cyber-Crime; Cyber-Espionage; Cyber-Terror; and Cyber-War," *Aspen Security Forum*, July 18, 2013, http://www.nsa.gov/public_info/_files/speeches_testimonies/ GEN_A_Aspen_Security_Forum_Transcript_18_Jul_2013.pdf.
86. Ron Nixon, "U.S. Postal Service Logging All Mail for Law Enforcement," *The New York Times*, July 3, 2013, http://www.nytimes.com/2013/07/04/us/monitoring-of-snail-mail.html?pagewanted=all.
87. The data retention policies of the U.S. telecommunication giants vary from company to company and depending on the type of information. In 2011, the ACLU of North Carolina obtained through a FOIA request a chart created by the Department of Justice that details how long six major cellular service providers kept their data. Cell tower information was kept on a rolling one-year basis by Verizon; for 18 to 24 months by Sprint; and indefinitely since 2008 by AT&T. In contrast, the content of text messages was not retained at all by four of the companies, and kept for 3 to 5 days by Verizon and 90 days by Virgin Mobile (but only accessible to law enforcement with a warrant). See Allie Bohm, "How Long Is Your Cell Phone Company Hanging On To Your Data?" *American Civil Liberties* Union, September 28, 2011, http://www.aclu.org/blog/technology-and-liberty/how-long-your-cell-phone-company-hanging-your-data. Similarly, on *Washington Week* with Gwen Ifill, Pete Williams said that, "the phone companies only keep this data for 30 to 90 days. They don't have any reason. There's no business reason for the phone company to keep six-month old phone records. So they throw it away. Unless the government gets it, it's not going to keep it." See Pete Williams as quoted in "'Transcript,' *Washington Week with Gwen Ifill*," June 7, 2013, http://www.pbs.org/weta/washingtonweek/watch/transcript/39902.
88. Mike Rogers, "'This Week' Transcript: Sen. Dianne Feinstein and Rep. Mike Rogers," *ABC This Week*, June 9, 2013, http://abcnews.go.com/Politics/week-transcript-sen-dianne-feinstein-rep-mike-rogers/story?id=19343314&page=4#.Udsm2jtilJl.
89. Legal Information Institute, "Fourth Amendment," *Cornell University Law School*, http://www.law.cornell.edu/wex/fourth_amendment.
90. American Civil Liberties Union "ACLU Motion for Preliminary Injunction in ACLU v Clapper," (2013): 4, https://www.aclu.org/national-security/aclu-v-clapper-legal-documents.
91. Eve Brensike Primus, "Disentangling Administrative Searches," *Columbia Law Review* 111 (2011): 256, http://www.columbialawreview.org/wp-content/uploads/2011/03/111-2_Primus.pdf.
92. Ibid., 263.
93. *Illinois v. Lidster*, 540 U.S. 419, 427 (2004).
94. See *Michigan Department of State Police v. Sitz*, 110 S. Ct. 2481 (1990).
95. See: *United States v. Hartwell*, 436 F.3d 174, 180 (3d Cir. Pa. 2006); and *Electronic Privacy Information Center v. United States Department of Homeland Security*, 653 F.3d 1, 10–11 (D.C. Cir. 2011).
96. Primus, "Disentangling Administrative Searches," 263–64.
97. *Michigan Department of State Police v. Sitz*, 496 U.S. at 455.
98. Ibid., 451.

99. See, for example, *Illinois v. Lidster*, 540 U.S. 419, 427 (2004) (quoting *Brown v. Texas*, 443 U.S. 47, 51 (1979)).
100. *United States v. Hartwell*, 436 F.3d 174, 180 (3d Cir. Pa. 2006).
101. Ibid.
102. *United States v. Davis*, 482 F.2d 893, 908.
103. *United States v. Pulido-Baquerizo* 800 F.2d 899, 901.
104. Jeffrey Rosen, "The Naked Crowd: Balancing Privacy and Security in an Age of Terror," *Arizona Law Review* 46 (2004): 613.
105. United States Foreign Intelligence Surveillance Court, "In Re Application of the Federal Bureau of Investigation for an Order Requiring the Production of Tangible Things from [Redacted]," *American Civil Liberties Union* (2013): 13–14, https://www.aclu.org/files/assets/br13-09-primary-order.pdf.
106. Ibid., 15.
107. Ibid.
108. Robert Litt, "Privacy, Technology, and National Security: An Overview of Intelligence Collection," *Brookings Institution*, July 19, 2013, http://www.dni.gov/index.php/newsroom/speeches-and-interviews/195-speeches-interviews-2013/896-privacy,-technology-and-national-security-an-overview-of-intelligence-collection.
109. Charlie Savage, "Senate Panel Presses N.S.A on Phone Logs," *The New York Times*, July 31, 2013, http://www.nytimes.com/2013/08/01/us/nsa-surveillance.html?pagewanted=all; and "Section 215 White Paper," U.S. Department of Justice, p. 3, http://www.nytimes.com/interactive/2013/08/10/us/politics/10obama-surveillance-documents.html?_r=0.
110. United States Foreign Intelligence Surveillance Court, "In Re Application of the Federal Bureau of Investigation for an Order Requiring the Production of Tangible Things From [Redacted]," 7.
111. Section 215 White Paper, 4.
112. Christopher Harress, "NSA Surveillance to Continue: Senate Votes Against USA Freedom Act," *International Business Times*, November 18, 2014.
113. Charlie Savage, "N.S.A. Phone Data Collection Could Go On, Even If a Law Expires," *New York Times*, November 19, 2014.
114. Barton Gellman et al., "In NSA-intercepted Data, Those Not Targeted Far Outnumber the Foreigners Who Are," *Washington Post*, July 5, 2014.
115. See, for example, Mark Udall and Ron Wyden, "The White House Should End the Bulk Collection of Americans' Phone Records," *The Washington Post*, July 26, 2013, http://articles.washingtonpost.com/2013-07-26/opinions/40864658_1_phone-records-collection-program-americans.
116. See 83.
117. Marc Rotenberg and Chris Jay Hoofnagle, open letter to Reps. Adam Putnam and William Clay, Electronic Privacy Information Center (2003), http://epic.org/privacy/profiling/datamining3.25.03.html; Arshad Mohammed and Sara Kehaulani Goo, "Government Increasingly Turning to Data Mining," *The Washington Post*, June 15, 2006, http://www.washingtonpost.com/wp-dyn/content/article/2006/06/14/AR2006061402063.html; and

Heidi Boghosian, "The Business of Surveillance," *Human Rights Magazine* 39 (2013), http://www.americanbar.org/publications/human_rights_magazine_home/2013_vol_39/may_2013_n2_privacy/the_business_of_surveillance.html.
118. Christopher Slobogin, "Government Data Mining and the Fourth Amendment," *The University of Chicago Law Review* 75 (2008): 317, 320.
119. Ibid.
120. "Rein in the Surveillance State," American Civil Liberties Union, accessed March 3, 2015 at https://www.aclu.org/rein-surveillance-state.
121. Jeff Mason, "Exclusive: Obama Sharply Criticizes China's Plans for New Technology Rules," Reuters, March 2, 2015.
122. Erin Kelly, "Tech Companies Say NSA Spying Harms Competitiveness," *USA Today*, October 7, 2014.
123. Sam_Frizell, "The FBI and NSA Hate Apple's Plan to Keep Your iPhone Data Secret," *Time*, September 27 2014.
124. Glenn Greenwald and Ewen MacAskill, "NSA Prism Program Taps in to User Data of Apple, Google and Others," *The Guardian*, June 6, 2013, http://www.theguardian.com/world/2013/jun/06/us-tech-giants-nsa-data.
125. "Cover Letter and 2009 Report on the National Security Agency's Bulk Collection Program for USA PATRIOT Act Reauthorization," Office of the Director of National Intelligence, Washington, DC (2013), http://www.dni.gov/files/documents/2009_CoverLetter_Report_Collection.pdf.
126. "Letters to the House Permanent Select Committee on Intelligence and the Senate Select Committee on Intelligence Leadership regarding Section 702 Congressional White Paper 'The Intelligence Community's Collection Programs Under Title VII of the Foreign Intelligence Surveillance Act,'" Office of the Director of National Intelligence, Washington, DC (2013): 6, http://www.dni.gov/files/documents/Ltr%20to%20HPSCI%20Chairman%20Rogers%20and%20Ranking%20Member%20Ruppersberger_Scan.pdf.
127. James Ball, "NSA Collects Millions of Text Messages Daily in 'Untargeted' Global Sweep," *The Guardian*, January 16, 2014.
128. Barton Gellman and Ashkan Soltani, "NSA Infiltrates Links to Yahoo, Google Data Centers Worldwide, Snowden Documents Say," *Washington Post*, October 30, 2013.
129. Glenn Greenwald and Ewen MacAskill, "NSA Prism Program Taps in to User Data of Apple, Google and Others," *The Guardian*, June 6, 2013, http://www.theguardian.com/world/2013/jun/06/us-tech-giants-nsa-data. With respect to the Americans whose data is collected, the *Washington Post* reports that "The surveillance may not 'intentionally target' an American, but the NSA can obtain the private communications of Americans as part of a request that officially 'targets' a foreigner" (Lee, "Here's Everything We Know about PRISM to Date").
130. Litt, "Privacy, Technology, and National Security."
131. *United States v. Verdugo-Urquidez*, 856 F.2d 1214, 1218 (9th Cir. 1988).

132. It was initially unclear whether *Verdugo* would evolve into a general rule or a fact-specific finding, so I think a clarifying point is in order. In order to draw the conclusion that the finding does in fact limit Fourth Amendment rights this broadly, it would be necessary to also provide evidence that the finding has since been interpreted as a general rule rather than a fact-specific finding. A wide range of dissenting and concurring opinions written by the various justices has apparently 'muddied the water' and led *Verdugo* to be understood to apply in a "diverse array" of situations.
133. This is a reference to the eight Nazis who came entered the United States via submarine with explosives and instructions to destroy vital war-time infrastructure. President Roosevelt set up a military commission for their prosecution. Stuart Taylor Jr., "The Bill to Combat Terrorism Doesn't Go Far Enough," *National Journal*, October 29, 2001, http://www3.nationaljournal.com/members/buzz/2001/openingargument/102901.htm.
134. Anderson makes a similar point. The constitutional rights and criminal protections granted to American citizens 'have developed *within* a particular political community, and fundamentally reflect decisions about rights within a fundamentally domestic, democratic setting in which all of us have a stake in both side of the equation . . . because we are part of the political community which must consider both individual rights and collective security . . . Terrorists who come from outside this society . . . cannot be assimilated into the structure of the ordinary criminal trial." (Kenneth Anderson, "What To Do with Bin Laden and Al Qaeda Terrorists?: A Qualified Defense of Military Commissions and United States Policy on Detainees at Guantanamo Bay Naval Base," *Harvard Journal of Law and Public Policy* [2001–2002]: 610.)
135. *United States v. Verdugo-Urquidez*, 856 F.2d 1214, 1218 (9th Cir. 1988).
136. Ibid.
137. Ibid.
138. Mary Lynn Nicholas, *United States v. Verdugo-Urquidez: Restricting the Borders of the Fourth Amendment*, Fordham International Law Journal 14/1 (1990): 270.
139. Ibid.
140. "H.R. 6304 (110th): FISA Amendments Act of 2008," http://www.govtrack.us/congress/bills/110/hr6304/text.
141. Ibid.
142. "50 USC § 1801 – Definitions," *Legal Information Institute*, http://www.law.cornell.edu/uscode/text/50/1801.
143. Barton Gellman and Laura Poitras, "U.S., British Intelligence Mining Data from Nine U.S. Internet Companies in Broad Secret Program," *The Washington Post*, June 6, 2013, http://www.washingtonpost.com/investigations/us-intelligence-mining-data-from-nine-us-internet-companies-in-broad-secret-program/ 2013/06/06/3a0c0da8-cebf-11e2-8845-d970ccb04497_story_1.html.
144. "Letter from the Honorable Reggie B. Walton to Senator Patrick Leahy" (2013), https://www.fas.org/irp/news/2013/07/fisc-leahy.pdf.

145. Ibid.
146. Ibid.
147. Ibid.
148. "The Universal Declaration of Human Rights," *The United Nations*, http://www.un.org/en/documents/udhr/.
149. Richard B. Lillich, as quoted in David Cole, "Are Foreign Nationals Entitled to the Same Constitutional Rights As Citizens?" *Georgetown Law Faculty Publications and Other Works* 297 (2003): 372, http://scholarship.law.georgetown.edu/facpub/297.
150. William A. Schabas, "Invalid Reservations to the International Covenant on Civil and Political Rights: Is the United States Still a Party?" *Brooklyn Journal of International Law* 21 (1995): 277, 280, as quoted in Kristina Ash, "U.S. Reservations to the International Covenant on Civil and Political Rights: Credibility Maximization and Global Influence," *Northwestern Journal of International Human Rights* (2005), http://scholarlycommons.law.northwestern.edu/cgi/viewcontent.cgi?article=1018&context=njihr.
151. For more on this "tu quoque" argument, see Jack Goldsmith, "Spying on Allies," *Lawfare*, July 1, 2013, http://www.lawfareblog.com/2013/07/spying-on-allies/. Goldsmith notes that there is even some reason for thinking that widespread spying provides a normative and legal defense of privacy violations, quoting a 1999 Department of Defense Report wherein it was contended that "the lack of strong international legal sanctions for peacetime espionage may also constitute an implicit application of the international law doctrine called 'tu quoque' (roughly, a nation has no standing to complain about a practice in which it itself engages)." This claim would also defuse more specific criticisms that PRISM is spying even on our allies. See, for example, Steven Erlanger, "Outrage in Europe Grows Over Spying Disclosures," *The New York Times*, July 1, 2013, http://www.nytimes.com/2013/07/02/world/europe/france-and-germany-piqued-over-spying-scandal.html?pagewanted=all.
152. John Napier Tye, "Meet Executive Order 12333: The Reagan Rule That Lets the NSA Spy on Americans," *Washington Post*, July 18, 2014.
153. In an editorial response, the "civil liberties protection officer for the Office of the Director of National Intelligence" defended the order, noting that "Oversight is extensive and multi-layered," but this oversight appears to be essentially internal to the Executive branch. See Alexander W. Joel, *The Truth About Executive Order 12333*, *Politico*, August 18, 2014.
154. One issue with Executive Order 12333 is the lack of oversight. Sen. Dianne Feinstein (D-CA), the Senate Intelligence Committee chair, said in August 2013 that the committee is less well-informed on "intelligence gathering that relies solely on presidential authority," and "said she planned to ask for more briefings on those programs." A "senior committee staff member" likewise noted that "the committee is far less aware of operations conducted under 12333," as the committee cannot ask questions about programs of which it is unaware, and the NSA is not obliged to volunteer such information. See Barton Gellman and Ashkan Soltani, "NSA Collects Millions of e-mail Address Books Globally," *Washington Post*, October 14, 2013.

155. Ben Jacobs and Tim Mak, "Boehner May Not Have the Ability to Sue Obama After All," *The Daily Beast*, June 26, 2014; see also Richard Wolf, "High Court Rules against Obama on Recess Appointments," *USA Today*, June 26, 2014.
156. "H.R. 6304 (110th): FISA Amendments Act of 2008," http://www.govtrack.us/congress/bills/110/hr6304/text.
157. "DNI Statement on Activities Authorized Under Section 702 of FISA," Office of the Director of National Intelligence, http:/www.dni.gov/index.php/newsroom/press-releases/191-press-releases-2013/869-dni-statement-on-activities-authorized-under-section-702-of-fisa.
158. "NSA Slides Explain the PRISM Data-Collection Program," *The Washington Post*, June 6, 2013, http://www.washingtonpost.com/wp-srv/special/politics/prism-collection-documents/.
159. Ibid.
160. Ibid.
161. Ibid.
162. Spencer Ackerman and James Ball, "NSA Loophole Allows Warrantless Search for U.S. Citizens' Emails and Phone Calls," *The Guardian*, August 9, 2013, http://www.theguardian.com/world/2013/aug/09/nsa-loophole-warrantless-searches-email-calls#.
163. Ron Wyden and Mark Udall, open letter to Keith Alexander, June 24, 2013, http://www.fas.org/irp/congress/2013_cr/wyden-nsa.pdf.
164. Ellen Nakashima, "NSA Gathered Thousands of Americans' e-mails before Court Ordered It to Revise Its Tactics," *The Washington Post*, August 21, 2013, http://articles.washingtonpost.com/2013-08-21/world/ 41431823_1_court-opinion-chief-judge-government-surveillance.
165. Barton Gellman, "NSA Broke Privacy Rules Thousands of Times Per Year, Audit Finds," *The Washington Post*, August 15, 2013, http://www.washingtonpost.com/world/national-security/nsa-broke-privacy-rules-thousands-of-times-per-year-audit-finds/2013/08/15/3310e554-05ca-11e3-a07f-49ddc7417125_story.html.
166. Benjamin Wittes, "The NSA, the Washington Post, and the Administration," *Lawfare*, August 18, 2013, http://www.lawfareblog.com/2013/08/the-nsa-the-washington-post-and-the-administration/. This point also made by Jennifer Rubin who argues: "If there are 20 million inquiries each month over a year span that works out to 240,000,000. That equates to an error rate of .00001156666. If the NSA figures are accurate this is the most airtight surveillance program in history ("NSA Scandal or Near-Perfection?" *The Washington Post*, August 18, 2013, http://www.washingtonpost.com/blogs/right-turn/wp/2013/08/18/nsa-scandal-or-near-perfection/).
167. Wittes, "The NSA, the *Washington Post*, and the Administration."
168. Gellman, "NSA Broke Privacy Rules Thousands of Times per Year, Audit Finds."
169. Wittes, "The NSA, the *Washington Post*, and the Administration."
170. Andrea Peterson, "LOVEINT: When NSA Officers Use Their Spying Power on Love Interests," *The Washington Post*, August 24, 2013, http://www.washingtonpost.com/blogs/the-switch/wp/2013/08/24/loveint-when-nsa-officers-use-their-spying-power-on-love-interests/.

171. Wittes, "The NSA, the *Washington Post*, and the Administration."
172. Litt, "Privacy, Technology, a National Security"; and Sean Mirski and Benjamin Wittes, "The NSA Documents Part VI: The 2011 Minimization Procedures," *Lawfare*, August 23, 2013, http://www.lawfareblog.com/2013/08/the-nsa-documents-part-vi-the-2011-minimization-procedures/.
173. Gellman, "NSA Broke Privacy Rules Thousands of Times per Year, Audit Finds."
174. Corey M. Then, "Searches and Seizures of Americans Abroad: Re-examining the Fourth Warrant Clause and the Foreign Intelligence Exception Five Years After United States v. Bin Laden," *Duke Law Journal* 55 (2005): 1064.
175. Ibid., 1065–68.
176. Zeke J. Miller, "Obama Administration Declassifies Details On 'PRISM,' Blasts 'Reckless' Media and Leakers," *TIME*, June 8, 2013, http://swampland.time.com/2013/06/08/obama-administration-declassifies-details-on-prism-blasts-reckless-media-and-leakers/.
177. Edward Liu, "Reauthorization of the FISA Amendments Act," *Congressional Research Service*, Washington, DC, April 2013, p. 5, http://www.cfr.org/intelligence/crs-reauthorization-fisa-amendments-act/p30877.
178. Ackerman and Ball, "NSA Loophole Allows Warrantless Search for U.S. Citizens' Emails and Phone Calls."
179. Gellman and Poitras, "U.S., British Intelligence Mining Data from Nine U.S. Internet Companies in Broad Secret Program."
180. "H.R. 6304 (110th): FISA Amendments Act of 2008," http://www.govtrack.us/congress/bills/110/hr6304/text.
181. *United States v. Ramsey*, 431 U.S. 606, 616 (1977).
182. *Almeida-Sanchez v. United States*, 413 U.S. 266, 272, (1973).
183. "Will the Fourth Amendment Protect Your Laptop at the Border?" American Bar Association, September 17, 2013, http://www.americanbar.org/publications/gp_solo/2012/november_december2012privacyandconfidentiality/will_fourth_amendment_protect_your_laptop_border.html.
184. Yule Kim, "Protecting the US Perimeter: Border Searches Under the Fourth Amendment," *Congressional Research Service* (2009), http://www.fas.org/sgp/crs/homesec/RL31826.pdf.
185. See Michael Riley, "NSA Said to Exploit Heartbleed Bug for Intelligence for Years," *Bloomberg*, April 12, 2014; David Sanger, "Obama Lets N.S.A. Exploit Some Internet Flaws, Officials Say," *New York Times*, April 12, 2014; Michael Daniel, "Heartbleed: Understanding When We Disclose Cyber Vulnerabilities," *White House Blog*, April 28, 2014.
186. Glenn Greenwald and Ewen MacAskill, "Boundless Informant: The NSA's Secret Tool to Track Global Surveillance Data," *The Guardian*, June 11, 2013.
187. Barton Gellman and Ashkan Soltani, "NSA Surveillance Program Reaches 'Into the Past' to Retrieve, Replay Phone Calls," *Washington Post*, March 18, 2014.
188. James Ball, "NSA Collects Millions of Text Messages Daily in 'Untargeted' Global Sweep," *The Guardian*, January 16, 2014.
189. Gellman and Soltani, "NSA Tracking Cellphone Locations Worldwide."

230 NOTES

190. Gellman and Soltani, "NSA Collects Millions of e-mail Address Books Globally."
191. Glenn Greenwald, "XKeyscore: NSA Tool Collects 'Nearly Everything a User Does on the Internet,'" *The Guardian*, July 31, 2013; see also Barton Gellman et al., "In NSA-intercepted Data, Those Not Targeted Far Outnumber the Foreigners Who Are," *Washington Post*, July 5, 2014.
192. Hendrik Hertzberg, "Snoop Scoops," *The New Yorker*, June 24, 2013, http://www.newyorker.com/talk/comment/2013/06/24/130624taco_talk_hertzberg; for the opposing view, see Katherine Strandburg, "Membership Lists, Metadata, and Freedom of Association's Specificity Requirement," *ISJLP* 10: 327 ("relational surveillance using so-called metadata implicates the First Amendment right to freedom of association," which "imposes specificity requirements on government acquisition of associational information that are not met by the NSA's comprehensive and undifferentiated collection and scrutiny of associational information.")
193. Luke Johnson, "Obama Defends NSA Programs, Says Congress Knew About Surveillance," *The Huffington Post*, June 7, 2013, http://www.huffingtonpost.com/2013/06/07/obama-nsa_n_3403389.html.
194. Ellen Nakashima, "NSA Gathered Thousands of Americans e-mails before Court Ordered It to Revise Its Tactics."
195. Trevor Timm, "President Obama claims the NSA has Never Abused Its Authority. That's False," *The Guardian*, December 31, 2013.
196. Chris Strohm, "Lawmakers Probe Willful Abuses of Power by NSA Analysts," *Bloomberg*, August 24, 2013.
197. Siobhan Gorman, "NSA Officers Spy on Love Interests," *Wall Street Journal*, August 23, 2013.
198. Kyle Balluck, "Former CIA Official Admits to 'Very Minor' NSA Abuses," *The Hill*, January 19, 2014.
199. Barton Gellman, "NSA Broke Privacy Rules Thousands of Times per Year, Audit Finds," *Washington Post*, August 15, 2013.
200. Carol D. Leonnig, "Court: Ability to Police U.S. Spying Program Limited," *Washington Post*, August 15, 2013.
201. Ibid.
202. John D. Bates, "April 2011 Submissions," as published in *The Washington Post*, http://apps.washingtonpost.com/g/page/national/fisa-court-documents-on-illegal-nsa-e-mail-collection-program/409/ p. 16, note 14.
203. Scott Shane, "Court Upbraided N.S.A. on Its Use of Call-Log Data," *New York Times*, September 10, 2013, http://www.nytimes.com/2013/09/11/us/court-upbraided-nsa-on-its-use-of-call-log-data.html?pagewanted=all.
204. Ibid.
205. Eyder Peralta, "Senators Announce Bill That Ends NSA Phone Records Collection," *NPR*, September 25, 2013, http://www.npr.org/blogs/thetwo-way/2013/09/25/226263270/senators-announce-bill-that-ends-nsa-phone-records-collection.
206. Such demands came not only from rights advocates such as the American Civil Liberties Union (see, for example, ACLU, "Bringing Transparency to the

FISA Court," 2013, https://www.aclu.org/bringing-transparency-fisa-court), but also from affected tech firms (see, for example, Alanna Petroff, "Marissa Mayer Calls for More NSA Transparency," *CNN Money*, January 22 2014) and academia (see, for example, Bryce Clayton Newell, "The Massive Metadata Machine: Liberty, Power, and Secret Mass Surveillance in the U.S. and Europe," *ISJLP* 10: 481).

207. Peter Baker, "After Leaks, Obama Leads Damage Control Effort," *The New York Times*, June 28, 2013, http://www.nytimes.com/2013/06/29/us/politics/after-leaks-obama-leads-damage-control-effort.html?pagewanted=all.
208. Trevor Timm, "The NSA Leaks Are Forcing More Transparency on Both Companies and the Government," *Freedom of the Press Foundation*, June 15, 2013, https://pressfreedomfoundation.org/blog/2013/06/nsa-leaks-are-forcing-more-transparency-both-companies-and-government.
209. Ellen Nakashima, "Bipartisan Group of Senators Urges Transparency on Phone Record Surveillance," *The Washington Post*, June 28, 2013, http://articles.washingtonpost.com/2013-06-28/world/40251889_1_phone-records-bulk-collection-senators.
210. Scott Shane, "U.S. is Urged to Consider Releasing Data on Calls," *The New York Times*, September 14, 2013, A10.
211. Ibid.
212. Scott Shane, "New Leaked Document Outlines U.S. Spending on Intelligence Agencies," *The New York Times*, August 29, 2013, http://www.nytimes.com/2013/08/30/us/politics/leaked-document-outlines-us-spending-on-intelligence.html?pagewanted=all.
213. Intelligence official reports that a leak to the press regarding the government's capability to intercept al Qaeda's electronic communications prompted the group to immediately and dramatically change the way in which they communicated and the sorts of information that passed through electronic channels to avoid U.S. surveillance. See, Eric Schmitt and Michael S. Schmidt, "Qaeda Plot Leak has Undermined U.S. Intelligence."
214. Scott Shane and David E. Sanger, "Job Title Key to Inner Access Held by Snowden," *The New York Times*, June 30, 2013, http://www.nytimes.com/2013/07/01/us/job-title-key-to-inner-access-held-by-snowden.html?pagewanted=all.
215. Vindu Goel and Claire Cain Miller, "More Data on Privacy, but Picture Is No Clearer," *The New York Times*, June 17, 2013, http://www.nytimes.com/2013/06/18/technology/more-data-on-privacy-but-picture-is-no-clearer.html.
216. Spencer Ackerman, "Senators Press NSA Director for Answers on Secret Surveillance Program," *The Guardian*, June 12, 2013, http://www.guardian.co.uk/world/2013/jun/12/senate-nsa-director-keith-alexander.
217. Andrea Peterson and Scott Wilson, "Former U.S. Officials to Assess Surveillance Policy," *The Washington Post*, August 23, 2013, A2.
    Such a board might also take the form of something along the lines of the Privacy and Civil Liberties Oversight Board. See Garrett Hatch, "Privacy and

Civil Liberties Oversight Board: New Independent Agency Status," *Congressional Research Service*, RL34385 7-5700 (2012), http://www.fas.org/sgp/crs/misc/RL34385.pdf.
218. Janet Hook and Carol E. Lee, "Obama Plan to Revamp NSA Faces Obstacles," *The Wall Street Journal*, August 12, 2013, A4; see also, Dan Roberts, "US Must Fix Secret FISA Courts, Says Top Judge Who Granted Surveillance Orders," *The Guardian*, July 9, 2013, http://www.theguardian.com/law/2013/jul/09/fisa-courts-judge-nsa-surveillance. President Obama, himself, proposed such a measure. See "President Obama Weighs In On Information-Gathering," *The Washington Post*, August 9, 2013, http://articles.washingtonpost.com/2013-08-09/opinions/41237761_1_president-obama-government-surveillance-technologies.
219. Andrea Peterson, "The House is Divided Over Almost Everything. But FISA Court Reform Might Be Able to Unite It," *The Washington Post*, October 1, 2013, http://www.washingtonpost.com/blogs/the-switch/wp/2013/10/01/the-house-is-divided-over-almost-everything-but-fisa-court-reform-might-be-able-to-unite-it/. This proposal would have the advocate assist communications companies and analyze all requests sent before the FISA court—though judges could exclude the advocate from certain cases. The advocate would have the option to appeal cases to the FISA Court of Review.
220. Shayana Kadidial, "NSA Surveillance: The Implications for Civil Liberties," *ISJLP* 10: 433: arguing more broadly that "many reform proposals [. . .] are merely 'tinkering with the machinery of mass surveillance' [. . .] the overbroad scope of the FAA statute and the statutes governing third-party records requests (NSLs, Section 215 orders, and their like) is the true problem, and one that would go unaddressed even if the public had an in camera advocate, the judges sat in banks of three, were not hand-picked by the Chief Justice, and the court enjoyed more transparency than exists now."
221. See, for example: Matthew C. Waxman, in an interview with Jonathan Masters, "Has the FISA Court Gone Too Far?" *Council on Foreign Relations*, July 12, 2013, http://www.cfr.org/intelligence/has-fisa-court-gone-too-far/p31095.
222. Such a measure might resemble the Whistleblower Protection Enhancement Act. See Government Accountability Project, "Whistleblower Protection Enhancement Act (WPEA)," http://www.whistleblower.org/program-areas/legislation/wpea.
223. See 50 U.S.C.S. §§ 413, 413a, 413b(c), (e). (2007).
224. Bruce Ackerman, "Surveillance and the FISA Court," *Los Angeles Times*, September 24, 2013, http://www.latimes.com/opinion/commentary/la-oe-ackerman-fisa-reform-20130924,0,5246449.story.
225. Dianne Feinstein, "Make NSA Programs More Transparent," *The Washington Post*, July 30, 2013, http://articles.washingtonpost.com/2013-07-30/opinions/40893423_1_nsa-analyst-national-security-agency-fisa-court.
226. Ken Dilanian, "Russian Spies Were Succeeding, FBI Official Says," *Los Angeles Times*, October 31, 2011, http://articles.latimes.com/2011/oct/31/nation/la-na-russian-spies-20111101.

227. Such a measure is proposed in: Kenneth L. Wainstein, "Memorandum for the Attorney General," November 20, 2007, 9, http://www.emptywheel.net/wp-content/uploads/2013/06/111120-Wainstein-memo.pdf. However, it has been noted that the efficacy of audit trails can be compromised through the introduction of loopholes. For more on this point, see Patrick C. Toomey, "Raiding the 'Corporate Store': The NSA's Unfettered Access to a Vast Pool of Americans' Phone Data," *American Civil Liberties Union*, August 2, 2013, https://www.aclu.org/blog/national-security/raiding-corporate-store-nsas-unfettered-access-vast-pool-americans-phone-data.
228. Leonard H. Schrank and Juan C. Zarate, "Data Mining, Without Big Brother," *The New York Times*, July 2, 2013, http://www.nytimes.com/2013/07/03/opinion/data-mining-without-big-brother.html?_r=0.
229. Ibid.
230. Ibid.
231. In 2001, six men from Buffalo, New York, took a trip to Pakistan for a spiritual retreat sponsored by Tablighi Jamaat—a group that, while associated with radicalism, was not designated as a terrorist organization. While there, however, the six men were accused of attending a terrorist training camp called Al Farooq and supposedly listened to a speech delivered by Osama bin Laden. No evidence was presented of a forthcoming plot on their part. There were no weapons found, no history of violence uncovered, nor was there any 'clear and convincing evidence' that the six men were planning any sort of terrorist act. Yet they were still charged under the Antiterrorism and Effective Death Penalty act with a possible fifteen years in prison and $250,000 fine for their activities. JoAnn Wypijewski, "Living in an Age of Fire," *Mother Jones*, March/April 2003, http://www.motherjones.com/politics/2003/03/living-age-fire.
232. Greg Miller and Sari Horwitz, "Boston Case Highlights Limitations of U.S. Counterterror Network," *The Washington Post*, May 4, 2013, http://articles.washingtonpost.com/2013-05-04/world/39025322_1_boston-marathon-national-counterterrorism-center-terrorist-bomb-plot/2.
233. Privacy And Civil Liberties Board, "Report On The Telephone Records Program Conducted Under Section 215 of the USA Patriot Act and on the Operations of the Foreign Intelligence Surveillance Court" 145, January 23, 2014, http://www.pclob.gov/siteassets/pages/default/pclob-report-on-the-telephone-records-program.pdf
234. Privacy and Civil Liberties Oversight Board, "Report on the Surveillance Program Operated Pursuant to Section 702 of the Foreign Intelligence Surveillance Act," July 2, 2014.
235. Spencer Ackerman, "NSA Reformers Dismayed after Privacy Board Vindicates Surveillance Dragnet," *The Guardian*, July 2, 2014.
236. Kim Dotcom, "Prism: Concerns over Government Tyranny Are Legitimate," *The Guardian*, June 13, 2013, http://www.guardian.co.uk/commentisfree/2013/jun/13/prism-utah-data-center-surveillance.
237. Conor Friedersdorf, "All the Infrastructure a Tyrant Would Need, Courtesy of Bush and Obama," *The Atlantic*, June 7, 2013, http://www.theatlantic.com/politics/archive/2013/06/all-the-infrastructure-a-tyrant-would-need-courtesy-of-bush-and-obama/276635/.

238. Micahel Gerson, "Rand Paul Masks His True Worldview," *The Washington Post*, March 12, 2013, http://articles.washingtonpost.com/2013-03-11/opinions/37621773_1_rand-paul-drone-policy-drone-program.
239. Shayana Kadidal, "NSA Surveillance: The Implications for Civil Liberties," *ISJLP* 10: 433.

Chapter 10

1. I am indebted to Professors Sonia Suter, Mark Rothstein, Hank Greely, and George Annas for comments on previous drafts, and to Erin Syring, Renee Souris, and Rory Donnelly for research assistance.
2. Amitai Etzioni, "NSA: National Security vs. Individual Rights," *Intelligence and National Security* 29 (2014): 1; Amitai Etzioni, *How Patriotic is the Patriot Act? Freedom Versus Security in the Age of Terrorism* (2004); Amitai Etzioni, "Public Health Law: A Communitarian Perspective," *Health Affairs* 21 (2002): 102; Amitai Etzioni, "Who Will Guard the Guardian?," *The Atlantic*, February 3, 2014; Amitai Etzioni, *The Limits of Privacy* (2000).
3. David Lazer and Viktor Mayer-Schönberger, "Statutory Frameworks for Regulating Information Flows: Drawing Lessons for the DNA Data Banks from Other Government Data Systems," *Journal of Law, Medicine, and Ethics* 34 (2006): 371.
4. Nancy Beatty Gregoire, "Federal Probation Joins the World of DNA Collection," *Federal Probation Journal* 66 (2002): 30; Frederick R. Bieber, "Turning Base Hits into Earned Runs: Improving the Effectiveness of Forensic DNA Data Bank Programs," *Journal of Law, Medicine, and Ethics* 34 (2006): 222.
5. Russ Hoyle, "The FBI's national DNA database," *Nature Biotechnology* 16 (1998): 987.
6. Nathan James, "DNA Testing in Criminal Justice: Background, Current Law, Grants, and Issues," *CRS Report for Congress* (Dec. 6, 2012), http://fas.org/sgp/crs/misc/R41800.pdf. See also Kelly Ferrell, "Twenty-First Century Surveillance: DNA 'Data-Mining' and the Erosion of the Fourth Amendment," *Houston Law Review* 51 (2013): 253.
7. "CODIS—NDIS Statistics," *FBI Laboratory Services*, July 2014, http://www.fbi.gov/about-us/lab/biometric-analysis/codis/ndis-statistics.
8. "Collection and use of DNA identification information from certain Federal offenders," § 3(a)(2), 42 U.S.C.A. § 14135a(a)(2).
9. Valerie Ross, "Forget Fingerprints: Law Enforcement DNA Databases Poised To Expand," *PBS Nova*, January 2, 2014.
10. Maryland v. King, 569 U.S. __ (2013).
11. H. M. Wallace et al., "Forensic DNA Databases: Ethical and Legal Standards: A Global Review," *Egyptian Journal of Forensic Sciences*, June 7, 2014, http://www.sciencedirect.com/science/article/pii/S2090536X14000239; "All UK 'Must Be on DNA Database,'" *BBC News*, September 5, 2007, http://news.bbc.co.uk/2/hi/uk_news/6979138.stm.

12. For more on the EU ruling, see George J. Annas, "Protecting Privacy and the Public—Limits on Police Use of Bioidentifiers in Europe," *New England Journal of Medicine* 361 (2009): 196–201, http://jeeg.webhost4life.com/page Documents/G2SBTU15QR.pdf; see also "DNA and Fingerprint Guidelines 'Unlawful,'" *BBC News*, May 18, 2011.
13. "Protection of Freedoms Act 2012: How DNA and Fingerprint Evidence is Protected in Law," *U.K. Home Office*, April 4, 2013, https://www.gov.uk.
14. Helena Machado and Susana Silva, "Informed Consent in Forensic DNA Databases: Volunteering, Constructions of Risk and Identity Categorization," *BioSocieties* 4,4 (2009): 335–48.
15. Hank Greely, "Amgen Buys DeCODE—Reflections Backwards, Forwards, and on DTC Genomics," *Stanford Center for the Law and Biosciences*, December 13, 2012, http://blogs.law.stanford.edu/lawandbiosciences/2012/12/13/amgen-buys-decode-reflections-backwards-forwards-and-on-dtc-genomics/.
16. FBI Laboratory Services, *Frequently Asked Questions (FAQs) on the CODIS Program and the National DNA Index System*, http://www.fbi.gov/about-us/lab/biometric-analysis/codis/codis-and-ndis-fact-sheet.
17. "Sensitive information" is a complex, contested term. For the purposes of this chapter, however, it can be construed to generally refer to information that societal norms dictate should be kept to oneself or revealed only with a select group of people for one reason or another. This might include health information, information about relationships, information that is used for important government purposes, financial information, and more. For a rough definition of "sensitive information," see Amitai Etzioni, "A Cyber Age Privacy Doctrine: A Liberal Communitarian Approach," *ISJLP* 9 (2014), http://papers.ssrn.com/sol3/papers.cfm?abstract_id=2348117.
18. Candice Roman-Santos, "Concerns Associated with Expanding DNA Databases," *Hastings Science and Technology Journal* 2 (2011): 267.
19. George J. Annas, "Privacy Rules for DNA Databanks: Protecting Coded 'Future Diaries,'" *Journal of the American Medical Association* 270 (1993): 2346.
20. Subbaya Subramanian, Rakesh K. Mishra, and Lalji Singh, "Genome-wide Analysis of Microsatellite Repeats in Humans: Their Abundance and Density in Specific Genome Regions," *Genome Biology* 4 (2003): R13; see also Harvey Lodish et al., *Molecular Cell Biology*, 224 (2008): Simple-sequence DNA, which includes satellite DNA, minisatellites, and microsatellites, comprises about 6 percent of the human genome.
21. Rebecca Laird, Peter M. Schneider, and Silvana Guadieri, "STRs as Potential Disease Markers: A Study of VWA and von Willbrand's Disease," *Forensic Science International: Genetics* 1 (2007): 253.
22. P. Bennett, "Demystified . . . microsatellites," *Molecular Pathology* 53 (2000): 177: SSRs can either be protein-coding or noncoding, and only about 3 percent of the human genome codes for proteins. Meanwhile, functional DNA, which regulates gene transcription and helps to maintain the structure of chromosomes, "is thought to comprise less than a sixth of the total human genome." The sum of all DNA with any known function represents only about 30 percent of the human genome. All forensic loci are chosen from the remaining 70 percent.); see also Gábor Tóth, Zoltán Gáspári, and Jerzy Jurka, "Microsatellites

in Different Eukaryotic Organisms: Survey and Analysis," *Genome Research* 10 (2000): 957.
23. Natalie Ram, "Fortuity and Forensic Familial Identification," *Stanford Law Review* 63 (2011): 751.
24. Maryland v. King, 569 U.S. __, (2013).
25. *Brief of Genetics, Genomics and Forensic Science Researchers as Amici Curiae in Support of Neither Party* in Maryland v. King, 569 U.S. __ (2013).
26. "Full DNA Samples to be Destroyed," *Express*, December 13, 2012.
27. "S and Marper v. United Kingdom," *European Court of Human Rights* (2008): 1581.
28. For a discussion of the critical difference between limiting secondary usages and limiting collection, see Amitai Etzioni, "A Cyber Age Privacy Doctrine: A Liberal Communitarian Approach," *ISJLP* 9 http://papers.ssrn.com/sol3/papers.cfm?abstract_id=2348117.
29. Tracey Maclin, "Is Obtaining an Arrestee's DNA a Valid Special Needs Search Under the Fourth Amendment? What Should (and Will) the Supreme Court Do?," 34 *Journal of Law, Medicine and Ethics* 166 (2006).
30. The CODIS website states that "CODIS was designed to compare a target DNA record against the DNA records contained in the database. Once a match is identified by the CODIS software, the laboratories involved in the match exchange information to verify the match [. . .] to establish probable cause to obtain an evidentiary DNA sample from the suspect. [. . .]The casework laboratory can then perform a DNA analysis on the known biological sample so that this analysis can be presented as evidence in court. See FBI Laboratory Services, *Frequently Asked Questions (FAQs) on the CODIS Program and the National DNA Index System,*, 2011, http://www.fbi.gov/about-us/lab/biometric-analysis/codis/codis-and-ndis-fact-sheet.
31. Aaron P. Stevens, "Arresting Crime: Expanding the Scope of DNA Databases in America," *Texas Law Review* 79 (2001): 921.
32. New York State Division of Criminal Justice Services, "DNA Frequently Asked Questions," http://www.criminaljustice.ny.gov/forensic/dnafaqs.htm.
33. United States v. Stewart, 532 F.3d 32 (1st Cir. 2008).
34. Maryland v. King, 569 U.S. __ (2013).
35. Amitai Etzioni, "The Privacy Merchants: What Is to Be Done?" *University of Pennsylvania Journal of Constitutional Law* 14, 4 (2012).
36. U.S. Department of Justice Office of the Inspector General, "Compliance with Standards Governing Combined DNA Index System Activities at the Southwestern Institute of Forensic Sciences at Dallas County, Texas," (December 2009), http://www.justice.gov/oig/grants/2009/g8010002.pdf.
37. State v. Maxfield, 125 Wash.2d 378, 392, 886 P.2d 123 (1994).
38. Sonia M. Suter, "All in the Family: Privacy and Familial DNA Searching," *Harvard Journal of Law & Technology* 23, 2 (2010): 323.
39. Robin Williams and Paul Johnson, "Inclusiveness, Effectiveness and Intrusiveness: Issues in the Developing Uses of DNA Profiling in Support of Criminal Investigations," *Journal of Law, Medicine and Ethics* 34 (2006): 234; see also Sonia M. Suter, "All in the Family," 309.

40. Jeremy W. Peters, "New Rule Allows Use of Partial DNA Matches," *The New York Times*, January 24, 2010, http://www.nytimes.com/2010/01/25/nyregion/25dna.html.
41. Sonia M. Suter, "All in the Family," 309, 318.
42. Ibid., 309, 312.
43. Dane C. Barca, "Familial DNA Testing, House Bill 3361, and the Need for Federal Oversight," *Hastings Law Journal* 64 (2013): 518; see also Rebecca Dresser, "Families and Forensic DNA Profiles," *Hastings Center Report* 41 (2011): 12; Rori V. Rohlfs et al., "The Influence of Relatives on the Efficiency and Error Rate of Familial Searching," *PLoS One* 8 (2013): 9; Henry T. Greely et al., "Family Ties: The Use of DNA Offender Databases to Catch Offenders' Kin," *Journal of Law, Medicine, and Ethics* 34, 2 (2006): 254.
44. Joyce Kim, Danny Mammo, Mami B. Siegel, and Sarah H. Katsanis, all of the Center for Genome Ethics, Law, and Policy at Duke University, point out that partial match searches often generate unnecessarily large suspect pools. See Joyce Kim et al., "Policy Implications for Familial Searching," *Investigative Genetics* 2, 1 (2011): 4.
45. Michael Naughton and Gabe Tan, "The Need for Caution in the Use of DNA Evidence to Avoid Convicting the Innocent," *International Journal of Evidence and Proof* 15 (2001): 245–57.
46. Erin E. Murphy, "Familial DNA Searches: The Opposing Viewpoint," *Criminal Justice* 27 (2012): 20.
47. For example, false positives can be reduced by increasing the number of loci analyzed in a DNA profile. Performing additional types of DNA analysis that more accurately predict relationships between individuals and including this information in DNA profiles would also decrease the probability of false positives. Moreover, refining the computer algorithms used to suggest partial matches would also help to separate random matches from true relatives. See Henry T. Greely et al., "Family Ties," 254; Jianye Ge et al., "Developing Criteria and Data to Determine Best Options for Expanding the Core CODIS Loci," *Investigative Genetics* 3, 1 (2012).
48. Sonia M. Suter, "All in the Family," 309, 385–94.
49. Joyce Kim et al., "Policy Implications for Familial Searching," 4.
50. Office of the Attorney General, "Brown's Forensic Experts Identify Grim Sleeper Serial Killer Suspect Through Unexpected Use of Familial DNA," *State of California Department of Justice*, July 8, 2010, https://oag.ca.gov/news/press-releases/browns-forensic-experts-identify-grim-sleeper-serial-killer-suspect-through.
51. Sepideh Esmaili, "Searching for a Needle in a Haystack: The Constitutionality of Police DNA Dragnets," *Chicago-Kent Law* Review 82 (2007): 495.
52. Ibid.
53. Jeffrey S. Grand, "The Blooding of America: Privacy and the DNA Dragnet," *Cardozo Law Review* 23 (2002): 2280; Christopher Slobogin, "Government Dragnets," *Law & Contemporary Problems* 73 (2010): 123: "Privacy violations [are] inherent in the DNA dragnet"; Fred W. Drobner, "DNA Dragnets: Constitutional Aspects of Mass DNA Identification Testing," *Capital University*

Law Review 28 (2000): 479; Sepideh Esmaili, "Searching for a Needle in a Haystack," 495.
54. Mark A. Rothstein and Meghan K. Talbott, "The Expanding Use of DNA in Law Enforcement: What Role for Privacy?" *Journal of Law, Medicine, and Ethics* 24 (2009): 156.
55. Sepideh Esmaili, "Searching for a Needle in a Haystack," 495, 498–99.
56. Kevin Hartnett, "The DNA in Your Garbage: Up for Grabs," *Boston Globe*, May 12, 2013, http://www.bostonglobe.com/ideas/2013/05/11/the-dna-your-garbage-for-grabs/sU12MtVLkoypL1qu2iF6IL/story.html; see also Holly K. Fernandez, "Genetic Privacy, Abandonment, and DNA Dragnets: Is Fourth Amendment Jurisprudence Adequate?" *Hastings Center Report* 35 (2005): 21.
57. California v. Greenwood, 486 U.S. 35 (1988).
58. Holly K. Fernandez, "Genetic Privacy, Abandonment, and DNA Dragnets: Is Fourth Amendment Jurisprudence Adequate?" *Hastings Center Report* 35 (2005): 21.
59. Elizabeth E. Joh, "Reclaiming 'Abandoned' DNA: The Fourth Amendment and Genetic Privacy," *Northwestern University Law Review* 100 (2006): 874, 875.
60. State v. Galloway and Hoesly, 109 P.3d 383 (Or. App. 2005).
61. This includes Hawaii and New Jersey (see Dennis Hevesi, "New Jersey Court Protects Trash From Police Searches," *New York Times*, July 19, 1990); New Hampshire (Robert E. Williams, "New Hampshire and the Methodology of the New Judicial Federalism," *New Hampshire Bar Journal* [Summer 2004]); New Mexico (Deborah Baker, "Court Says Privacy of Garbage Is Protected," *Associated Press*, June 11, 2006); Vermont (State v. Morris (94-299); 165 Vt 111; 680 A.2d 90); and Washington (Hope Lynne Karp, "Trash: A Matter of Privacy?," *Pace Law Review* 20 (2000): 541).
62. Kristy Holtfreter et al., "Public Perceptions of White-Collar Crime and Punishment," *Journal of Criminal Justice* 36, 1 (2008): 50.
63. Duana Fullwiley, "Can DNA Witness Race," *Council for Responsible Genetics* (2004), http://www.councilforresponsiblegenetics.org/genewatch/GeneWatchPage.aspx?pageId=59&archive=yes.
64. See, for example, Tim Alamenciak, "OPP Faces Scrutiny over DNA Testing Sweep That Brought Racial-Profiling Complaint," *The Star*, March 3, 2014, http://www.thestar.com/news/gta/2014/03/03/police_watchdog_investigates_opp_over_dna_testing.html.
65. Howard Cooke, "DNA and Police Files," *Lancet* 342, 8864 (1993): 130.
66. Michael Purtill, "Everybody's Got a Price: Why Orange County's Practice of Taking DNA Samples from Misdemeanor Arrestees is an Excessive Fine," *Journal of Criminal Law and Criminology* 101 (2011): 311; David Skinner, "The NDNAD Has No Ability in Itself to be Discriminatory: Ethnicity and the Governance of the UK National DNA Database," *Sociology* 47 (2013): 977.
67. Mark Berman, "Texas Man Exonerated through DNA Testing He Didn't Know was Going to Happen," *Washington Post*, July 25, 2014, http://www.washingtonpost.com/news/post-nation/wp/2014/07/25/texas-man-exonerated-through-dna-testing-he-didnt-know-was-going-to-happen/.

68. Carole McCartney, "Forensic DNA Sampling and the England and Wales National DNA Database: A Sceptical Approach," *Critical Criminology* 12 (2004): 157; Michael E. Smith, "Let's Make the DNA Identification Database as Inclusive as Possible," *Journal of Law, Medicine, and Ethics* 34 (2006): 288; Robert Williamson and Rony Duncan, "DNA Testing for All," *Nature* 418, 6898(2002): 585; Christine Rosen, "Liberty, Privacy, and DNA Databases," *The New Atlantis* (Spring 2003), http://www.thenewatlantis.com/publications/liberty-privacy-and-dna-databases; D. H. Kaye and Michael E. Smith, "DNA Databases for Law Enforcement: The Coverage Question and the Case for a Population-wide Database," in D. Lazer, ed., *DNA and the Criminal Justice System: The Technology of Justice*, 247–84 (Cambridge, MA: MIT Press, 2004); Akhil Reed Amar, "A Search for Justice in Our Genes," *The New York Times*, May 7, 2002, http://www.nytimes.com/2002/05/07/opinion/a-search-for-justice-in-our-genes.html; Kathleen M. Donovan and Charles F. Klahm IV, "Prosecuting Science: The Rational Defence of Mandatory DNA Databases," *Howard Journal of Criminal Justice* 48 (2009): 412.
69. D. H. Kaye and Michael E. Smith, "DNA Databases for Law Enforcement," 247–84.
70. Ibid.
71. Etzioni, Amitai, "A Cyber Age Privacy Doctrine."
72. Along the lines suggested by Sonia Suter in "All in the Family," 309.
73. Jeremy Gans, "Something to Hide: DNA, Surveillance and Self-Incrimination," *Current Issues in Criminal Justice* (2001) 13: 168–84, http://papers.ssrn.com/sol3/papers.cfm?abstract_id=1030450.
74. Janet C. Hoeffel, "The Dark Side of DNA Profiling: Unreliable Scientific Evidence Meets the Criminal Defendant," *Stanford Law Review* 42 (1990): 465, 533; Dan L. Burk and Jennifer A. Hess, "Genetic Privacy: Constitutional Considerations in Forensic DNA Testing," *George Mason University Civil Rights Law Journal* 5 (1994): 17.
75. Schmerber v. California, 384 U.S. 757, (1966), cited in Paul C. Giannelli, "ABA Standards on DNA Evidence: Nontestimonial Identification Orders," *Criminal Justice* 24 (2009): 24.
76. Nicholas Soares, "The Right to Remain Encrypted: The Self-Incrimination Doctrine in the Digital Age," *American Criminal Law Review* 49 (2012): 2001, 2004.
77. Nicholas Soares, "The Right to Remain Encrypted," 2001, 2004–5.
78. Michael S. Pardo, "Disentangling the Fourth Amendment and the Self-Incrimination Clause," *Iowa Law Review* 90 (2005): 1870: "Non-verbal conduct, however, may be testimonial: For example, the act of responding to a subpoena by providing a requested object discloses one's (1) knowledge that the object exists, (2) possession of it, and (3) belief that the provided object is the one demanded. Physical evidence, by contrast, is not 'testimony' and hence an individual forced to disclose it is not protected, even if the evidence is compelled and incriminating. This includes evidence (including DNA evidence) taken from a suspect's body."
79. Nita A. Farahany, "Incriminating Thoughts," *Stanford Law Review* 64, 2 (2012): 351.

80. Schmerber v. California, 384 U.S. 757, (1966), cited in Paul C. Giannelli, "ABA Standards on DNA Evidence," 25.
81. Sonia M. Suter, "All in the Family," 309; Henry T. Greely et al., "Family Ties," 254; Jianye Ge et al., "Developing Criteria and Data to Determine Best Options for Expanding the Core CODIS Loci."
82. Butler v. Michigan 352 U.S. 380 (1957).
83. Andromachi Tseloni et al., "Exploring the International Decline in Crime Rates," *European Journal of Criminology* 7 (2010): 377.
84. Mike Weisser, "It's Clear Violent Crime Is Decreasing, But Less Clear Why," *Huffington Post*, February 10, 2014, http://www.huffingtonpost.com/mike-weisser/violent-crime-cities_b_4760996.html.
85. Terry Frieden, "U.S. Violent Crime Down for Fifth Straight Year," *CNN*, October 29, 2012, http://www.cnn.com/2012/10/29/justice/us-violent-crime/.
86. Federal Bureau of Investigation, "Crime in the United States,", http://www2.fbi.gov/ucr/cius2009/data/table_01.html.
87. Federal Bureau of Investigation, "Crime in the United States 2011: Clearances,", http://www.fbi.gov/about-us/cjis/ucr/crime-in-the-u.s/2011/crime-in-the-u.s.-2011/clearances: The FBI defines a case as "cleared" when at least one person has been arrested in connection with a crime, charged with the offense, and turned over to the court for prosecution. This does not necessarily mean that an individual is convicted of having committed the offense. Alternately, situations in which law enforcement has identified the probable offender, has probable cause for an arrest and prosecution, and knows the probable offender's exact location—but an "exceptional circumstance" such as the suicide of the probable offender prevents the actual arrest and prosecution are considered to be "cleared by exceptional means."
88. Ibid.
89. Chain of custody refers, for DNA and forensics in general, to "a record of individuals who have had physical possession of the evidence. Documentation is critical to maintaining the integrity of the chain of custody. Maintaining the chain of custody is vital for any type of evidence. In addition, if laboratory analysis reveals that DNA evidence was contaminated, it may be necessary to identify persons who have handled that evidence." See National Institute of Justice, *DNA Evidence: Basics of Identifying, Gathering and Transporting*, August 9, 2012, http://nij.gov/topics/forensics/evidence/dna/basics/Pages/identifying-to-transporting.aspx.
90. Ricky Ansell, "Internal Quality Control in Forensic DNA Analysis," *Accreditation and Quality Assurance* 18 (2013): 280.
91. Innocence Project, "Wrongful Convictions Involving Unvalidated or Improper Forensic Science that Were Later Overturned through DNA Testing" (February 1, 2009) http://www.innocenceproject.org/docs/DNA_Exonerations_Forensic_Science.pdf.
92. William C. Thompson, "Subjective Interpretation, Laboratory Error and the Value of Forensic DNA Evidence: Three Case Studies," *Genetica* 96 (1995): 153.

93. Michael Doyle, "FBI Announces Review of 2,000 Cases Featuring Hair Samples," *McLatchy DC*, July 18, 2013, http://www.mcclatchydc.com/2013/07/18/197069/fbi-announces-review-of-2000-cases.html.
94. "How Accurate Is Forensic Analysis?" *The Washington Post,* April 16, 2012, http://www.washingtonpost.com/wp-srv/special/local/forensic-analysis-methods/.
95. Sandra Laville, "Forensic Lab Errors in Hundreds of Crime Cases," *The Guardian*, February 21, 2007, http://www.theguardian.com/politics/2007/feb/22/topstories3.ukcrime.
96. "How Accurate Is Forensic Analysis?" *The Washington Post.*
97. National Academy of Sciences, "Strengthening Forensic Science in the United States: A Path Forward, Committee on Identifying the Needs of the Forensic Sciences Community," (August 2009), https://www.ncjrs.gov/pdffiles1/nij/grants/228091.pdf.
98. David Grann, "Trial by Fire," *The New Yorker*, September 7, 2009, http://www.newyorker.com/reporting/2009/09/07/090907fa_fact_grann?currentPage=all.
99. Innocence Project, "Wrongful Convictions Involving Unvalidated or Improper Forensic Science that Were Later Over turned through DNA Testing."
100. Steven B. Duke, "Eyewitness Testimony Doesn't Make It True," *Yale Law School News Archive*, June 12, 2006, http://www.law.yale.edu/news/2727.htm.
101. Joan Biskupic, "Supreme Court Examines Reliability of Eyewitness Testimony," *USA Today*, November 2, 2011.
102. Innocence Project, "Eyewitness Misidentification" (July 2014), http://www.innocenceproject.org/understand/Eyewitness-Misidentification.php.
103. David A. Schroeder and Michael D. White, "Exploring the Use of DNA Evidence in Homicide Investigations," *Police Quarterly* 12 (2009): 319: Although Schroeder and White found that "[when] DNA evidence was available for use, clearance rates were low," Schroeder and White both offer explanations for this result that were rooted in the low rates with which DNA analysis was used. They suggested that many cases clear before DNA analysis was completed due to detectives continuing to work the case while evidence was at the laboratory. (In short, they lacked controls.) They thus acknowledge that their methodology for this section of the paper was insufficient to fully explore the value or lack thereof of DNA analysis for criminal investigations.
104. Federal Bureau of Investigation, "Rapid DNA or Rapid DNA Analysis" (2014), http://www.fbi.gov/about-us/lab/biometric-analysis/codis/rapid-dna-analysis: Rapid use DNA testing is an automated process of developing a CODIS profile using a sample of saliva. "The 'swab in—profile out' process consists of automated extraction, amplification, separation, detection and allele calling without human intervention.
105. J. K. Roman et al., "The DNA Field Experiment: Cost-effectiveness of the Analysis of the Use of DNA in the Investigation of High-Volume Crimes," *Urban Institute Justice Policy Center* (April 2008), cited in David B. Wilson et al., "Does

Forensic DNA Help to Solve Crime? The Benefit of Sophisticated Answers to Naïve Questions," *Journal of Contemporary Criminal Justice* 26 (2010): 463.
106. W. T. Dunsmuir, C. Tran, and D. Weatherburn, "Assessing the Impact of Mandatory DNA Testing of Prison Inmates in NSW on Clearance, Charge, and Conviction Rates for Selected Crime Categories," (2008) cited in David B. Wilson et al., "Does Forensic DNA Help to Solve Crime?," 463.
107. David B. Wilson et al., "Use of DNA Testing in Police Investigative Work for Increasing Offender Identification, Arrest, Conviction and Case Clearance," *2011 Campbell Systematic Reviews* (2011).
108. Matthew Gabriel et al., "Beyond the Cold Hit: Measuring the Impact of the National DNA Data Bank on Public Safety at the City and County Level," *Journal of Law, Medicine, and Ethics* 38 (2010): 399; John K. Roman et al., "The DNA Field Experiment," 346.
109. "DNA Links Longtime Boston Strangler Suspect to Murder," *Associated Press*, July 11, 2013, http://www.cbc.ca/news/world/dna-links-longtime-boston-strangler-suspect-to-murder-1.1329562.
110. Amitai Etzioni, "A Cyber Age Privacy Doctrine."
111. Philip Hunter, "All the Evidence," *EMBO Reports* 7 (2006):4
112. Ricky Ansell, "Internal Quality Control in Forensic DNA Analysis," *Accreditation and Quality Assurance* 18 (2013): 281.
113. Ibid., 285.
114. Federal Bureau of Investigation "Standards for Forensic DNA Testing Laboratories," http://www.fbi.gov/about-us/lab/biometric-analysis/codis/stds_testlabs.
115. Ibid.
116. William C. Thompson, "Are Juries Competent to Evaluate Statistical Evidence?" *Law and Contemporary Problems* 52 (1989): 9–10, 41; Jason Schklar and Shari Seidman Diamond, "Juror Reactions to DNA Evidence: Errors and Expectancies," *Law and Human Behavior* 23 (1999): 159; Dan Frumkin, Adam Wasserstrom, Ariane Davidson, and Arnon Grafit, "Authentication of Forensic DNA samples," *Forensic Science International: Genetics* 4 (2010):102.
117. Mark Nelson et al., "Making Sense of DNA Backlogs, 2012—Myths vs. Reality," *National Institute of Justice, United States Department of Justice Office of Justice Programs* (December 2013), https://www.ncjrs.gov/pdffiles1/nij/243347.pdf.
118. This is not the total number of cases received in 2011; it is a snapshot of the cases that were pending at the laboratories at that point. Other cases had already been given final reports. See Mark Nelson et al., "Making Sense of DNA Backlogs, 2012 – Myths vs. Reality."
119. "Women Express Concern over Police Rape Kit Backlogs," *Associated Press*, March 19, 2012, http://www.washingtonpost.com/blogs/crime-scene/post/women-express-concern-over-police-rape-kit-backlogs/2012/03/19/gIQATVRhMS_blog.html.
120. See, for example, Rajendrani Mukhopadhyay, "Forensic Flow," *Chemistry World* (April 2011): 50–53.
121. Jim Ridley, "Demetria Kalodinos Tells the Story of Jeffrey Womack, the Boy Who Didn't Kill Marcia Trimble," *Nashville Scene*, November 15, 2012,

http://www.nashvillescene.com/nashville/demetria-kalodimos-tells-the-story-of-jeffrey-womack-the-boy-who-didnt-kill-marcia-trimble/Content?oid=3080150.
122. "Arrest in Girl Scout's 33-Year-Old Murder Jolts City," *FOX News*, September 22, 2008, http://www.foxnews.com/story/2008/09/22/arrest-in-girl-scout-33-year-old-murder-jolts-city/.
123. Jim Ridley, "Demetria Kalodinos tells the story of Jeffrey Womack, the boy who didn't kill Marcia Trimble."
124. Kevin Flynn, "Fighting Crime with Ingenuity, 007 Style; Gee-Whiz Police Gadgets Get a Trial Run in New York," *New York Times*, March 7, 2000.
125. Keith L. Alexander and Spencer S. Hsu, "Man Exonerated in 1982 D.C. Killing; DNA Reveals FBI Error in Conviction," *The Washington Post*, July 21, 2014, http://www.washingtonpost.com/local/crime/dc-man-exonerated-in-1982-rape-and-murder-dna-reveals-fbi-error-in-conviction/2014/07/21/ee7cc490-0ec8-11e4-8341-b8072b1e7348_story.html? wpmk=MK0000205.
126. Innocence Project, "DNA Exonerations Nationwide," (2014), http://www.innocenceproject.org/; see also Molly Hennessey-Fiske, "DNA Evidence Exonerates 300th Prisoner Nationwide," *Los Angeles Times*, October 1, 2012, http://articles.latimes.com/2012/oct/01/nation/la-na-dna-evidence-20121001.
127. Greg Hampikian et al., "The Genetics of Innocence: Analysis of 194 U.S. DNA Exonerations," *Annual Review of Genomics and Human Genetics* 98 (2011):104.
128. Sean Gardiner, "'Central Park Five' Settlement Eyed In Similar Cases," *Wall Street Journal*, July 7, 2014, http://online.wsj.com/articles/central-park-five-settlement-with-new-york-city-eyed-by-wrongful-conviction-lawyers-1404785297.
129. Steve Mills and Juan Perez Jr., "$40M Wrongful Conviction Settlement: 'The Money Is Almost Beside the Point,'" *Chicago Tribune*, June 25, 2014, http://www.chicagotribune.com/news/local/breaking/chi-40m-wrongful-conviction-settlement-the-money-is-almost-beside-the-point-20140625,0,3363955.story.
130. Greg Hampikian et al., "The Genetics of Innocence: Analysis of 194 U.S. DNA Exonerations," *Annual Review of Genomics and Human Genetics* 98 (2011): 104.
131. Amitai Etzioni, *The Limits of Privacy* (2000): 14.

Index

accountability, 34–35, 46, 72, 107–108, 109–111, 144–145, 148–149, 151–154, 161, 173
administrative searches, 42, 106, 134
advocacy model, 102, 124–125
Alexander, Keith, 35, 94, 110, 133, 151
Alito, Samuel, 2, 11, 27, 57–58, 70
al-Zawahiri, Ayman, 126, 131
Angwin, Julia, 80
arrest records, 17

Bates, John, 144, 149
big data, *see* privacy merchants
bin Laden, Osama, 126, 130–131
Blair, Tony, 159
Blitz, Marc Jonathon, 3–4
Brandeis, Louis, 2
Bush, George W., 35, 93, 97–98

California v. Ciraolo, 57
California v. Greenwood, 55, 165
Camara v. Municipal Court, 134
Cate, Fred, 20
CCTV, 11, 17, 43–44
cell phones
 location tracking of, 17, 75, 84, 144
 smart phones, 71
 wiretapping of, *see* wiretaps
Clinton, Hillary, 114
Clapper, James, 143, 150
cloud storage, 17–18, 21–22, 132; *see also* digital age
common good
 threats to, 6, 46, 53, 104
 tradeoff with individual rights, 103–104, 105–107, 170–177

communitarianism
 authoritarian, 5, 101, 124
 civil society, 47, 155
 liberal, 5, 24, 101–103, 124–125, 157–158, 168, 170
containers, 69
cookies, 75, 77
crime
 difference between terrorism and crime, 128–129
 rates of, 9, 108, 171
 recidivism, 116–117
 see also right to be forgotten
cybernation, 2, 11–12, 32–36, 71–72
 deriving sensitive information through, 15, 76
 distinction from volume, 28, 38
cybersecurity, 93–100, 138, 147

democracy, 53, 109, 154
digital age, 21–22, 54–55, 58, 67–68, 86, 89, 106–107, 114, 116–117, 136
digital personhood, 40,
digitization of records, 17, 19, 32, 114, 118
 social media, 77–78, 81
 data collection, 14
 versus secondary usages, 1–2, 19–21, 25, 161
 spot collection, 2, 12, 20, 28
databases, 33, 46, 87, 117–118, 137, 157–177; *see also* privacy merchants
DeVries, WIll Thomas, 21
distribution, 33–34

Domain Awareness System, 11, 43–44, 58
Dow Chemical Company v. United States, 3, 55, 57
DNA, 18, 46, 157–177

Easton, Raymond, 163–164
Entick v. Carrington, 63
Epstein, Richard A., 21, 49
European Union Data Protection Directive, 13–14, 22–23, 85–86, 120
expectation of privacy, 8, 23–24, 49–54

Feinstein, Dianne, 96,148, 152
feminism, 3, 64–65
Fifth Amendment, 169–170
financial information, 21
Florida v. Jardines, 41
Florida v. Riley, 39
fundamental rights approach, see European Union Data Protection Directive

general searches, 106, 133–135; see also administrative searches

Harlan, Marshall, 54, 56–57, 69
Hoboken, Jaris van, 23
Holder, Eric, 98, 125
homes, 3–4, 38–39, 41, 56–59, 61–73, 134
  history of housing exceptionalism, 62
  homelessness, 66–67
  curtilage, 41

Illinois v. Lidster, 134
individual rights
  balance with common good, 5–7, 103–106, 175–176
information as privacy approach, see European Union Data Protection Directive
intimate information, see sensitivity
intrusiveness, 4, 7

Johnson v. United States, 62

Katz v. United States, 23, 40, 49–59, 61, 68–69
Kerr, Orin, 6–7, 11, 15
Kyllo v. United States, 8–9, 38–39, 68

law
  case, see court cases by name
  international, 142
  statutory, see privacy, statutory protections of
Lawless, Matthew, 13
libertarianism, 5, 29–30, 46, 83, 102–103, 111–112

MacKinnon, Catharine, 3
McClain, Linda, 3
Mayer-Schönberger, Viktor, 20, 115
Maryland v. King, 159, 160
Maynard v. United States, see United States v. Jones
metadata, 44, 123, 131
Michigan Department of State Police v. Sitz, 134
minimization, 16, 161–162
mosaic theory of the Fourth Amendment, 2, 11, 42–43
Mundie, Craig, 20, 56

national security, 34–35, 44, 46, 53, 98–100, 104–105, 106, 110–111, 124–156
New York Times Co. v. United States, 125
Nojeim, Greg, 13
normative considerations, 4–5, 25–26, 81–82

Obama, Barack, 93, 97–98, 100, 103, 125–126, 132, 143, 148
Olmstead v. United States, 3, 62

Paul, Rand, 155
Payton v. New York, 63
Perry, Rick, 114

Persistent Surveillance Systems (PSS), 43–44, 58; *see also* Domain Awareness System
personally-identifiable information, *see* sensitivity
poverty, 66
PRISM, 105, 110, 112, 123, 130, 139–146
privacy, personal sphere of, 70
Privacy and Civil Liberties Oversight Board, 103, 130, 154
protection-of-personhood version of, 4
public opinion about, 82–83; *see also* normative considerations
statutory and regulatory protections of, 9–10, 15, 27, 30–31, 34–35, 56, 71, 76, 79, 83–85, 87, 88, 96–97, 135, 141–142, 143–144
technology and, 67–68; *see also* digital age
privacy merchants, 15, 22, 28, 55–56, 67, 80–91, 114–115, 137–138
privacy violating triangulation (PVT), 76, 89–90
public-private distinction, 3–4, 51, 54–55, 58, 64–66, 67–68, 78–80, 87–88, 94–100, 136–138; *see also* privacy merchants

racial profiling, 166–169
reasonableness, 54, 103, 124–125
retention of information, *see* storage
revealing information, *see* sensitivity
right to be forgotten, 17, 107–108, 115, 118–122
Riley v. California, 71

Scalia, Antonin, 3, 41, 57–58, 76
Schmerber v. California, 38, 169
secondary usages, 86–87
   versus data collection, 1–2, 19–21, 25
Sedley, Stephen, 159
Semayne's Case, 63
sensitivity, 7–8, 15, 29–32, 71, 76, 88–89, 159–160
   social construction of, 30, 53

sharing, *see* distribution
Silverman v. United States, 3, 62
Slobogin, Christopher, 4, 15, 52, 76
Smith v. Maryland (1979), 131–132
Smith v. Maryland (2012), 21, 42–43, 57, 63
Snowden, Edward, 35, 105, 147
Solove, Daniel J., 29, 79
Sotomayor, Sonia, 31–32, 58
State v. Galloway and Hoesly, 166
Stevens, John Paul, 39
Swire, Peter, 6–7, 16, 56
storage, 32–33

terrorism, 125–127; *see also* national security
third party doctrine, 9, 12–13, 21, 55–56, 131–132
Total Information Awareness (TIA), 16
totalitarianism, 154–155
transparency, 109–111, 150–151
trespass doctrine, 3, 57
Tsarnev brothers, 130, 154

United States v. Bin Laden, 145
United States v. Davis, 134
United States v. Hartwell, 125, 134
United States v. Jones, 2, 11, 27, 31–32, 40, 57
United States v. Karo, 57
United States v. Knotts, 57
United States v. Miller, 21, 55, 131
United States v. Pulido-Baqeruizo, 134
United States v. Rumely, 32
United States v. Verdugo-Urquidez, 140
United States v. White, 41–42

vehicles, 69, 70
volume, 10–11, 26, 70–71
   bandwidth, 28
   distinction from cybernation, 28, 38
   quantity, 26–28

warrants, 69, 140
Warren, Samuel, 1
Wilkes v. Wood, 63
wiretaps, 45, 130, 132–133

Womack, Jeffrey, 175–176

Zazi, Najibullah, 105
Zuckerberg, Mark, 81

The manufacturer's authorised representative in the EU is Springer Nature Customer Service Centre GmbH, Europaplatz 3, 69115 Heidelberg, Germany. If you have any concerns regarding our products, please contact ProductSafety@springernature.com

Printed and bound by CPI Group (UK) Ltd, Croydon, CR0 4YY
23/03/2026
02076449-0017